FORMOSA
TODAY

THE PRAEGER CONTEMPORARY WORLD SERIES: *No. 11*

The Praeger Contemporary World Series

FORMOSA
TODAY

Edited by

MARK MANCALL

FREDERICK A. PRAEGER, *Publisher*

New York · London

FREDERICK A. PRAEGER, Publisher
64 UNIVERSITY PLACE, NEW YORK 3, N.Y., U.S.A.
77-79 CHARLOTTE STREET, LONDON W.1, ENGLAND

Published in the United States of America in 1964
by Frederick A. Praeger, Inc., Publisher

Most of the material in this book was first published
in Great Britain in 1963 in *The China Quarterly*

Library of Congress Catalog Card Number: 64-13491

Printed in the United States of America

Preface

THE ESSAYS in this volume represent, in their totality, an attempt to survey Taiwan today. With two exceptions, they all appeared in Volume 15 (July–September, 1963) of *The China Quarterly*. The authors for the most part have had personal experience of Taiwan. Sheppard Glass, John Israel, Maurice Meisner, Jonathan Mirsky, and I studied or worked on the island. Lucy H. Chen and Ong Joktik are themselves from Taiwan, and Mei Wen-li is a mainlander long resident there. Lewis Gilbert, Joyce K. Kallgren, Donald Klein, Akira Iriye, and Shinkichi Eto are specialists in their own fields who have taken time to study particular problems relating to Taiwan. The essays represent, therefore, a cross section of the knowledge generally available in academic and journalistic circles in the United States and elsewhere concerning the Republic of China today. The shortcomings of this volume are the shortcomings, unfortunately, of a subject all too little studied, despite its current importance to the interests of America and the free world.

Two points must be made: First, these essays are, in a special fashion, highly personal. None of them is necessarily scholarly in the strictest tradition of academic discipline. Rather, they are meant to provide a relatively comprehensive picture of particular subjects. In many cases, they are the distillation of personal experience and observation. Some readers may quarrel with the choice of contributors, particularly because none appears to have provided an adequate defense of the Nationalist Government's position. The authors were invited to contribute because they had recently been on Taiwan and/or were familiar with their subject. Everyone was given total freedom to express himself as he saw fit. Apparent uniformity of opinion in the broad sense was never intended; that it generally exists, however, represents a widespread reaction of scholars and journalists working on Taiwan. Nor was any effort made to induce uniformity of fact. It would have been improper to have done so, particularly in an area like Taiwan where fact itself may be subject to dispute. Where the authors disagree with each other, constructive discussion and further research should develop.

Second, with the exception of the introduction, all the essays were completed by the beginning of 1963. The introduction to this volume, which was completed at the end of 1963, is therefore intended to give a broader survey of Taiwan than was possible in any individual essay and, where attainable, to update the information presented.

Finally, a note on terminology. There is much confusion between the names "Taiwan" and "Formosa." The island is called Taiwan in both Kuo-yü (the Chinese national dialect) and in the dialects of the island. Islanders themselves, when speaking English, often prefer to use the name Formosa. British usage tends toward Formosa, whereas American usage emphasizes Taiwan. Because most of these essays first appeared in *The China Quarterly,* which is published in London, British usage was followed. However, whether Formosa or Taiwan is used, no political connotations are intended.

M.M.
Hong Kong
December, 1963

Contents

FORMOSA
TODAY

Introduction:
Taiwan, Island of Resignation
and Despair

By MARK MANCALL

THE VAST majority of specialists on contemporary China have devoted their attention during the years since 1949 to the study of Communist China. They are naturally impelled to this by the overwhelmingly important role mainland China, with its organized population of 700 million, plays in world politics. By comparison, Taiwan, with its population of only 11 million, has been almost totally ignored in academic research and in the public press. In the United States, this neglect approaches a national calamity.

There are few American client states today as intimately associated with the United States as is Taiwan. Taiwan, or the Republic of China, as its government prefers it to be known, has been the object of vast American military and economic aid. Its chief defense today is the presence of the American Seventh Fleet in the Straits of Taiwan and the Western Pacific. There are more than 10,000 American residents on Taiwan, including diplomats and other government servants, military personnel, missionaries, students, businessmen, and their dependents. American information agencies represent Nationalist China's propaganda interests in Southeast Asia and elsewhere. Chiang Kai-shek and his Nationalist Party regime have played in the past, and continue to play today, a key role in American politics.

Taiwan is also a major international problem. It is America's continued support for the Nationalist Chinese seat in the United Nations that, to a large extent, keeps Communist China out of that international body. Chiang Kai-shek's policy of "counterattack" against mainland China introduces a further unstable element into the already unstable East Asian situation. It is the United States which, to an important degree, prevents Chiang from attempting to carrying out his threats. Chiang has, in fact, surrendered a degree of his sovereignty to the United States in his treaty arrangements with Washington: He has conceded that any offensive action against the mainland will be the subject of "joint agreement." Perhaps most important, public debate in the United States on the question of recognition of the Chinese Communist regime has often missed the point: Any eventual policy of *rapprochement*

1

with Peking, or even the establishment of diplomatic or cultural relations, assuming such were possible, would have to begin with Taipei, not Peking. Peking has time and again indicated its unwillingness to enter into any fundamental relationship with the United States until the "Taiwan question" is solved, or, for that matter, to enter the United Nations until Chiang's representatives are expelled.

In supporting the Chiang regime, the United States supports a one-party dictatorship that has alienated most of Taiwan's population, tramples on political freedoms, stifles intellectual expression, and maintains itself in power through the exercise of overwhelming police force and a subdued terror. The current situation on Taiwan has built-in elements of instability, which could erupt at any time. Is it in America's best interests to wait until the process of breakdown begins before reconsidering our policy toward Taiwan, or would the national interest be better served by a reformulation of policy before the breakdown confronts us with a crisis? To what extent does the Chiang regime really serve the free world's interests? What, to suggest a fundamental question, do we mean by "internal stability" and "international stability" in the Far East? These and many other questions must be asked about Taiwan today.

TAIWAN AND THE MAINLANDERS

Taiwan was turned over to Chinese Nationalist control at the end of World War II in accordance with the Cairo Declaration of 1943, which said that "All the territories Japan has stolen from the Chinese, such as Manchuria, Formosa, and the Pescadores, shall be restored to the Republic of China." Americans were the first allied representatives to land on the island after the Japanese surrender, but by the end of 1945 the Chinese had arrived in force.

Japan's Taiwan: a modernizing society. The Chinese confronted on Taiwan a society and an economy considerably more advanced and modernized than any they knew on the mainland. The literacy rate alone, which was about 80 per cent, was second only to Japan in Asia and considerably higher than the mainland. By 1943, some 70 per cent of children of legal school age were officially enrolled in schools.[1] While secondary and higher education were less acceptable to Taiwanese,

---

[1] Chen Shao-hsing, "Population growth and social change in Taiwan," *Bulletin of the Department of Archeology and Anthropology, National Taiwan University,* 5 (May 1955), 76–103; 6 (November 1955), 86–119. All references are to the first part of the article. For supplementary and sometimes conflicting statistics, see George W. Barclay, *Colonial Development and Population in Taiwan* (Princeton, 1954). See Chen, p. 96.

universal compulsory primary education put Taiwanese society on the path to modernization. Medical education, one of the few advanced fields open to Taiwanese, provides a good example of modernization. In 1906, 90 per cent of the death certificates required by law on Taiwan were issued by doctors of traditional Chinese medicine. By 1935, 90 per cent of the death certificates were issued by doctors of western medicine.[2] Another important factor in the social maturation of the island's society was the development of an efficient transportation system, including railroads, roads, bridges, buses, automobiles, and bicycles. Geographical mobility and social uniformity were thus encouraged.[3]

Universal education led to the development of a sophisticated intellectual life. In the 1920's, under the influence of Japanese liberalism, Wilsonian ideals, and the May Fourth Movement on the China mainland, vigorous social and political movements developed on the island. Before 1920, opposition to the Japanese had largely taken the form of revolt; after that date the "resistance of the people changed gradually from revolt by force to organized political and social movements."[4] Labor and peasant unions, political parties, and literary movements mushroomed, to be put down only after the rise of Japanese militarism in the 1930's. Perhaps the most remarkable intellectual phenomenon of the period was the formation of the Taiwan Culture Association, through which students returning for summer vacations from Japan and elsewhere spread out into the countryside and lectured on nationalism, culture, and history to the peasants in the villages. A leading Taiwanese sociologist, Professor Chen Shao-hsing of Taiwan National University, summarized Taiwan's social modernization:

> The 1920's is [sic] the turning point in the social history of Taiwan. Epidemics were wiped out, prevention of malaria had improved, the doctors of western medicine exceeded the doctors of Chinese medicine, and even the cattle pest was wiped out. Political and social movements began for the first time. Primary education spread, the conservative farmer began to adopt new strains and new technics, and increase production. Mobility of the people had increased, more bicycles, automobiles, and trucks were used, and the level of living was raised somewhat.[5]

Taiwan's social and intellectual development was encouraged by economic modernization. The years from 1926 to 1940 saw a "tremendous increase in the output of agricultural products,"[6] which, reaching

[2] *Ibid.,* p. 100.
[3] *Ibid.,* pp. 91–92, 97–98.
[4] *Ibid.,* p. 86.
[5] *Ibid.,* p. 102.
[6] *Ibid.,* p. 83.

3

peak production on the eve of World War II, subsequently fell. During the War, the value of industrial products produced on Taiwan exceeded the value of agricultural products, and the tempo of urbanization quickened.[7] In 1942, for instance, the value of the total output of all forms of production on Taiwan amounted, according to Professor Chen, to Y515,627,000. Of this, manufactured goods accounted for 46 per cent, agricultural goods for 42 per cent, and other forms of production, including processed agricultural items, for 12 per cent.[8] In 1945, therefore, the Chinese found on the island an economy that was capable of producing a surplus of agricultural products and could produce, albeit in limited quantities, such items as refined petroleum, cement, steel, aluminum, and various consumer goods.

The restoration to China. Despite economic and social advancement, the Taiwanese were restive under Japanese colonial rule and sharply resented the political, social, and economic restrictions that kept Taiwan a colony. Consequently, they welcomed the return to China with great enthusiasm. The first Chinese officials and troops to land at the end of 1945 at Keelung, Taipei's harbor, were greeted by cheering and flag-waving crowds that lined the highway from the port to the capital. Within eighteen months, however, the population of Taiwan was in open revolt against Chiang Kai-shek's Nationalist administration.

Between September 1945 and February 1947, large numbers of carpetbaggers arrived on the island from the mainland. Together with remarkably ruthless administrators, they exploited the Taiwanese and brought not only former Japanese properties but Taiwanese properties as well under mainlander control. Widespread corruption developed, with the profits largely going to relatives of the Generalissimo's, such as the Kung family. Mainlander troops often misbehaved. The island that had welcomed the mainland Chinese as liberators and brothers was treated, in short, as if it were occupied territory. The tension finally exploded on the night of February 27–28, 1947, when mainlander police clubbed to death an elderly woman who was presumably selling cigarettes without a license. (Cigarettes were made a government monopoly after the "restoration.") Demonstrations began throughout the island, and large areas were taken over by local revolutionary committees. Chinese soldiers were brought in from the mainland to put down the revolt. In the process they killed an estimated 10,000 Taiwanese, including a large percentage of the leadership class.[9]

[7] *Ibid.*, p. 84.

[8] *Ibid.*, p. 93.

[9] An important Taiwanese leader in Taipei at the time, who later cooperated with the KMT regime, has estimated privately that at least 17,000 were killed. The Taiwanese were also betrayed time and again in the course of negotiations.

At the end of 1949 (and continuing into 1950 and 1951), Chiang Kai-shek and his Kuomintang regime, together with some 1,500,000 to 2,000,000 refugees from the mainland, fled to Taiwan after their defeat at the hands of the Communists. Martial law was declared and remains in force today.

American aid for survival. How long the Chiang regime could have survived on Taiwan in the face of Communist victory on the mainland and popular opposition on the island is a moot point. Before the Korean War, Washington's policy toward China had been uncertain. While the United States had publicly and definitely abandoned Chiang, it was not yet clear what kind of relationship would develop with the Communists. The Korean War, which was in fact though not officially a war between the United States and Communist China, rescued Chiang and his Kuomintang from extinction. Chinese Communist participation in the Korean conflict gave Chiang the appearance of being an important, though not necessarily attractive, ally in the Far East. Massive American military and economic assistance was given to the Republic of China and, subsequently, a Sino-American mutual defense treaty was concluded between Washington and Taipei.

One of the most remarkable and idealistic assistance projects, the Joint Commission on Rural Reconstruction (JCRR), illustrates the way in which the Kuomintang was able to use American aid to maintain its control over Taiwan. JCRR was established in 1948 on the mainland at the behest of the American and Chinese Nationalist governments. Later, on Taiwan, it had the strong backing and support of Ch'en Ch'eng, presently Vice-President, who recognized its value to the KMT. A group of dedicated and forward-looking Americans and Chinese carried out a wide-scale land-reform and extension-service program in Taiwanese agriculture. Staffed by the two governments (and largely U.S.-financed), JCRR succeeded in carrying out a "land-to-the-tillers" program, and in raising the efficiency of the island's agriculture. Formosan leadership was largely concentrated in the landlord class, which was most disadvantageously affected by the land-reform program. Consequently, while the government tried on the one hand to win the support of the island's peasantry, it destroyed on the other the economic base of the only class capable of providing effective political opposition to the Kuomintang regime.

THE IDEOLOGY OF COUNTERATTACK

Generalissimo Chiang Kai-shek has, to all intents and purposes, staked the existence of his regime since 1949 on a policy of "counterattack against Communist China." He has spent the fourteen years since his flight from the mainland in 1949 on Taiwan ostensibly reorganizing his forces, reforming and revitalizing Chinese society, and preparing a base for the expected counterattack. His government claims that it has controlled corruption, created a democratic and vigorous society united in pursuit of the "national goal" of counterattack, created a growing economy with a rising standard of living for its people, and established an effective fighting force of more than 600,000 men, the world's fifth largest armed force. Whether or not Chiang is willing and able to carry out such a policy, the ideology of counterattack provides the rationale both for the existence of the regime itself and for the specific policies it seeks to carry out.

The "ideology of counterattack" is explained today in several basic documents: (1) the President's annual "Double Tenth Message," issued on Nationalist China's national day, October 10; (2) "The Six Freedoms" and (3) "The Three Assurances," both dated October 10, 1957; (4) "The Four Principles" and (5) "The Ten Pledges," both dated October 10, 1962.[10] These documents sum up the government's concept of "counterattack," and the appeal the government makes to its people on Taiwan as well as to the vast population on the mainland.

According to the ideology of counterattack, China's present sufferings are the result of foreign aggression. In his book *China's Destiny,* published in 1943, the Generalissimo castigated all "imperialist powers" for aggression against China. Now, however, with the mainland under Communist control and with Japan trying to normalize relations with Peking, at least commercially, this year Tokyo has become the chief villain. "The over-all cause of this catastrophe was foreign aggression which began with the Mukden Incident. If it had not been for the Mukden Incident, the Chinese mainland would not have fallen and there would be no Communist threat to other Asian nations," the Generalissimo declared in his Double Tenth Message for 1963.

Communist China is the chief threat to peace and stability in Asia, according to Chiang, and it is the mission of the Government of the Republic of China (GRC) to "liberate" the mainland by all means possible, including force. "To us recovery of the mainland is a *sacred mission* and to end Communist aggression in Asia is to remove the danger of a nuclear war. *It is our duty to launch a punitive expedition against the rebels,* to deliver our compatriots from under tyranny, and to recover the mainland."[11] This will be accomplished in a variety of

---

[10] For the full text of these documents, including the latest presidential Double Tenth Message, see *The China Post* (hereafter *CP*), Taipei, October 11, 1963. Also see, for equally pertinent documents, the President's annual New Year messages and the platform of the IX. Kuomintang Party Congress.

[11] See the Double Tenth Message, *CP*, October 11, 1963.

ways, but fundamentally it is an internal Chinese problem: "As this is our internal war against the Communist rebels, we need not, and will not, involve other nations."[12] In the anti-Communist struggle, the entire nation must be united under the government:

> Our principles, our country, and our duty constitute the spiritual standards for all six hundred million Chinese people to observe. It is incumbent upon every Chinese to participate in, and support, the national revolutionary movement based on the Three Principles of the people! Everyone has the right to participate in the counteroffensive. . . . As long as we all maintain the noble revolutionary spirit characteristic of our people, remain united in spirit and singular in purpose, and mobilize our resources for the sake of our national task, we shall be able to destroy the enemy's morale and overpower him with both frontal and flank attacks, thus shortening the duration of our war of liberation.

History itself ensures the victory of the Kuomintang, and there can be no questioning of history: "History bears ample witness to the fact that a revolutionary war fought for righteousness, justice, freedom, against tyranny and in answer to the unanimous wish of a people for survival and freedom cannot fail. It has been so in the past and it will be so in the future." This historical optimism re-enforces the conviction that the counteroffensive and national recovery "is not a case of wishful thinking, but the consensus of aspirations burning in the hearts of our 600 million compatriots."

The counterattack, therefore, is not an abstract idea. It involves military action as well as political and economic maneuvers. However, the GRC recognizes that it does not exist in a political vacuum and that there are limitations imposed on its freedom of action by the outside world. "The world situation today is complicated and unpredictable," Chiang declared on October 10, "and the revolutionary path is seldom smooth. In other words, it may not be possible for us to attain our goal in one leap." A month later, at the Ninth Congress of the ruling Kuomintang party on November 12, 1963, the Generalissimo further elaborated on the problem of limitations on freedom of action by stating that had a military attack been launched against the mainland in 1961, it would have succeeded. "We did not do so because we took into consideration many other factors contributing to the success of total war."[13]

In the same speech, the Generalissimo repeated his 1958 redefinition of the concept of counterattack—a redefinition originally urged upon him by Washington. Military factors, he said, account for only 30 per

---

[12] *Ibid.*
[13] *CP,* November 13, 1963.

7

cent of final victory in modern warfare. The other 70 per cent consists of diplomatic maneuverings and economic development and potential.

The basis of the ideology of counterattack, therefore, is a declaration of the need for military action against the Communists, limited by the nature of modern warfare and the international scene. The entire military and economic policy of the GRC on Taiwan has been aimed directly at creating the potential for armed conflict with Communist China. Annually, the Generalissimo and other GRC officials declare that the moment for counteroffensive action is at hand. This year the Generalissimo declared that the "time to begin counteroffensive action may now come at any minute." In order to give credence to this statement, and to maintain faith in counterattack, the Taipei newspapers play up alleged Nationalist guerrilla action against the mainland. Exactly what "any minute" means, however, is unclear. The closest Chiang came to defining it was his statement that, "though some people abroad[14] maintain that no important change will come to the Chinese Communist regime in the next three to five years, we firmly believe that both subjective and objective conditions for our return to the mainland are ripening so fast that we do not have to wait that long before we can bury Mao's regime."

The future society. The other four basic documents in the canon of the ideology of counterattack are in many ways more interesting and important than the Double Tenth Message: They provide a closer look at the type of society the Kuomintang hopes to establish on the mainland, and at the nature of this society's appeal to the Chinese on the mainland.

"The Six Freedoms" and the first part of "The Ten Pledges" describe the society the Kuomintang plans to establish on the mainland after its return. The general objective of the government will be to "restore to the people the free way of life and to ensure the continuity of Chinese cultural heritage." In order to achieve this, the Kuomintang guarantees freedom of speech, residence, assembly, publication, worship, academic study, association, and movement. Furthermore, "all political groups or civilian organizations that now *take part in the anti-Communist task* shall be able to enjoy equality and legitimate rights and interests within the constitutional framework." (Italics added.) Everyone is guaranteed food, clothing, and daily necessities "free of control." Chinese history and culture will be preserved, ethical and moral standards re-established, the family system protected, and the sanctity of marriage restored.

Certain social classes receive specific pledges. For instance, the

[14] This refers to Japanese Prime Minister Ikeda.

worker is promised the "fundamental right to choose employment," to organize trade unions freely, and to enjoy the "fruits of his honest labor without interference from the government." The peasant is promised the dismantling of the commune system; he will be allowed to retain the land he tills and will be entitled to his own harvest. The businessman is promised abolition of the "public-private–joint-ownership system" and "monopolized buying and selling" of daily necessities. He is also guaranteed the protection of "private ownership and lawful profitmaking." To the intellectual, the Kuomintang promises to "re-establish respect for rationality and reason, and encourage free academic pursuit."

The Kuomintang program, however, contains both explicit and implicit limitations on the development of democratic institutions in the future China, at least as those institutions are understood today in the "free world." For instance, the program specifically limits the enjoyment of equality and "legitimate rights and interests within the constitutional framework" to those political groups and organizations that are currently taking part in the "anti-Communist task." At no place does the program define what those "legitimate rights and interests" are, and it obviously leaves it up to the Kuomintang regime to determine who is now taking part in the "anti-Communist task." Furthermore, the program implicitly limits the very pledges it makes. Article 5 of "The Six Freedoms," for instance, states that, "in order to restore to the people their security of life and *to consolidate the foundation of society*" (italics added), the government will ban all forms of class struggle and "other like activities that tend to create hatred among the people, such as liquidation, mass trials, etc." Therefore, while guaranteeing the workers the right to organize unions, the government implicitly denies them the right to strike (a right denied them on Taiwan too, incidentally), and reserves to itself the right to determine what activities, political or otherwise, "tend to create hatred among the people." Furthermore, at no point in the program does the government guarantee free elections or any other form of free political competition. In short, the program that the Kuomintang hopes will rally support on Taiwan and appeal to the masses on the mainland does not really differ significantly from its program on the mainland before 1949. What might have been considered innovations, such as the "freedoms" the government will guarantee the people, are institutionally limited by the program itself.

The KMT's appeal to the mainland. "The Three Assurances" and the second part of "The Ten Pledges" summarize the specific methods whereby the Kuomintang hopes to rally support among the mainlanders. The appeal is more to material reward than to idealism or to ideology; it re-enforces the impression that, in fact, the KMT remains "unreconstructed" and has failed either to develop new techniques or ideas in the realm of government, or to analyze the causes for its original catastrophic defeat. For instance, officers and enlisted men who defect from the Chinese Communists "shall be generously rewarded according to [their] merits, and shall receive the same treatment as the government troops." Anyone leading a military unit against the Communists will be assigned as the commanding officer of his unit and will be guaranteed promotion and appointment as the "administrative chief of the area he has recovered for the Government." (While these may be temporary provisions operative while recovering the mainland, this latter pledge is a clear and distinct echo of the warlord system in the pre-Communist era. It also negates the possibility of the establishment of a civil service based on merit.)

It is difficult to understand how any of these pledges would appeal to personnel who undoubtedly remember, or have heard about, the oppressive and corrupt KMT military system on the mainland, or who remember the Generalissimo's relationships with many of the warlords. The same lack of imagination can be seen in the political appeal to the mainlanders: "All political and civic organizations which will have joined the Government in anti-Communist activities" are guaranteed the "opportunity under the Constitution and the principle of fair competition to contribute their efforts towards the reconstruction of a new China of the people, by the people, and for the people." They are not guaranteed free elections, and once again the KMT implicitly reserves the right to determine who has joined it and who has not.

Ideological assumptions and current policy. The ideology of counterattack is grounded on certain assumptions which dictate both domestic and foreign policy. These assumptions may be summarized briefly as follows: (1) There is only one China, and the Kuomintang regime is the legal government of that China. Two Chinas, on the model of two Germanies, Koreas, or Vietnams, is an historical, cultural, and political "absurdity." It is China's great historical tradition of unity, lacking in the other states, that dictates China's current unity. (2) Because there is only one China, and consequently only one legitimate government of China, the Communists are "rebels" or "bandits" who must be suppressed.[15] Any development on the international scene that might tend to prejudice the opportunity or the ability of the GRC to suppress the "bandits" is anathema. This includes any lessening in Cold War tensions.

The assumption that there is only one China is continually challenged from two directions. First, it is challenged by the existence of

---

[15] It is customary in Taiwan to refer, both in published materials and in speech, to the Chinese Communists as "kung-fei," or "Communist bandits."

commercial or diplomatic relations between Peking and other states. Consequently, the GRC opposes strenuously, and deems an unfriendly act, any extension of recognition in any form whatsoever to the Peking government by other nations. Japan, for instance, was a source of major irritation to Taipei in the latter half of 1963. The outstanding GRC-Japan problems are fundamentally three: Prime Minister Ikeda's public doubts concerning the possibility of Chinese Nationalist counterattack; increased Japanese trade with mainland China as exemplified by the Kurashiki Rayon Company's contract to sell a vinolyn plant to the Communists; and the disposition of Chou Hung-ching, a defector from the mainland now in Tokyo.[16] Because all three of these issues directly challenged the Kuomintang's concept of "one China," the government reacted with near hysteria to the Japanese positions. During late summer and early fall, as one problem followed the other, the government tried, unsuccessfully, to whip up public sentiment against the Japanese. Announcements of spontaneous demonstrations, many of which never actually took place, filled the newspapers. The Nationalist ambassador was recalled from Tokyo "for consultations." The newspapers tried to create a crisis atmosphere. A typical dispatch read: "The government and the ruling Kuomintang have been trying, so far successfully, to suppress any mass demonstration of anti-Japanese feelings." "We are so fed up with the Japanese that we may heed the government advice no more," one public figure announced.[17] There was much talk of a break in relations and economic retaliation. The level of hysteria indicated the government's sensitivity to the issue.

The second constant challenge to the assumption of "one China" is the unclear legal status of Taiwan. Neither the Japanese surrender documents nor the Japanese Peace Treaty clearly settles the issue. Furthermore, the government is morbidly afraid of Taiwanese self-consciousness. Consequently, it reacts with vigor to any suggestion that Taiwan may not be part of China, since if it is not, the GRC itself is an illegal organization usurping power in territory not rightfully belonging to it. An editorial in the *China Post* for August 5, 1963, illustrates the fine point of detail the regime observes on this issue. "That Taiwan is a province of the Republic of China is an elementary fact which should be known to all those who have visited this island or have had any official or non-official dealings with Free China," it began. It then

---

[16] The designation to be used by the Chinese Nationalist Olympic Team at the 1964 Tokyo Olympics is also an issue, but one not directly affecting Sino-Japanese bilateral relations. Except for the initials ROC (i.e., Republic of China), which will appear on the athletes' jerseys, the island will be designated "Taiwan," which, to the GRC, is a direct affront.

[17] *CP*, October 29, 1963.

11

proceeded to praise the United States Armed Forces Radio and Tele-
vision Service for always being "meticulously careful to emphasize that
it serves the American military community in the Republic of China
and is located in Taiwan 'with studios' . . . in downtown Taipei."[18]
What ired the government was a press release by the U.S. AID mission
to China, dated August 1, which identified Taiwan "as a country along
with the Philippines and Thailand." To quote: "Taiwan has been chosen
as one of three Far East countries for a U.S. AID-supported private
investment survey. . . . If the survey findings are favorable, one of the
three countries—Taiwan, Philippines, or Thailand—may be selected for
investment in the field of plastics manufacture." No one should blame
the Chinese people, the paper commented, for being so sensitive on this
point. "They are sensitive because they know only too well that many
people in foreign countries have been insisting that the so-called status
of Taiwan is still an open question, and that there are others who would
like to see the emergence of an 'independent Taiwan' or a 'Formosan
Republic' as a possible solution of the 'China Question.' " The paper
concluded, "We do not like to see the continuance of a questionable
practice, especially if it is remembered that it is fraught with political
undertones."

Because the ideology of counterattack explicitly includes prepara-
tions for an eventual armed attack on mainland China, the GRC must
oppose any trends toward a lessening of international tension in the
Cold War. Any lessening of international tension, it reasons, might result
in the slacking off of American military aid, and might even destroy the
rationale of counterattack itself. Consequently, to cite one example, the
China Post, which faithfully represents the Kuomintang point of view,
severely criticized Walter Lippmann's article "Dealing With the Soviet
Union," originally published in *Newsweek* on July 22, 1963. The primary object of criticism was Lippmann's statement that the "vital national interest of the Russians is to check the expansion of the Chinese
into Russian Siberia, and, because the Russians are Westerners, to make
peace with the West." The *China Post* insisted that Russians are not
Westerners because, "If the Russians are Westerners, the conventional
references to the cold war as one between West and East would be
meaningless." Furthermore, "To say that it is the vital interest of the
Russians to check Chinese Communist expansion into Siberia is to
engage in daydreaming and to indulge in wishful thinking." The Chinese,
the *China Post* insisted, had never had any interest in expanding into
Siberia. Furthermore, Lippmann's position that nationalism was perhaps
as important if not more important a motivating factor than Communism

[18] *Ibid.,* August 5, 1963.

in the Soviet Union was simply false. Lippmann was also accused of being a bad historian. He erred in suggesting that the Chinese Communists had conquered the mainland without significant Soviet aid, and he erred in suggesting that the United States was involved in the Quemoy crisis of 1958. "Doesn't Mr. Lippmann know that the offshore islands have not been defended by American troops, but by government troops of the Republic of China?," asked the *Post*. (Of course, there is an American Military Assistance and Advisory Group team on Quemoy, although it has no defensive functions.) The extent of the GRC's exasperation with Lippmann can be seen in the epithets it used to attack him: "dangerous," "pure fancy," "ridiculous." But what most disturbed the GRC was the belief that Lippmann's ideas "seem to reflect the official policy that is being followed by Washington."[19]

The GRC fear of a Soviet-American detente influences policy decisions as well as policy theory. The regime was seriously disturbed by the Partial Nuclear Test Ban Treaty which, it felt, might lead to future accords that would prejudice its plans for a comeback against the Chinese Communists. The Taipei press, on the day after the initialing of the Treaty, expressed fears that it might lead to a new spirit of Yalta, and recalled the conference toward the end of World War II at which China was pressured into signing a treaty with the Soviet Union granting the latter certain privileges on Chinese soil. Consequently, the regime debated the Treaty for more than a week before agreeing, probably under American pressure, to sign.[20]

President Kennedy's announcement in mid-November that the United States "is not wedded to a policy of hostility to Red China" also disturbed the regime. The statement "has taken every sensible person by surprise," a government organ stated. If the United States hesitates in taking the lead in eliminating the Chinese Communist regime, "she is either aiding the enemy or bring [*sic*] trouble to herself."[21]

The ideology's institutional implications. The ideology of counterattack also has certain specific institutional implications for the government in addition, of course, to its military posture. Justifying itself on the grounds that with most of China under "bandit" control it is impossible to hold national elections (the government continues to hold provincial elections on Taiwan), the regime has abrogated all national electoral procedures for the duration of the "civil war." The last elections for the two most important national legislative bodies, the Legislative Yuan (the national legislature) and the National Assembly (the elec-

[19] *Ibid.*, August 12, 1963.
[20] The initial coincidence of opinions between Taipei and Peking concerning the treaty should be noted.
[21] *CP*, November 11, 1963.

toral college with power to elect the president and amend the constitution), were held in 1947. The regime believes, understandably, that to hold new national elections in only one section of China would be tantamount to the recognition of the existence of two Chinas.

The natural consequence of the electoral-abrogation policy is the inability of the government to renew its elective offices (with the exception of the president, who is not constitutionally elected by popular vote, anyway). While, theoretically, electoral procedures will be reinstated once the regime returns to power on the mainland, in reality, in the absence of such a return, the regime has embarked on a policy that must inevitably lead to electoral suicide. As members of the various national legislative bodies disappear through death or illness brought on by old age, the institutions themselves will disappear from the national context. The position of the president must itself eventually fall vacant, since the disappearance of the National Assembly would leave no constitutional procedures available for selection of the president. This does not apply, of course, to appointive offices or the civil service, where it remains possible to introduce younger blood.[22]

The authoritarianism that permeates the island's entire political structure, together with the inability to introduce new blood into national elective institutions, has led to the growing impotency and functional atrophy of specific institutions, as well as to a loss of interest in their activities among the members themselves.[23] In June, 1962, for instance, some sixty members of the Legislative Yuan held a tea party to discuss the functioning of that body. They were worried because they felt that the Legislative Yuan was "on the verge of paralysis," and that too many of the members found its meetings "more and more uninteresting." As an example, they cited a scheduled joint meeting on June 7 of the judicial, laws, education, and internal affairs committees to discuss the regulations controlling the motion picture industry. The meeting had been called for 3:00 P.M., but by 4:30 only six of the 130 members of the four committees had appeared and the meeting had to be canceled for lack of a quorum.[24]

In November, 1962, the Control Yuan, which is the highest supervisory and "watch dog" organ of the national government, announced that it was unable to perform its duties effectively. Impeachments and

[22] Actually, of course, some constitutional solution to this problem could be found. However, although this problem is recognized by many thinking Chinese, public discussion of it is out of the question since such a discussion would itself connote a long-term stay for the regime on the island, and this would contradict its present policy of return.

[23] This is also the result of the abrogation of their powers to the president under certain "emergency provisions" appended to the constitution.

[24] *Cheng-hsin hsin-wen pao* (hereafter *CHHWP*), June 8, 1962.

14

accusations of illegal activities or misdeeds on the part of members of other branches of the government brought no response.[25] In the Control Yuan's annual meeting in 1962, one member claimed that the Yuan was a "dog which barks but cannot bite." A judge who had been accused by the Control Yuan of misdeeds was not only not punished or degraded, the Yuan claimed, but even received a special promotion, "thus proving that the authorities are consciously acting against the Control Yuan."[26]

In 1963, the Control Yuan found a similar situation in other government organs. On November 9, it accused the government of negating and nullifying its civil-service system. Out of 200,000 civil servants on Taiwan (approximately 40,000 in the central government and 160,000 in provincial and local governments), only 9,000 had passed the government's own qualifying examinations. Although some 600 persons annually passed the state civil-service exams, the Yuan claimed, "most government agencies have their own way of hiring personnel, and they are not interested in hiring persons who have passed the government examinations."[27] The Yuan also claimed that it was subjected to "obstructions and pressures" from outside in carrying out its constitutional functions. One member cited the case of a judge who was investigated for tax evasion. The judge, in return, threatened the members of the Control Yuan with a countercharge. In a stagnant constitutional situation such as exists on Taiwan, personal pressures obviously play a larger role than they ordinarily would, even in a society as highly oriented toward personal relationships in politics as China.

The concepts of "one China" and counterattack also prevent the government from allowing Taiwanese personnel to fill the number of positions that would proportionally and normally be their due, given the fact that they make up nine-elevenths of the effective population of the Republic of China today. The Taiwanization of the regime would contradict the government's claim to be representative of all China, it feels. (Consequently, even though membership in the ruling Kuomintang party may now be about 30 per cent Taiwanese, the party does not like to admit this and keeps control firmly in the hands of mainlanders, even in the provincial party apparatus.) The fact that even the Taiwan provincial government administration is overwhelmingly mainlander on its higher levels is a source of social friction. The director of the Taiwan Provincial Personnel Department announced on November 5, 1963, that the number of Taiwanese in the provincial government service had more

---

[25] Under the constitution, the Control Yuan has powers of investigation and impeachment, but disciplinary powers fall under the Judicial Yuan.

[26] *CHHWP,* November 16, 1962.

[27] *The China News* (hereafter CN), November 9, 1963.

than doubled since 1945, the end of Japanese colonial administration.[28] What he failed to point out, of course, was that the Taiwanese population (as opposed to mainland-born Taiwanese) had also almost doubled since 1945, and that proportionally, therefore, there had been much less of an increase in Taiwanese participation in the provincial civil service than would have been expected, given the fact that Taiwanese now have legal equality with mainlanders (rather than colonial status, as they had under the Japanese) and that they make up the overwhelming majority of the population in the province. This phenomenon on the provincial level, however, must be explained by the regime's unwillingness to allow the Taiwanese, whose dedication to the goals of the central government is considered questionable, any more access to administrative positions than is absolutely necessary.

The cult of personality. The GRC's entire political and ideological posture is shored up by a remarkably highly developed cult of Chiang Kai-shek's personality. Larger than life-sized statues of the President stand at major crossroads. Twenty-foot photographs and paintings of him cover public structures on national holidays. His image appears on postage stamps. Buildings are painted with such slogans as "President Chiang, our nation's star of salvation." On October 31, 1963, he celebrated his seventy-sixth birthday with all the fanfare of a Stalinesque cult of personality. Special cigarettes, the "Presidential Brand," were issued this year, as in the past, to signify the occasion. The newspapers sang paeons of praise. Calling him an "indispensable source of hope and strength," the "beloved leader," the "supreme leader," the *China Post* declared that, "With such a great leader as President Chiang at the helm of the Chinese ship of state, those of us who have come from the mainland cannot but be quite confident that the day is not far distant when we shall be able to return to our homes to be reunited with our beloved ones."[29] Even foreign diplomats got into the act. The Turkish ambassador publicly praised the Generalissimo as a man "whose life has been spontaneously devoted to the destiny of his nation." The Spanish ambassador described the President as "one of the greatest statesmen of the world and his colossal stature derives both from his political genius and his being the Apostle of Chinese nationalism." And the Vatican's Apostolic Internuncio declared, through his representative, that Chiang "personifies the very soul of the Chinese race."[30]

The omnipresent cult of personality lends itself to the conclusion that the Generalissimo is more interested in holding on to power for its own sake than in really attempting a return to the mainland at the risk

[28] *CN,* November 16, 1963.
[29] *CP,* October 31, 1963.
[30] *Ibid.*

of losing his power should he fail. Former intimates of the President suggest that he is the type of person who would rather go down in history as the "hero who never gave up" than as the man who tried but failed. The passage of time, the rigors of old age, and continued American reluctance to give the KMT the logistic support to attempt a counter-attack make the eventual return of the present regime to the mainland less and less likely. As a consequence, the "ideology of counterattack" becomes more and more a means of justifying, no matter how illogically, the continuation of the present regime in power. It is no longer a description of the regime's realistic objectives.

THE VIABILITY OF THE KUOMINTANG REGIME

The growing realization and acceptance, both internationally and on the island itself, of the unlikelihood of the KMT regime's return to the mainland make it necessary to evaluate the viability of the regime against a different frame of reference than its announced goals. The viability of the regime will be its ability to remain in power through inevitable and accidental crises. Inevitably, the Generalissimo, now 76, will die or disappear from the political scene due to ill health or the infirmities of old age.[31] This will open the way for a power struggle and an eventual readjustment of power relationships within the party and the government. Accidentally, the tension between the islanders and the mainlanders could erupt into overt conflict, as it did on February 28, 1947. Such an eruption could coincide with the Generalissimo's death. The economic, social, and intellectual health of the island will, to a large extent, determine the viability of the regime in such crises. An evaluation of the state of Taiwan's health should also contribute to the assessment of the contribution Taiwan, and the Kuomintang regime, can make to the free world's defenses in the Far East.

Economic viability. A healthy economy on Taiwan is a *sine qua non* for both the maintenance of the Kuomintang's internal strength, and the mounting of a counterattack against mainland China. In recognition of this, the United States has poured vast amounts of economic aid into the island. Since 1951, Washington has given Taipei about $3.5 billion in military and economic assistance. The result, according to Howard L. Parsons, Director of the U.S. Agency for International Development Mission to the Republic of China, is that the "economy of the Republic of China is lively and growing rapidly." Parsons, in a speech before the American Chamber of Commerce in Manila on

---

31 The regime's doubts about its own viability can be seen in the fact that the problem of succession to the Generalissimo is a taboo subject in the nation's press and in public discussion.

November 4, 1963, stated that Taiwan's gross national product has annually increased by 6 per cent and that, "despite a high rate of population growth," there has been an annual increase in per capita income of 3-4 per cent. "Population growth is slowing down a little," Parsons continued, "so per capita gains in the future may be even better." Industry continues to grow by more than 12 per cent a year, according to Parsons, and, since 1956, exports have more than doubled.

Taiwan's agriculture also shows important improvements. As a result of JCRR's land-reform program, from 1949 to 1959 the number of farmers owning their own land jumped from about 210,000 to more than 470,000 and agricultural output rose about 40 per cent. Parsons, in the same Manila speech, stated that "agricultural production has kept ahead of population increase" on Taiwan.[32]

The United States considers, therefore, that its program of economic aid to Taiwan has brought the island to the "take-off point" from where it can begin "to go it alone." The economy, again according to AID Director Parsons, "has now [November 1963] reached a degree of development, and it is achieving a credit-worthiness, which will make it possible for the Republic of China to secure its needs for external capital from the traditional international sources drawn upon by developed economies." Consequently, Parsons continues, the "Agency for International Development foresees that within a short time the Republic of China will no longer need assistance on concessional terms from the United States." Consequently, an American delegation, headed by Joseph A. Yager of the State Department's Policy Planning Staff, began talks with Chinese officials in mid-November in Taipei on the future of American assistance to Taiwan.

The assumption which appears to underlie American assessment of the economic aid program is that the economy's growth is an important basis for political stability. This would undoubtedly be true if large sectors of the population—the peasants and the urban working class—participated in economic growth, actually or psychologically. Despite the rosy statistical picture, however, there are signs that the actual economic outlook on Taiwan provides less grounds for optimism. The rise in income has been offset, it would appear, by rising taxes to meet the government's enormous defense budget, as well as by a slow but steady inflation unaccompanied by a proportionate increase in wages, particularly in the cities. People of all but the highest class continue to complain that they have to work harder to maintain a lower standard of living now than before. Furthermore, the economy may be much less stable

---

[32] For Parsons' speech, see USIS Press Release, Taipei, Taiwan, PR-63-524, November 4, 1963.

than either the Americans or the Chinese will admit. An AID film on private industry in Taiwan, for instance, had to be delayed not long ago because six of the twenty firms chosen as examples of economic success either failed or were drastically reorganized during the film's shooting schedule. Another indication of economic difficulty is that the average marriage age among the Taiwanese appears to have risen recently. While this may be part of the modernization process, the Taiwanese themselves explain it in terms of growing economic hardships.

Agriculture, statistically one of the healthiest sectors of the economy, also contributes to the doubts concerning the island's economic success. A growing population, rising prices, and rising taxes may have prevented any real increase in the peasants' standard of living.[33] The size of private farms has begun to diminish;[34] there are also widespread rumors of the recreation of old landed estates, particularly in the southern part of the island. Even the press had to admit that, at the end of 1961, increased special "defense taxes" lowered the peasants' standard of living almost to where it had been ten years before. The eventual abolition of the defense surtax did not, as had been expected, result in relief.[35] Furthermore, in many rice-growing and rice-consuming areas, peasants still consume more sweet potatoes than rice.[36] This is particularly significant in a culture where sweet potatoes are usually considered animal fodder and are consumed by humans only in time of famine.[37] Too many peasants simply cannot afford to consume their own rice. In addition to paying high taxes, the peasant must purchase his fertilizer from the government on unfavorable terms.[38] The peasants find it difficult to obtain relief through farm loans. Confusion of offices, conditions, rates, terms, and amounts makes the farm-loan situation difficult. Furthermore, there have been serious charges of corruption. "The real farmers who are badly in need of loans are not in a position to get those loans," a Taipei paper remarked.[39]

[33] This appears to be particularly true psychologically. While there are visual signs of agricultural prosperity—more brick houses, some electrical appliances, and so forth—peasants complain widely that they have not benefited from the economy's growth.

[34] *CHHWP,* November 18, 1962.

[35] *CP,* November 15, 1963.

[36] See *Lien-ho pao* (hereafter *LHP*), November 18, 1962, which states that in Tainan County, for instance, the average peasant consumes 320.9 grams of rice per day and 355.5 grams of sweet potatoes per day.

[37] According to one informant, a private survey recently showed that the average calorie intake of a Taiwanese peasant today is only 1,300 calories as against the official figure of 2,000.

[38] See Sheppard Glass's article in this volume. See also *CHHWP,* June 13, 1962. which gives another, less favorable, view of this problem.

[39] *Ibid.,* November 15, 1962.

Perhaps one of the most graphic illustrations of the economic problem is the fact that, according to the Taipei city health office, primary school children in the capital between six and twelve years of age are shorter and lighter than Japanese students of the same age. "This is an alarming signal," one paper commented; "the next generation will be less well than the previous one. . . . We have always humiliated the Japanese for being shorter; how can we face the next generation?"[40]

Unemployment or underemployment evidently is also a worrisome problem for the regime. According to statistics issued at the beginning of 1963 for the year 1961, the total population of Taiwan was 11,149,139 at the end of 1961. Of this figure, 6,775,146 were included in the "labor force," though precisely what constitutes the labor force in a still largely agrarian economy is not clear. Of the government-defined "labor force," 3,428,525, or 49.4 per cent were employed at the end of 1961.[41] While the precision of these statistics (that is, exactly who were included in the labor force, how long they were "unemployed," and so forth), is not verifiable, the statistics indicate an important problem. One of Taipei's leading papers pointed out that "further analysis shows that our employment of labor is dropping."[42] While one may argue that high rates of underemployment are characteristic of developing societies, it is, at the same time, important to recognize that high unemployment is not conducive to political stability.

Another problem confronting the government is the low salary scale of its own employees. "The pay problem of government employees and servicemen," the *China Post* said, "has become more and more serious because of the constantly upward movement of commodity prices, especially the prices of daily necessities. The pinch is particularly keenly felt by those belonging to the low-income brackets, who have to devote all their earnings to such daily articles."[43] A low-ranking officer in the armed forces may receive only NT$300 to NT$400 (NT$1.00 is approximately US$0.04) a month, in addition to certain quantities of rice, oil, and so on, while enlisted men and noncommissioned officers receive even less. "Yet he has to feed a family of five persons," the *Post* continued.[44] At the same time that salaries are low in the government service, enormous differences exist between the lower and the upper echelons of the government. "Complaints are also heard against unfair treatments with a small number of high-ranking personnel enjoying various privileges," the *Post* pointed out. Ma Kung-chen, a member

[40] *Ibid.*, October 24, 1963. See also *CP*, November 10, 1963.
[41] *LHP*, January 14, 1963.
[42] *Ibid.*
[43] *CP*, November 18, 1963.
[44] *Ibid.*, November 8, 1963.

of the Control Yuan, announced that his body had discovered that "key post holders" draw special allowances of NT$100,000 or more per month. He also said that many of the nation's top military officers, "live like princes," and that their relations with their men are becoming "remote."[45] While this may not be corruption in the same sense of the naked corruption prevalent in the Kuomintang regime on the mainland before 1949, it is not dissimilar in its demoralizing effects upon the government bureaucracy.

The GRC, aware of political implications of economic stability, is opposed to the American policy, now under consideration, of bringing concesssional aid to a close. This concern shows that the GRC is less sanguine than Mr. Parsons about the success of the AID program. The continuing defense-budget burden (which the government cannot afford to decrease without weakening the GRC's political position vis-à-vis "counterattack"), the growing population problem, and the basic economic instability will continue to "tighten the nation's purse-strings." Taking issue with Parsons' statement that exports have more than doubled since 1956, the Chinese government pointed out that "much of Taiwan's export value was inflated by the soaring world sugar price and that the boom may not last very long."[46] What has been left unsaid, of course, is that American concessional aid has also been a source of psychological stability for the KMT regime, an important symbol of American political support which, if lost, could seriously jeopardize the GRC's image of total power over the island.

Corruption. Economic difficulties may go a long way toward explaining the widespread corruption that afflicts Taiwan. Today, corruption is rife in public service, the school system, and private industry. While the regime apparently has been successful, since its arrival on the island in 1949, in avoiding the *grand* corruption that was so much a part of it on the mainland, it has been unsuccessful in controlling widespread corruption on most levels of government, national and local. At one point toward the end of 1962, for instance, the magistrates and mayors of several important counties and cities on the island, including the capital, were either in jail or before the courts.[47] Corruption affects such programs as public housing,[48] heavy industry,[49] and national resources.[50] It also affects the tax system. The Control Yuan stated last year that the tax burden falls most heavily on the poorer

---

[45] *Ibid.,* November 7, 1963. To what extent this is generally true is not clear.
[46] *CN,* November 18, 1963, and *CP,* November 19, 1963.
[47] *CHHWP,* November 16, 1962.
[48] *CN,* November 18, 1963.
[49] *CHHWP,* November 16, 1962.
[50] *Ibid.,* June 13, 1962.

segments of the population, since many rich people and military welfare organizations engaged in commercial business avoid paying taxes.[51] Corruption, therefore, seriously affects the efficiency of government. The mayor of Chiayi City, Su Yü-heng, himself before the courts for bribing high Kuomintang officials in connection with his nomination as mayor, confessed that once, when his city treasury was so empty that he was unable to pay employees' salaries, he had had to bribe the magistrate of Chiayi County in order to get an advance on funds for the daily running of his administration. In order to obtain an advance of NT$300,000, he had had to pay a "commission" of NT$25,000 to the magistrate.[52]

The police are also subject to corruption. A member of the Provincial Assembly in 1962 pointed out, for instance, that police personnel use bribes to obtain more advantageous assignments. In the P'ing-tung district in the southern part of the island, policemen were accused of paying between NT$20,000 and NT$30,000 for assignment to prostitution areas, which were considered "goldmines" for bribery. The P'ing-tung Chief of Police himself ran a prostitution house. Although he was accused, he was not punished but was transferred to another post; he later returned to threaten his accuser.[53] Even the Foreign Affairs Police, in charge of foreigners resident on Taiwan, are involved in smuggling, bribery, and other forms of corruption.[54]

High position, party connections, and personal influence can also affect the outcome of judicial proceedings. One of the most notorious cases in recent Taiwan history involved the mayor of Taipei, Huang Chi-jui, who was involved in a bribery case in the City Bus Administration. Although convicted by lower courts, Huang and the director of the Bus Administration were acquitted by the High Court. Two of the judges of the High Court were later promoted to the Supreme Court, and Mrs. Huang, who was convicted of receiving NT$300,000 in bribes, was given a deferred jail sentence. As one member of the Control Yuan pointed out, the wife of the director of the Provincial Forestry Administration, who had previously been involved in a similar case, was given a sentence of eight years for the same offense.[55]

Perhaps one of the most socially demoralizing forms of corruption involves the school system. Promotion or transfer of teachers often depends on bribes. One provincial assembly member estimated that

[51] *Ibid,* November 16, 1962.
[52] *LHP,* November 21, 1962.
[53] *Ibid.,* July 10, 1962.
[54] See, for instance, *CP,* November 19, 1963.
[55] *CN,* November 16, 1963. The director himself was also jailed, since the court held that he must have been a party to the case.

some 53,000 primary school teachers on Taiwan have had at one time or another to pay bribes to obtain or retain their positions.[56] In one famous case, a primary school teacher in Hsin-chu, outside of Taipei, obtained permission to transfer to Changhua, in central Taiwan. Upon arriving in Changhua, she was informed that she would be appointed to a school the quality of which would depend on the size of the bribe she could offer.[57] School directors have asked for, and received, commissions for the building of school facilities. Furthermore, principals and headmasters often live far beyond their official incomes, raising serious corruption questions.[58] The demoralizing effects of this on both teachers and students is great. Education Minister Huang Chi-lu, avoiding the fundamental moral questions, has urged "all schools to pay more attention to the personalities and private lives of teachers." According to Minister Huang, for instance, murders committed by teachers are a "very serious problem." The chairman of the Legislative Yuan's education committee also stated that educational authorities paid too little attention to "character guidance education," which, he says, "is the reason why there have been so many accidents involving teachers."[59]

Petty corruption in Chinese society is often explained away by specialists in terms of historical tradition and cultural phenomena. It can also be interpreted as a form of social mobility. However, on Taiwan at least, corruption must be considered against the background of the policy objectives of the regime and its claims to success. The KMT evidently finds it impossible to control corruption. Furthermore, the failure to punish corruption once it is discovered leads to more corruption. In the school system, it has a distinct demoralizing effect on the next generation. In general, it is a serious flaw in a society which, officially at least, is prepared to carry out a counterattack against mainland China.

A divided society. Economic problems and corruption form only the background to the two great divisions that rend the island's society today.

Taiwan is deeply divided between the islanders and the mainlanders. Except for the small aboriginal tribes, Taiwan was originally settled by mainlanders—chiefly from Fukien province across the Straits from Taiwan. The most important first wave of settlement came in the seventeenth century, at the end of the Ming and the beginning of the Ch'ing dynasties. While the Taiwanese dialect is today approximately the same as Amoy or Minnan-hwa on the mainland opposite, the islanders, in the

[56] *CHHWP,* October 22, 1963.
[57] *CHHWP,* August 16, 1963.
[58] *Tzu-li wan-pao* (hereafter *TLWP*), August 4, 1963.
[59] *CP,* November 5, 1963.

course of about 300 years of physical (and, under the Japanese, 50 years of political) separation from the mainland, developed certain distinctive characteristics. Nevertheless, until February 28, 1947, the islanders remained conscious of their Chinese origins and strongly identified with the mainland, as witness their joyous reception of the Chinese "liberators" in 1945. A great deal of Taiwan's active intellectual life in the 1920's and 1930's was influenced by developments on the mainland and sought identification with mainland culture and intellectual movements. Consequently, the communal feeling that has developed since 1947 is, in many respects, a *negative* reaction. The result of discrimination and persecution, it has led to a deep-seated self-consciousness of Taiwanese as Taiwanese. Nevertheless, Taiwanese communalism is a most important political and intellectual phenomenon on the island today.

Growing Taiwanese self-consciousness has been fed, and continues to be fed, by the Kuomintang's administrative practices and political objectives. Many Taiwanese feel that they are discriminated against in public administration and education. They are politically disenfranchised on the national level and intellectually silenced. They are not allowed to form political organizations, even on the provincial level, where the Governor himself is a mainlander. Nor are they allowed what they feel is their proportional due in appointments to high civil or military positions. They dislike their island being used as a base for a policy of return to a mainland few of them have ever seen—a policy which, since February, 1947, they have grown to resent deeply. Many Taiwanese will admit that they wanted to be Chinese, but they add that the Chinese would not let them. Instead, the mainlander regime has consistently and methodically tried to wipe out all vestiges of Japanese cultural influence on the Taiwanese, an influence that many older Taiwanese now feel was beneficial, and that brought intellectual flowering and social modernization to the island.

The adult mainlander, in his turn, looks down on the Taiwanese as a provincial who was denied the benefits of Chinese civilization for a generation. On the one hand, he resents finding himself in an alien environment far from home with receding hopes of returning. For a decade or more, the mainlander lived in Taiwan "temporarily," usually refusing to buy land, even if he could afford it, or to purchase furniture or other more or less permanent items. He has looked on Taiwan as a way station back to the mainland. His declining economic situation— many government-employed mainlanders were wealthy on the mainland —has embittered him. Part of his bitterness is directed against the Taiwanese who, he feels, have been favored by American AID policies.

As prospects for returning to the mainland fade, his hopelessness and bitterness grow, and he thinks only of sending his children away from Taiwan. Taiwan may be politically part of China, from the mainlander point of view, but it is not part of the China the mainlander would like to live in. America is preferable.

Institutional contact between Taiwanese and mainlanders is minimal. Intermarriage is a much less common phenomenon than one would expect under the circumstances, and where intermarriage has taken place, it is usually among exsoldiers and other comparatively "lowclass" groups, from the Chinese point of view. Most commercial organizations are either Taiwanese or mainlander, rarely mixed.[60] On the whole, little social contact is found between Taiwanese and mainlanders, regardless of age or social level. Even in schools, Taiwanese and mainlanders evidently tend to group together. In Taipei, certain regions of the city have been taken over by the mainlanders, who moved into those areas and buildings formerly occupied by the Japanese (a move which, psychologically, at least, transformed some of the anti-Japanese resentment into anti-Mainlander resentment). Within both groups, of course, social and economic distinctions are fairly clearly drawn. In a sense, Taiwan has two parallel societies: Both the Taiwanese and the mainlanders have their class distinctions, their rich and their poor, their powerful and their weak. One important difference, however, is that the island's peasantry is overwhelmingly Taiwanese, a fact the regime cannot afford to forget. Nor can it forget that the vast majority of important private business organizations are Taiwanese-owned or -controlled.

Both parallel societies—islander and mainlander—are in turn riven by differences between the generations, the problems of "fathers and sons." Differences in generations are a problem in many modern societies, but rarely is the experience of one generation so different from that of the next as on Taiwan. The younger generation—islander or mainlander, but under thirty years of age—speaks of itself as "cut off" from its fathers. The issues are clear.

The mainlander "fathers" came to Taiwan in midcareer or midlife, having lived through the war with Japan and the subsequent Civil War. Many of them experienced only flight; many experienced flight and idealism: Mainland China held, and continues to hold, their only hopes for a return to normality, if they would have it, or for the construction of a "New China," if they are liberals. Taiwan is neither home nor hope. Nieh Hua-ling, perhaps the most talented young woman writer on Taiwan today, put the problem of the "father" generation among main-

---

[60] Even among the mainlanders, commercial organizations tend to be specialized, i.e., they may be Mainlander-Cantonese, Mainlander-Shanghai, and so forth.

landers on Taiwan very poignantly in her short story "The Purse."[61]
Li Huan, the heroine, is thirty-four, and therefore old enough at the
time the story takes place (1961 at the latest) to have graduated from
college on the mainland. But, in the course of her moving to Taiwan,
she has acquired a friend's name and identity card, together with the
friend's age, forty-two. Li Huan's great problem is fundamentally this:
Her identification card, and therefore her identity, are false, and this
poisons her relationships with her friends and the world in general. In
the end she resolves it in the only way she can:

> The Taipei City Court was some blocks away, on Chungking South Road,
> but she would walk instead of taking a pedicab. And when she got there,
> she would lay the identity card on the desk and tell them it was false and
> she wanted a new one for herself. . . . It wouldn't be pleasant. But when
> it was over, she would be thirty-four again. And maybe this time she
> would be able to do more with the eight years that would be given back
> to her.

Li Huan's position on Taiwan (and the author seems to imply the
same of the position of the entire older generation) is essentially false.
They have both left their identification at home on the mainland and,
consequently, have failed to build constructive lives, or to contribute to
social reconstruction, on the island.

The younger mainlander generation, the "sons," have no false
identity. In fact, they have no identity at all; their identity cards clearly
state that they are Szechwanese or Hunanese or Cantonese—all the
mainland provinces that they, for the most part, have never seen, or of
which they retain only the dimmest recollections. Many are born, and
more have been educated, on Taiwan, but they are not allowed legally
or psychologically to identify with the island. Officially, their attention
is riveted on the mainland and on the hope of returning to it. Actually,
they recognize the hollowness of the "ideology of return." "The swelling
of the silken afternoon opens to the steps of horses on expedition/Which
rise and fall like the fizzling of firecrackers/In celebration of the Chinese
New Year. The refrain of expedition/Lingers/In the glory of boundless
ashes," writes the young poet Yeh Wei-lien.[62] "We are the desperate
generation, with no hope," a young mainlander remarks.

Among the Taiwanese, the break in continuity between generations
is even sharper. In effect, there are two cultures, which often do not
speak the same language. The Taiwanese "fathers" were for the most

[61] Nieh Hua-ling, "The Purse" (Taipei, 1962), pp. 3–22.
[62] In Lucian Wu, *New Chinese Writing* (Taipei, 1962), p. 141.

part born, and all were raised, under the Japanese. They were to a significant extent assimilated in the Japanese culture; through it they started on the path to modernization. They studied in Japanese language schools in a modern educational system established by the Japanese. In the 1920's and 1930's, the intellectuals among them participated in the anti-Japanese movements, and in 1945 they welcomed the Chinese from the mainland as brothers and liberators from the yoke of Japanese colonialism. But the Taiwanese "fathers" also went through the agony of February 28, 1947. They experienced the humiliation of seeing their hopes, and their identities as Chinese, violated by corruption and oppression and physical violence by rulers who came from a region in many ways less highly developed than their own island. Pushed to the breaking point, they rose in a chaotic revolt that was systematically suppressed. In the course of suppression, the Taiwanese lost a whole generation of leaders; many families lost fathers, brothers, and sons. The agony transformed their view of Japan. They began to think of their former oppressor with nostalgia and longing. Today, many of the older generation of Taiwanese look back to the Japanese period as the "good old days," and speak Japanese in preference to Mandarin Chinese, if they can speak the latter at all. Given free political choice, they would most likely choose independence first and reunion with Japan second.

The younger Taiwanese generation—those under thirty—remember the Japanese period vaguely. Only the oldest among them may have been in grammar school during the Japanese era. They were educated largely under the Chinese in Mandarin; and Chinese traditions, Sun Yat-sen, and Chiang Kai-shek replaced Japanese culture and the Emperor as focal points in their political universe. Most of them do not read or speak Japanese, and they have little or no nostalgia for the Japanese period. This is one of the great dividing points between them and their fathers, one of the great breaks in the island's cultural continuity. At the same time that they escaped the agony of disappointment of the February 28 revolt, however, they also escaped the decades of identification with the mainland that characterized Taiwanese intellectual life in the last two decades of Japan's half-century rule over Taiwan. The point of departure from the mainlanders for them is social and political discrimination, unequal treatment in the armed forces (Taiwanese may not hold responsible military positions), discrimination in obtaining bureaucratic appointments, and so forth. The idea of returning to the mainland is for them, as for their fathers, meaningless, but for different reasons: The majority find themselves treated like a minority on their own island. They know that the better jobs in most fields, except in private industry and commerce, will be reserved for mainlanders. They reject the idea of fighting for a mainland China whose representatives on Taiwan have rejected them. At the same time, the impact of fifteen years of Chinese education on Taiwan has been to break the cultural continuity. Given the opportunity, many of them would like to be part of a new and democratic China, rejecting both Communists and Nationalists. Short of this—and most realize how short of this goal reality falls—they would choose independence as the solution for Taiwan's problem of identity. Few, if any, look to Japan, as do their fathers.

No bridge of tradition crosses the chasm that separates the young generation of both societies from their fathers. Among the mainlanders, particularly among the intellectuals, the Confucian tradition of Imperial China was rejected in their own youth in the days of the May Fourth Movement. The government has tried to revive this tradition among today's youth, but with little apparent success. The students study the Confucian classics in school, but Confucian precepts have become more cant than belief. Among the Taiwanese, the continuity of tradition is also lacking. The young Taiwanese today simply is not interested in Confucianism or the Chinese tradition: He appears to absorb much less of it from the educational system than the mainlander of the same age. But, at the same time, the heady intellectual tradition of Taiwan in the 1920's and 1930's, when Taiwan received the impact of the ideologies then current in the world, is also a historical memory rather than a current reality. Even the political, social, and often the creative literature of that period, which was mostly written in Japanese, is now lost to the young Taiwanese.

Intellectual and moral stagnation. The island's intellectual life today is a combination of stagnation, despair, and resignation. The Kuomintang regime has cut the island off from contact with the more vital aspects of modern Chinese culture, largely because the Chinese Communists have claimed the best of China's modern writers, painters, and poets as their own. Consequently, few if any people under thirty have read Lu Hsün or Mao Tun or other great Chinese writers of the twentieth century. (One student remarked, "If the Communists made the eating of rice part of their dogma, we on Taiwan would be required to eat bread.") No new writers have appeared or dared to write anything at all important about the problems of Taiwanese society or China's recent history. The subjects are politically too dangerous. The young writer today despairs of the present and is resigned to a future that holds no hope. He cannot grow from the literary roots of modern China on the mainland; he finds the Confucian tradition inapplicable to his current situation; and he finds only meaninglessness in the im-

28

mediate future. In the poem "Where Quietude Reigns," Yeh Wei-lien expresses the resignation of the younger generation:[63]

> Where quietude reigns a tract
> of watery sensations adrift
> to and from the still floor
> Autumn falls abruptly by the eaves
> As the syllables of voices flame
> out of the uncouth chambers of the heart
> The enveloping night mystifies
> the eye and the visible
> Autumn falls in where quietude reigns
> The room sinks into a trance in brew
> Rustling of leaves from distant provinces
> Rustling of silk gliding over strings of a lute
> So we go into a rainy season
> Rains that drip and drip
> Rains that have a downward cadence
> downward down-a-down
> In the faraway provinces
> a shower beats a city in an afterglow
> stirs up a flight of white cranes
> from the marshes
> In an afterglow they say one senses
> a pavilion of brightness of the past
> screened in a sunny shower
> undertones in time of war
> gold winds winding down the cornfield
> wafting a flowing of glimmering hair
> downward down-a-down
> a canticle of bones
> rises from where quietude reigns
> Drums and heads of martyrs from the plain
> flow here and away
> with a downward cadence
> downward down-a-down

> (Unknowing of full dawn's advent   That
> comes like the wheel   Comes in mourning
> drapery   Where the door opens   The
> shouting of peddlers of the well known yester-
> day.)

[63] *Ibid.*, pp. 139–140.

Hsiu Tao, another young poet, pinpoints the hopelessness and the inertia of the island's youth in "Winter Evening":[64]

> Such a tar-colored winter evening.
>
> Open remained my door
> That kept a dubious gesture
> Between waving a farewell
> And extending a welcome.
>
> Out I went and in I came;
> Yet open remained the door.
>
> Out I threw a button that had
> Long nuzzled in a corner of my drawer.
> I threw a story into history.
>
> Hours passed without an ice-breaker
> Plowing by.
> Open remained my door.

In art, the same break in cultural continuity persists in the conflict between young experimental painters and artists of the old Chinese tradition. In 1957, when they held their first show, the members of the Tung Fang group, described by Shiy De Jinn, himself a leading young artist, as the "real vanguard" of modern painting in Taiwan, issued a manifesto in which they attacked "popular prejudice against the new painting," and sought to relate contemporary international trends with Chinese tradition, and called for a revitalization of the native heritage. One of their members, Hsiao Ming-hsien, won a prize at the Biennial International Art Exhibition at Sao Paulo, Brazil. But their work is rejected by the older and more important painters of the traditional school as "pretentious foreign nonsense."[65]

The stagnation of traditional art on Taiwan may perhaps best be illustrated by the work of Kao Yü-hung, who has risen to public prominence as the painting teacher of Madame Chiang Kai-shek. Kao, who had a large exhibition in Taipei in the fall of 1963, tries to combine the techniques of Walt Disney with the Chinese tradition and ends up with garish colors, insipid wildlife, and uninteresting wooden figures.

Nor does academic life escape the general malaise. Outside of the natural and physical sciences, where the regime has wisely abstained from interfering, the intellectual tone is largely set by old-fashioned

[64] *Ibid.*, p. 65.
[65] *Ibid.*, p. v. For manifesto, see pp. 79–82.

teaching methods and research techniques. The approach to subject matter is often set by the regime's ideology, particularly in the field of history. Too many professors read their lectures from old textbooks, which the students follow in class line by line. Professors at Taiwan National University and older researchers at Academia Sinica, the nation's highest research body, have not kept up very well with the latest developments in research and methodology abroad, follow traditional patterns, and stifle originality in their students. The approach to particular subjects, such as recent Chinese history, the history of Taiwan, or the study of certain problems in international relations, is strictly circumscribed by the regime, and objectivity, in the Western academic sense of the word, is not permitted.

Perhaps the only spark of life in Taiwan's intellectual world today is a monthly journal, *Wen Hsing* (Literary Star), published by one of Taipei's leading bookstores and edited by a young firebrand, Li Ao.[66] *Wen Hsing,* most recently under Li's direction, has not hesitated to attack the shibboleths of Taiwan's intellectual and academic environment; it is also an important vehicle for the introduction into the island of current developments in the West. Unfortunately, it too often gets involved in arid and acrid personal feuds, and Li Ao delights in making violent attacks on the leaders of the older generation, such as Hu Ch'iu-yuan of the Institute of Modern History at Academia Sinica and Li Chi, the great archeologist. Often these disputes are personal vendettas, encouraged by faculty members of the universities. Throughout *Wen Hsing*'s more recent issues there seems to run an element of nihilism that lacks hope of reconstruction after destruction.

Taiwan's intellectual and moral stagnation is encouraged, even if indirectly, by the KMT regime, which discourages originality and reform lest they lead to movements that might question the regime itself. In the first part of 1963, an American student, with the Chinese name of Ti Jen-hua, wrote a letter to the leading Taipei newspaper, the KMT party organ, criticizing Chinese students for· discourtesy, mentioning such things as inconsiderateness of others, cheating on exams, pushing ahead in lines, and the like. The students were shamed into starting a "Self-Consciousness Movement" for moral reform,[67] which included such things as getting up in buses for pregnant women and crippled men. The government, evidently fearing any mass movements not under

[66] Sometimes spelled Li Ngao
[67] There is some debate in Taipei concerning the origins of the movement. Some observers believe the government started it but that it soon got out of hand. Others believe that the students themselves were shamed by Ti's letter into starting the movement, which the government, disturbed by its possible consequences, eventually took over. There were half-hearted attempts to revive it in the fall of 1963, without much success.

its direct control, appears to have taken over the movement in order to squelch it with official enthusiasm. As one commentator remarked, "We must carry out this movement with care. We should not be lost in a bewildering maze of slogans and rumors,"[68] and the *China Post* declared editorially, "We believe the actual issues involved are quite subtle. Young people may be lost in a perplexing maze of slogans." It called upon the university authorities to "give a helping hand so as to guide the students in the right direction."[69] What was most remarkable about the movement, however, was the students' inability (for political or intellectual reasons) to discuss the social and economic origins of corruption and despair in Taiwan today. In a collection of sixty-nine essays written during and about the "Self-Consciousness Movement" by students and faculty members, none penetrated Taiwan's social, moral, or intellectual problems.[70] By and large, the volume calls upon the youth to return to traditional virtues and patriotic sentiments.

The Generalissimo's response to the moral and intellectual stagnation of Free China has been the creation of a Confucius-Mencius Study Society to revive the "old virtues." A similar attempt by him in the 1930's, the "New Life Movement," totally failed. The new Confucius-Mencius Study Society has not evoked much popular enthusiasm. Instead, Taiwan, like East Germany before the "wall," is quickly losing its intellectuals and technicians. Older professors will take any chance to leave the island and remain abroad. Students stream to the United States and Japan and, to a lesser extent, to Europe. The regime lets them go lest they become troublesome at home. Since 1950, less than 7 per cent of them have returned to Taiwan.[71] Consequently, while the better minds seek economic opportunity and intellectual freedom abroad, second-rate minds are left at home to try to keep the ship afloat. One satirical journal recently remarked, with astonishing bravery, that the only movement worth joining on the island today is the movement to America.

The depression that lies heavily over Taiwan and that results from the island's stagnation and despair was graphically illustrated recently by Taipei's reactions to the film "Liang Shan-po and Chu Ying-t'ai," a Hong Kong production. The slightly preposterous story concerns a girl, Chu Ying-t'ai, who wants to go to school, a privilege reserved in ancient times for boys. She dresses as a boy and goes off to the big city

[68] *CP*, June 9, 1963.
[69] *Ibid.*, June 2, 1963.
[70] For the essays, see *Jen-ch'ing-wei yü Kung-te-hsin* (Taipei, 1962). For Ti Jen-hua's letter, see *ibid.*, pp. 1–6.
[71] Even the leadership tries to get its children off what it must consider to be a sinking ship. The members of Ch'en Ch'eng's cabinet had, collectively, more children in the United States than in Taiwan, according to one estimate.

to attend school for three years. Chu Ying-t'ai becomes fast friends with Liang Shan-po, a boy (also played by a female) who is a student at the school, and for three years they live next to each other, Liang often taking care of Chu when he (she) is sick. Chu, of course, falls in love with Liang but cannot tell him that she (he) is a girl. Liang, who is also in love with Chu, discovers this only too late, when Chu is already betrothed to another. He wastes away and dies, and Chu visits his grave on her way to her own wedding. In a melodramatic ending, Chu disappears into Liang's grave and the two emerge as butterflies.

The film, shot in riotous color, is based on an old folk story, traditionally quite popular in Taiwan, and is presented in a modernized version of Chinese opera. It was, undoubtedly, the most popular entertainment to hit Taiwan in its entire history. Thousands went to see the picture over and over again, the audiences sang the music along with the actors, and special clubs were formed of people who had seen the picture more than fifty times. The text was published in countless editions, records of the music were issued, and the story was told and retold in print. Finally, the film won the "Gold Horse Prize," and Lin Po, a leading Hong Kong actress who played Liang Shan-po, came to Taiwan for a visit. The visit created such a stir that security precautions similar to those for a visiting head-of-state had to be taken, and various groups vied with each other in presenting her with awards and prizes, including expensive jewelry.[72]

Taipei's reaction to the film was so hysterical that one pro-KMT Hong Kong newspaper was moved to call the capital a "town gone crazy." One of Taipei's leading papers commented:

> The picture was so welcomed in Taipei not just because of the performance of the actress. It was welcomed because it is full of emotional depression and the songs are so sad. The people here after years of war are depressed. Once [hysteria] is touched off, it is uncontrollable; since we cannot laugh at our lives, the only way is to use a safety valve, crying and laughing madly. Dear people, if you are really depressed, hurry to awaken yourselves from these dreams.[73]

Social tension. The public's despair and resignation, the lack of hope for a constructive future, is mirrored in rising social tension, which is a serious problem for the regime. This social tension expresses itself in a wide variety of ways. Juvenile delinquency, for instance, appears

---

[72] The total expense for her two-and-a-half-day trip to Taipei was NT$400,000. It is amusing to note that the text of the film was plagiarized directly from a Communist text published on the mainland. See *TLWP*, October 23, 1963, for a textual criticism of the film. This embarrassed the government.

[73] *TLWP*, November 4, 1963.

to be on the rise. The Control Yuan reported that for the year July, 1961, to June, 1962, there were 1,869 criminal cases involving youth on Taiwan, an increase of 260, or almost 14 per cent over the previous twelve months.[74] Interestingly enough, juvenile delinquents in Taipei tend to divide themselves into two groups, *T'ai-pao,* who are chiefly mainlander, and *Liu-mang,* who are primarily Taiwanese. Although the differences are beginning to blur, the distinctions are important.[75] Tension between students and police has developed on many levels. On July 21, 1963, for instance, some forty Taipei high-school students besieged a branch police office in the early morning hours to protest the arrest of five of their fellow students on charges of disturbing the public order and peace.[76]

Tension between the police and the public is not limited to students. Demonstrations in front of police stations and even murders of policemen are frequently reported in the papers.[77] Nor are the police always blameless. Frequent public charges are made against the police for beating suspects and even innocent bystanders.[78] These charges are even made in the Legislative and Control Yuans.[79] Crime in general appears to be on the increase. In Hsinchu, a town of 150,000 outside of Taipei, police reported 148 theft cases during the month of October, 1963, despite a special theft-prevention campaign in that month. Of the 148 cases, only 74 were solved by the police. "The thieves seem to be able to outsmart the police and theft cases keep occurring in great numbers," the *China Post* reported. Actually, many citizens believe the police are often in alliance with the thieves and therefore hesitate to report crimes lest they be subjected to reprisals.

Nor are the courts able to deal effectively with the overwhelming business that comes their way. Between July, 1961, and June, 1962, according to the Control Yuan's report of November 14, 1962, the average judge on Taiwan had to deal with 121 civil cases a month, while in Taichung, the provincial capital, the average judge had to hear 166 civil cases per month. In the same period, criminal judges had to

---

[74] *LHP,* November 14, 1962.
[75] For a discussion of these groups, see Lin Tsung-yi's paper, "Two Types of Delinquent Youth in Chinese Society," delivered at the Tenth Annual Meeting of the World Federation for Mental Health, Copenhagen, August, 1957.
[76] *CP,* July 22, 1963.
[77] See, for instance, *TLWP,* March 23, 1963, and March 24, 1963; see also *LHP,* August 17 and 18, 1963.
[78] For a famous case involving police beating correspondents at the Taipei International Airport, see *CHHWP,* August 17, 1962.
[79] See, for instance, *CHHWP,* May 7, 1963. It has been suggested that the newspapers really only report a portion of known crimes, due to government disapproval of "yellow journalism," which would tend to emphasize the tensions existing in the island's society.

deal with an average of 64 cases per month, while in Taipei the figure stood at 88. For the same period, there were 229,682 civil cases and 98,508 criminal cases in the island's courts.[80]

Under martial law, the government often deals summarily with criminal cases. According to a report published on October 21, 1963, the police all over Taiwan picked up in September and October, as a result of "Operation 701," more than 900 "illegal elements," described as "thieves, Liu-mang, professional gamblers, and others." These "illegal elements" were exiled to Little Liu-ch'iu, a small island off Taiwan, for indeterminate periods without benefit of court procedures.[81] There is widespread belief in Taipei that the category of "and others" includes many political opponents of the regime on the village level, who, under martial law, can be dealt with in this way. A considerable amount of turbulence, fed by economic, social, political, and intellectual conditions, lies just below the surface of the island's society.

THE MAINTENANCE OF KUOMINTANG CONTROL

How do Chiang Kai-shek and his Kuomintang party continue to maintain their control over the island of Taiwan? Loyalty to and enthusiasm for the regime is not the answer. Nor is democracy. *The China News,* the more liberal of the two English-language dailies in Taipei, suggested by indirection, at the time of the Ninth Congress of the KMT in November, 1963, that all was not well with the party:

> Meeting at a time when the Communist Party has virtually ceased to hold congresses, and carefully suppresses what happens at them, the Kuomintang has the opportunity to trumpet to the world what it is, where it stands, and where it hopes to go. The fears and shackles of silence from the past should be thrown away for good and always. China's leading party should stand forth fearlessly as the champion of freedom and the rights of the people. Despite all the fancy oratory, that is the one way the Kuomintang can assure its perpetuation in growing strength and service.[82]

Except among a few thoroughly "educated" youth, it is difficult to find on Taiwan today many individuals who accept the KMT at its own face value.

An explanation of the regime's long continuity in power after its flight to Taiwan in 1949 must be sought, in part, in the nature of the power relationships between the regime and the two parallel mainlander and Taiwanese societies. The mainlanders depend to a remark-

[80] *LHP,* November 14, 1962.
[81] *Ibid.,* October 21, 1963.
[82] *CN,* November 12, 1963.

35

able extent on the government for their livelihood. In the vast civilian bureaucracy, in the army, or as retired servicemen living on government-sponsored farms or working in government factories, they look to the regime to maintain their economic existence as well as their "first-class-citizen status" on an island where they are a minority of only two out of eleven. Consequently, with the notable exception of a handful of educated mainlanders such as the group that attempted to organize the China Democratic Party in 1960, most mainlanders are unwilling to go into opposition, which might jeopardize their personal livelihood and, in the long run, the regime itself.

The Taiwanese, on the other hand, do not depend, for the most part, on the regime for their economic livelihood; while by conviction most of them are probably in the opposition, they remain silent by and large. Several factors contribute to this silence. The appearance of the regime's overwhelming military and police power, supported by the might and image of the United States (the GRC armed forces make up more than 5 per cent of the total population of the island; its paid police informers may number as many as 50,000 and part-time informers as many as 500,000), make most Taiwanese feel politically impotent, dependent on American policy changes for an improvement of their condition, and, therefore, unwilling to cross over into public opposition.

The image of the regime's overwhelming might re-enforces two conditions among the Taiwanese. First, there is a distinct sense of historical pessimism and exhaustion. The Taiwanese have a long history of revolt, first against the Ch'ing dynasty, later against the Japanese, and finally, in 1947, against the Kuomintang. Their revolts, however, consistently ended in failure, and this has led to a decline in political initiative and a sense of the historical inevitability of oppression. One contemporary Taiwanese writer described this feeling of pessimism succinctly:

All the incidents [of revolt in recent history] in Miaoli, Pei-p'u, Hsi-lai-an and other places relied on force to resist: they all met with tragic failure. Consequently there developed among the Taiwanese a feeling that resistence by force was of no avail. The Taiwanese understood that to resist the Japanese by force not only resulted in great sacrifices and little results, but it was also against the nature of the times.[83]

Secondly, the Taiwanese lost their more vigorous and less compromising leadership class in the months immediately after the 1947 revolt. Those Taiwanese leaders who did not join the KMT regime at that time

[83] Wu Cho-liu, *Ch'uang-pa chi* (A Collection of Scars), 2 vols. (Taipei, 1963), vol. 1, p. 196.

were liquidated or fled abroad. A second period of purge followed in 1949–51, after the regime's flight to Taiwan, when many active intellectuals and political or potential political leaders were shot. As a result of these several factors, revolt, when it has taken place, as in 1947, or as in scattered attacks on local police stations, has tended to be basically formless and leaderless.

The sense of political impotency on the part of most Taiwanese and mainlanders is further supported by geography. The geographic fact that Taiwan is an island is also a basic political fact of life. On the mainland, Chiang at no time succeeded in controlling the entire country, and many areas in which he had nominal control were in reality controlled by local warloads. Consequently, oppositionists always had, at least psychologically, a place to which they could escape when opposition led them into physical danger. (The foreign treaty concessions also played this role.) Taiwan's small size relative to the regime's might, however, has enabled Chiang to exert his control in every valley and on every mountaintop. There is no escape, even psychologically, and the waters of the Pacific are almost as strong as prison walls. It is not by chance, for instance, that the KMT's major concentration camp, euphemistically called a "re-education center," is located on Green Island, a dot off the coast of Taiwan, from which physical escape is virtually impossible.

This fundamental disposition to inaction and political apathy, supported as it is by an omnipresent secret police organization and armed might, is further re-enforced by a delicately balanced political mechanism that keeps the society in a state of suspended animation, politically. Taiwan is experiencing what might be called a form of "submerged totalitarianism." In other words, the Kuomintang regime is able to allow a certain degree of apparent freedom on society's surface because, just beneath the surface, it reserves the power and ability to isolate, paralyze, or liquidate its opponents. Opposition in a totalitarian society may often be a matter of calculated risks. An individual going into opposition knows that he faces two possibilities: Either he will survive or he will be punished in one fashion or another. A totalitarian regime will often, either by law or through demonstration, make fairly clear the penalties for opposition. Consequently, the individual trying to decide whether or not to go into opposition can weigh the possibilities of success, survival, and punishment and make his decision accordingly.

On Taiwan, however, the government has essentially deprived the individual, or group, of the opportunity to calculate the risk involved in opposition. This has been done by introducing a large random element into the government's own behavior. (Martial law, which permits the government total freedom of action in dealing with its opponents, is only the legal expression of randomness.) At no time since 1949 has the regime, for instance, defined the perimeters of acceptable opposition. Even the definition of a Communist has remained unclear, since it has never been defined in law and, consequently, the government can use the charge of being a Communist to justify action against individuals or groups. In other words, the limits of tolerable opposition appear to be undefined and always moving, and the individual can never be clear whether any given political act will be considered acceptable or unacceptable. A further random element is introduced by the absence of any rules of retribution. Even if the individual does suspect that a given act is unacceptable politically, he cannot tell beforehand, even within reasonable limits, what form the regime's retribution will take, when it will strike, or against whom the government will take action. In the absence, therefore, of what we call the "rule of law," or, again, in the absence of fairly clearly defined precedents as in the Soviet Union or Communist China, the individual or group on Taiwan is deprived of the opportunity to calculate reasonably the risk involved in opposition; he remains in a state of indecision and suspended animation, which deprives him intellectually and psychologically of the opportunity to oppose the regime.

The "Lei Chen case" is a good example. Lei Chen was the editor of the *Free China Fortnightly,* the leading opposition journal on the island, from November, 1949, to September, 1960, during which period the journal appeared approximately every two weeks. Although subject to constant pressures, the journal did not hesitate to criticize the regime on everything from military and fiscal policy to totalitarian methods of control, and was never completely shut down. During its initial period, moreover, it had financial support from the Asia Foundation and moral-financial support from USIS in the form of a large number of subscriptions. In late 1959 and the first half of 1960, Lei Chen and his supporters decided to organize an opposition political party that would include both mainlanders and Taiwanese. Although they may have suspected it, the party's organizers did not know definitely that this would be a totally "unacceptable" form of political opposition, since the regime still tolerated, and does today, two minor parties which it "keeps" to some extent. Nevertheless, on September 4, 1960, Lei was arrested together with some of his colleagues on charges of sedition, involving the "harboring" of a Communist agent. As specious as these charges were, Lei was tried by a military court, sentenced to ten years in jail, and his journal was suppressed.

The circumstances surrounding the Lei case are a clear example of the inability to calculate the consequences of an action that itself is not clearly an "unacceptable" form of opposition. This was further borne out by Mrs. Lei's efforts to find defense lawyers for her husband. She was refused, on several occasions, by leading lawyers in Taipei, not because they disagreed with her husband's position or condoned the regime's policies, but because—and they explicitly stated this to her—they could not determine what retribution they or their children might suffer immediately or in the future for their own defense of Lei, which might itself be considered an act of opposition.

Later developments in the Lei affair also illustrate the difficulties of opposition on Taiwan. *Shih yü Ch'ao* (Time and Tide), a well-known Taipei journal, published in its issue No. 166 on April 1, 1963, a poem written by Lei Chen in jail, together with an interview with Mrs. Lei concerning Lei Chen's life in jail and her own life. The poem, entitled "A Poem (epilogue appended) Written by Lei Chen in Jail," is as follows:

> Inspired by a dream in the night of Sept. 9 of Dr.
> Hu Shih's principle for toleration and freedom, I wrote
> this self-encouraging poem.
>
> Be kind to enemies and friends; listen more and speak less.
> Tolerate others, restrain yourself, freedom will be seen and democracy be practised.
> Accept criticism and correct mistakes, don't complain, don't blame, don't shirk, don't exaggerate, speak less and do more.
> Don't speak against others, don't speak highly of yourself.
> Let bygones be bygones, whatever will be will be.
> Be faithful and diligent.
> Tilling without harvesting.
> Keep yourself straight, ignore others' talk.
> Do whatever should be done, look upon death as going home.
> These are the principles for one to live by, to deal with people or to rule a nation.

My room was flooded by the typhoon on the night of Sept. 5. Things grew mildewed and spoiled. Ya-ying [Lei Chen's wife] came to see me on September 7 and brought me a bookshelf. Weather turned fine on the ninth, I moved everything outside to dry in the sun. Though someone tried to help me, I actually did most of the work. I ran back and forth almost a hundred times.

After taking a nap at noon, I wrote about 2,500 words. Then I put all the books on the shelf and placed other things in their proper places. I also

washed clothes after dinner. I felt awfully exhausted, so I went to bed at
9:00 P.M. without doing my evening exercises. I was too tired to sleep,
so I got up again at 11:30 and took a walk outside, ate two pieces of
biscuit, and went to bed again.

I was lost in a dream in which I realized the meaning of "toleration and
freedom" as explained by Dr. Hu Shih. Inspired by the dream, I wrote a
poem to encourage myself.

I jotted down and polished the poem first thing next morning. The word
"enemies" mentioned in the poem means people who hold different
opinions in political activities. For example, ruling party and opposition
party often refer to each other as "enemy." Here I want to make it clear
that the word does not refer to the enemy on the mainland [Chinese
Communists].[84]

The regime immediately moved against *Time and Tide* and Mrs. Lei
for publishing the poem and the interview. A suspension order dated
April 11, 1963, was issued by the Ministry of the Interior and signed
by Chou Pai-Lien, acting mayor of Taipei, prohibiting the publishing of
Time and Tide for one year and seizing all the journal's materials.[85]
The order specifically stated that the journal was being suspended
because of the publication of the poem and interview. "In these items
Lei's evil deeds are praised and this may influence others to do the same
evil deeds. Therefore, it seriously jeopardizes the public order." In
addition, Mrs. Lei, who is a member of the Control Yuan and who by
law has the right to visit her husband once a week, lost all visiting rights.
For more than five months, until the last part of October, she could not
visit her husband in prison. At the end of that time she was granted
a monthly visiting privilege, apparently due to domestic pressures and
the regime's fear of embarrassment abroad. (The question had been
raised with high officials by certain foreign dignitaries visiting Taiwan
during or shortly after the National Day celebrations on October 10.)
The editor and the publisher of *Time and Tide,* as well as Mrs. Lei,
all stated privately that they did not believe beforehand that the publication of Lei's poem and the interview with Mrs. Lei would lead to suspension of the journal or of Mrs. Lei's visiting rights. In fact, the
randomness of the definition of "opposition" and of retribution is so
obvious on Taiwan today that the editor and publisher felt that, if they
had only had a chance to explain their case directly to the Generalissimo,
Time and Tide would not have been suspended. In Taipei, this randomness is often called, privately of course, "the Old Man's whim," referring

---

[84] See *Shih yü Ch'ao* (Time and Tide), No. 166 (April 1, 1963), 5.
[85] The order was issued under the 1958 Press Law.

to Chiang Kai-shek and the role his personal inclinations play in the running of the government.

The regime has also time and again demonstrated its ability to manipulate electoral procedures to suit its own purposes. The case of Sung Lin-k'ang, a Taiwanese, is a good example. Running for office in Taipei in local elections on April 28, 1963, Sung was announced victor in fourth place (Taipei has multiple election districts) by one of the leading newspaper's electric news signs high above a large square in Taipei, by local radio stations and, significantly, by the Police Radio Station. Later, however, the election office announced that he had been defeated and, moreover, that he was only 7th in the list of defeated candidates. On April 29 and again on May 6, Sung asked for a recount of the votes for two reasons: (1) Throughout the province of Taiwan local elections had been completed and results announced by about 9:00 P.M. on election night. However, the Taipei election office, with the best communications on the island, did not announce its results until 2:00 A.M. the following morning. (2) Sung had nominated 123 election inspectors, as was his due under the law, to represent his interests at the polls and in the counting of votes. The Taipei election office, however, turned down his request to be given a list of the voting places where his nominees had been posted.[86] It is, therefore, difficult to avoid the suspicion that Sung lost his case in court due to great government pressure. Despite his loss, he held a parade in his district in the Taiwanese section of Taipei to thank the voters. The scale of the parade grew larger than Sung or the police expected, the crowd got out of hand, and a riot nearly ensued. Sung's case is simply one example of how the regime can manipulate voting procedures, and judicial appeals, to ensure the defeat of candidates it feels would be in opposition to its policies.

In addition to paralyzing potential opposition, demonstrating overwhelming police power, controlling the local press, and manipulating electoral procedures, the GRC is careful to prevent news from abroad entering the country if it would "jeopardize the public order." For instance, the Second Asian Press Conference, first scheduled to be held in Taipei in 1963, had to be transferred to Tokyo because the GRC vetoed its convening on Taiwan. Shen Chuang-huan, the Foreign Minister at the time, is said to have personally canceled the conference in Taipei "for fear of controversial political statements delegates from countries such as India and Indonesia might make in the conference."[87]

It has sometimes been said that the Kuomintang on the mainland before 1949 wanted to turn China into a totalitarian state but lacked

[86] *CHHWP,* May 7, 1963.
[87] *CP,* October 29, 1963.

the efficiency to do so. On Taiwan, the Kuomintang does not lack political efficiency. That it has not turned the island into a totalitarian society is due perhaps more to choice than to necessity. It can perpetuate its power without recourse to the more naked aspects of totalitarianism as known in Europe or on the China mainland. It believes, furthermore, that it is well served by the maintenance of a façade of democratic institutions. Without that façade, American aid might not be so readily forthcoming. Just beneath the surface of society, however, the regime maintains the entire panoply of political methods and institutions that characterize totalitarian or near-totalitarian states: secret police, concentration camps, controlled press, public fear, one-party dictatorship. Having paralyzed potential opposition and denied it access to effective political and judicial procedures, the regime can allow its opponents to rail against it in private, secure in the knowledge that the state cannot be challenged within the framework of existing institutions.

An Outline of Formosan History

By SHINKICHI ETO *

To the Portuguese navigators of the sixteenth century the sight of land after a long, hazardous and tiring voyage was a thing of beauty. Their cry, upon first sighting the fresh green of outlying islands, was often more poetic than nautical: "Ilha formosa!" or "Pretty island!" Today there are supposed to be more than ten such "formosas"; there is however only one *Formosa*. The name "Taiwan," literally "Terraced Bay" in Chinese, is a sinitic corruption of a Formosan aboriginal term *tayan* or *tayouan* applied first to the Chinese foreigners and later to their settlement on Anping Island in the harbour of the present city of Tainan. In time both the Chinese and Japanese came to refer to the whole island of Formosa as Taiwan. Together with the administratively constituent Pescadores Islands (Portuguese for "fishermen"), which lie off its west coast in the Straits of Formosa, and the several "off shore" islands (Matsu, Quemoy, and others), Formosa makes up the present *real* estate of the Republic of China. Its beginnings were more modest.

PRIOR TO CHINESE RULE

The Chinese migration to Formosa began in the sixteenth century, long after the Mongol Yüan dynasty (1271–1368) had in 1281 established its official presence in the Pescadores to control the Chinese fishermen, salt smugglers, pirates and merchants who had begun to call at and settle in the islands. And for almost a century before the first wave of Chinese settlers, Formosa and the Pescadores had been used by Chinese and Japanese privateers as bases for the thriving operations along the coastal sea lanes between north-east and south-east Asia. Both pirate and emigré however had to contend with a not always receptive native population consisting of a bewildering number of Malaysian and Indonesian aborigine tribes. These tribes—the Atayal, Saisiat, Bunun, Tsou, Tukai and Ami—migrated to Formosa in successive waves, maintained mutually exclusive cultural and linguistic traditions, and for three hundred years (actually well into the twentieth century) fought the foreigner, either Chinese or Japanese, for his land and his head. Their fate has been

* I would like to express my thanks to Mr. H. L. Kahn for his assistance in rendering this article into English.

similar to that of the American Indian: reduced in numbers, forced into the mountains and into poverty, and eventually controlled and " tamed " and in some cases even assimilated by the civilisation around them. Today more than 90 per cent. of Formosa's population is of Chinese not aboriginal descent, tracing its heritage to the south China provinces of Fukien and Canton.

The first Europeans to appear in Formosan waters were the Portuguese. They were soon followed by the Spanish and Dutch. This was the beginning of the age of mercantilism, and both the Portuguese and Spanish hoped to occupy Formosa in order to control trade in Chinese and Japanese waters. Unfortunately the Dutch beat them to the draw. In 1622 the Dutch East India Company built a fortress in the Pescadores, and, after an eight-month war with Chinese troops, agreed to a compromise plan whereby the Company would evacuate the Pescadores in exchange for a free hand in Formosa, where the Chinese did not claim sovereignty. As a result the first Dutch fort in Formosa was erected in 1624: Fort Zeelandia in Tayouan (present Anping). This was later followed by a second, Fort Provintia, in Saccam (present Tainan).

Surprised by the Dutch move, the Spanish hurried to occupy Keelung in northern Formosa, and in 1626 built Fort Salvador on Hoping Island in the bay of Keelung. Native diseases and tribal assaults took their toll however, and in 1642 the Spanish garrison was defeated by a Dutch force and expelled from Formosa.

The Spanish were not alone in opposing Dutch attempts to monopolise trade in Formosa. The Japanese opposed these efforts vigorously, and in 1628 sent an expedition of 470 men under Hamadaya Yahei against Fort Zeelandia. Hamadaya was promptly captured; he retaliated in kind by promptly seizing the Dutch governor and holding *him* hostage during his confinement! The two finally released one another and Hamadaya hurried home to report the affair to the Tokugawa Shogunate (1603–1868), which then ruled Japan. At the time the Shogunate was still unopposed to overseas trade and backed Japanese participation in the Formosan trade. Indeed, its embargo on Dutch ships at Nagasaki helped break the Dutch monopoly in Formosa, and the Japanese continued to share in the trade until 1636 when the Shogunate reversed its policy and " closed " Japan to the outside world. Thereafter Japanese were prohibited from leaving the country, or if they had already settled overseas, from returning. Consequently Japan soon disappeared from the entire arena of East Asian trade. In Formosa the Dutch were left unchallenged.

The Dutch East India Company was supreme in Formosa for over thirty years. During its first decade the chief domestic problem was to neutralise aborigine hostility. It was only after its garrisons defeated several of the more powerful tribes in 1635–36 that the Dutch sphere of influence around the forts expanded notably. Eventually it was said to include some seventy thousand subject aborigines. The Dutch encouraged Protestant missionary work in the hope of " civilising " the aborigines, and themselves sought to maintain friendly relations with the tribes. They also encouraged Chinese emigration from the mainland. By 1660 there were 25,000 Chinese in Formosa, mainly farmers, who cultivated rice, sugar cane, indigo, grain plants and potatoes. They also hunted deer and gray mullet (*mugil japonicus*), and fished the local coastal waters. Deer skin and sugar became major exports to Japan; dried fish and deer meat were shipped to China. The Dutch also encouraged certain manufactures while levying heavy taxes as well, chief among them being a poll tax and taxes on butter and alcohol. By the 1650s Formosa had, in fact, become one of the most profitable of the Dutch East India Company's entrepôts [or : bases] in Asia. All this came to an end when Cheng Ch'eng-kung (Koxinga) invaded Formosa in 1661.

UNDER CHINESE RULE

Koxinga was born in Japan in 1624. His father, Cheng Chih-lung, was a Chinese merchant-pirate whose power extended effectively over all of the Fukien coast in south-east China. The central government in Peking (the Ming Dynasty, 1368–1644), was helpless to rectify the situation and preferred appeasement to attempted military suppression. This was accomplished by conferring on Cheng high military rank and allowing him autonomous control of his merchant kingdom under the ostensible sovereignty of the Ming. The policy paid off. Cheng remained loyal to the Ming in its losing struggle against the Manchu invaders until the issue was clearly resolved. He only surrendered to the Manchu Ch'ing dynasty (1644–1911) in 1646, two years after the seizure of Peking by the new dynasty. His son, however, continued loyal to the lost Ming cause. He maintained his sea-power along the Fukien coast, and by developing trade with Japan, Dutch Formosa, Annam, Cambodia, Siam and the Philippines, secured the financial base of his war against the Manchus. Five times he requested reinforcements from the Tokugawa Shogunate, but the Japanese government had already decided upon its seclusionist policy and refused Koxinga aid.

The Ch'ing government in 1654 sought to settle its differences with Koxinga. The compromises they proposed as well as the repeated pleas by his father to surrender were made in vain. In 1658–59 he sent an expedition against Nanking and this, ultimately, was his undoing. His army was routed and he was forced to abandon his territorial base in the south and flee the country. To assure that his lines of support and logistics were cut, the Ch'ing government in 1661 ordered the evacuation of large stretches of the south China coast. Later that year Koxinga invaded Formosa to establish a new base of operations. His confrontation with the Dutch was brief and successful. They surrendered and were graciously permitted to leave the island with their muskets loaded and property in tow. This marked the end of the Dutch hegemony in Formosa and the beginning of a century-and-a-half of Chinese rule.

Koxinga died a year later, in 1662, at the age of thirty-eight. His régime, however, survived until 1683 when it finally surrendered to the Ch'ing. The Manchu policy of coastal evacuation had done its work. But for twenty years, and despite the ultimate success of that policy, Koxinga's Formosa had enjoyed a remarkable increase in its immigrant Chinese population and a concomitant growth in agricultural production and continental ways. Formosa was becoming " sinified." Tens of thousands of Chinese, including remnant Ming loyalists, famine victims, and criminals found their way to Formosa. With the application of their added man-power the production of the island's food staples—rice, sugar, grains, potatoes, and fish—grew rapidly. So, of course, did the spread of imported traditions, and soon Confucian ethics and education became a common feature of Formosa's cultural landscape.

With the final submission of Formosa to the Ch'ing the island and the Pescadores were placed under the provincial jurisdiction of Fukien, Koxinga's civil and military establishment broken up and removed from Formosa, and his grandson made a duke. The surrender was complete. And yet Koxinga's name lived on, and today enjoys with Sun Yat-sen the anomalous distinction of being honoured by both the Nationalist and Communist Chinese.

The evacuation of the south China coast was stopped in 1684, but the Ch'ing government continued to ban emigration to Formosa, primarily to prevent conflict between the aborigines and Chinese but also to limit absolutely the size of the Chinese community there. The ban failed, however, and clandestine Chinese settlement continued apace. Eventually this forced a realistic acceptance of the facts and the abrogation of the ban. It was not government fiat but native epidemics and civil disorders which held down population growth despite the heavy influx of Chinese settlers.

Ch'ing policy toward the aborigines was double-edged: to force them to assimilate with Chinese society or be expelled from the arable land to the mountains. By the eighteenth century, however, a myth of amelioration had grown up which reflected the gradual growth of amity between the two. It involved a just and wise Chinese official, Wu Feng, and the fierce, headhunting aborigine tribe over which he exercised financial and commercial jurisdiction. He defended native interests against the duplicity and animosity of the Chinese settlers and at the

46

same time sought to discourage tribal indulgence in head-hunting. He succeeded in getting a lengthy stay of decapitations by persuading the tribe that their present cache of forty heads was sufficient to meet their annual ritual demands for the next forty years. When the period was up and the supply exhausted they announced their intention of resuming the hunt. Wu Feng, ever helpful, suggested a likely and easy victim—a man who, he assured them, would pass a fixed spot the next morning wearing a red hood over his head. The advice was taken and so was the head. That it was Wu Feng's they learned too late. Stunned and grief-stricken they foreswore forevermore the practice that had taken the life of their trusted councillor and friend. Thereafter the tribe and the Chinese settlers in the area lived in peace, each worshipping the memory of a man who had, quite literally, given his head for a good cause. Long after, in the twentieth century, the Japanese resurrected Wu Feng and immortalised his deeds as an exemplary tale for schoolchildren in an authorised textbook They were, it is recalled, then having their own troubles domesticating these same aborigines.

Civil disorder in Formosa was not limited to disputes between the native tribes and the settlers. The Chinese fought among themselves as well. Private clan wars, especially between the Hakka Cantonese and the Fukienese occurred in Formosa with a frequency reminiscent of those in Fukien and Kwangtung on the mainland. And the popular saying, " Every three years a small revolt, every five a big one " (San-nien hsiao-p'an wu-nien ta-luan) seemed almost a statement of fact. Local government machinery was weak and the officials did little to improve social and economic conditions and to keep the peace. Scorn for the officials was widespread and vociferous—they were known as " tigerish old men "—and ultimately it fell to the clan and guild organisations and secret societies to maintain order and make whatever improvements were necessary.

It was not until 1887 that Peking realised the economic and political importance of Formosa and attempted for the first time to bring some kind of order to the chaos on the island. Administratively Formosa was declared a province, and her first Governor, Liu Ming-chuan, entrusted with the task of restoring order. He was an enthusiastic administrator and reformer and proved to be an able instrument of change in Formosa. The impetus for change, however, came from the West.

During the Opium War (1840–42) the British had attacked Formosa; after the Treaty of Peking (1860) the ports of Tamsui, Keelung, Anping and Takao had been opened to foreign trade. Thereafter a series of incidents marred Sino-Western relations in Formosa: in 1869 the British bombarded Anping; in the same year the United States sent a punitive force against an aborigine tribe which had massacred the crew of an

American ship, the *Rover*; and in 1884 the French occupied Keelung during the Sino-French war. Earlier, in 1873, Japan had sent a military expedition against another aborigine tribe after the Ch'ing government had refused jurisdiction of a case which involved the massacre of fifty-four Japanese. Meanwhile, and despite the bloodshed and riled foreign tempers, Formosa's trade continued to develop. By mid-century she was importing opium and cotton textiles in exchange for tea, sugar, rice and camphor, and the government in Peking was finally beginning to take notice.

Liu Ming-chuan undertook four major reforms on Formosa. He sought, with the assistance of foreign advisers, to strengthen and modernise the island's military establishment, up-date its equipment, and improve discipline; to develop a viable transport and communications system by encouraging road and rail construction and the introduction of modern navigation, telegraph, postal and mining systems; to reform and modernise the educational system; and to make an extensive land survey.

The purpose of the land survey was to determine and register for the first time the amount of land under cultivation and thereby ensure the government a reasonably accurate (and increased) revenue from the land tax. The results were promising, for where former annual revenue from this source had amounted to no more than 180,000 silver *tael* (Chinese ounces), the actual amount now determined payable was found to be some 670,000 *tael* per annum. Liu's own scrupulous fairness in fiscal matters however was no guarantee against corruption in the middle and lower ranks of the bureaucracy, and the increased land tax plus official "squeeze" resulted in several local revolts and political disturbances. And in 1892, before his reform programme was firmly established, Liu was transferred to another post. The modernisation of Formosa would have to await the Japanese.

In 1895 the Treaty of Shimonoseki ended the Sino-Japanese war and, among other things, ceded Formosa and the Pescadores to Japan. The provincial governor of Formosa was not pleased. He ignored the treaty, organised the armed forces to oppose the Japanese occupation, and on May 25, 1895, proclaimed Formosa an independent state and himself president of it. His forces, however, were no match for the Japanese and by June 6 he was in flight to mainland China. The remnants of his forces soon managed to alienate the population in the northern part of the island with their brigandage and violence, and as a result, the Japanese army was not entirely unwelcomed by the local Formosan leaders. Their collaboration with the occupation assured a peaceful transfer of power and order was quickly restored in the north. This was not the case in the south and in the mountains. There the resistance was bitter and it was not until the end of 1895 that the Japanese could safely occupy the major cities and towns in those areas.

Under Japanese Rule

At the beginning of his book, *A General Description of the Government of Taiwan*, published in 1905, Yosaburo Takekoshi, a leading historian of Meiji Japan, wrote, " The white people have long believed that it has been the white man's burden to cultivate the uncivilised territories and bring to them the benefits of civilisation. The Japanese people now have risen in the Far East and want to participate with the white people in this great mission. Will the Japanese nation, as a yellow people, be capable of performing this mission? The government of Taiwan may well provide the answer."

Formosa was not a promising colony. After the recall of Liu Ming-chuan the Ch'ing government made no further effort to continue or complete the programme of reform for Formosa. So bleak were its prospects that Ferdinand Richthofen, the German geographer and geologist, vetoed a suggestion by the Kaiser that Germany should occupy the island. Its inhabitants were too rebellious, he argued, and its harbours too poor. Instead he recommended the port of Kiaochow in the north-eastern Chinese province of Shantung. If Formosa then was an unpromising colony, it must be added that Japan at the time was an even more unpromising coloniser. She had little except an excess of nationalist zeal to bring to her new possession. Short of the necessary investment capital, the Japanese had even less of the specialised knowledge and experience necessary to run a colonial operation. The organisation of a colonial government, the pacification and assimilation of the aborigines, the solution of the opium problem, the handling of clan organisations—all were problems which had to be met by a new, untried and untrained colonial administration.

The chief financial prop of the new régime was to be a central colonial bank known as the Bank of Taiwan. It was to have been established in 1898 but failed to attract enough subscribers and had to wait until 1900 when the Japanese government agreed to guarantee it. The Japanese economy after the war with China was inflated and industrialising at a rapid rate, and with a high return on investments at home there was little incentive to invest in an unknown and highly unstable colony.

One reason for that instability was early administrative ignorance. Almost from the outset the Japanese colonial government—essentially a military government—antagonised and embittered the native population by its heavy-handed military solutions to most problems. This inevitably

set in motion a vicious circle of revolt and suppression whereby a show
of native discontent would be quashed by a force whose brutality would
lead to another uprising and yet another suppression. This was an
expensive way to run a colony and at least some Meiji leaders felt it
wasn't worth the effort. The Japanese government was at the outset
underwriting about 70 per cent. of the colonial budget (seven million
out of the ten million *yen* annual expenditures) and there were sugges-
tions from some that the island be sold and done with.

The problem was complicated by the lack of expertise of the colonial
administrative staff together with its lack of any esprit de corps. Officials
were generally of mediocre calibre and policemen, for example, were in
many cases former carpenters, plasterers and other workers who had
gone out to the new colony at government expense in the hope of
eventually making their fortunes as civilians. Not surprisingly they often
ignored or disobeyed regulations, since dismissal was the first step
toward that dream of civilian affluence.

GOTO'S REFORMS

Despite these early frustrations Japan retained the island and eventually
began to develop it. An economy-minded Diet in 1898 decreased
Formosa's subsidy from its previous high of seven million *yen* to an
annual four million and left the burden of economic development to
the colonial administration itself. The governor-general of Formosa
was left on his own to transform the colony into a self-sufficient economic
blessing to Japan.

Fortunately the governor-general at the time, the fourth in the brief
history of the colony, was a powerful and determined man. General
Gentaro Kodama was as influential in Japanese politics as he was in the
army and for eight years lent his reputation and support to the bold
and inspired policies of his subordinate, Shinpei Goto, the first civil
governor of Formosa. From 1898 to 1906 Goto put through a series
of reforms so successful that after 1905 no subsidy from the home
government was ever again needed. His three major reforms touched
on the most sensitive and pressing problems of Formosan life: security,
custom and law, and land.

In effect Goto reorganised the whole security system on Formosa. He
substituted a policy of pacification for the hated policy of suppression,
and leniency for the earlier code of harsh treatment of captured
"bandits." An efficient police system came to replace the military
security system and by 1902 organised " bandit " gangs were no longer
a problem. A variant of the Chinese system of group responsibility
for individual criminal acts (*paochia*) was reintroduced and eventually

every native Formosan was accounted for. The police were put in charge of household registrations and the census and recorded all births, deaths and changes of address. Thus there came to be little room for native " un-Japanese " activities in the colony. Peace and stability were assured.

To rectify the abysmal ignorance of Formosan law and custom with which the Japanese first approached their new colony, Goto sponsored extensive research into these and related fields. The Provisional Commission for Research on Customs in Formosa, the main research organ, was inaugurated in 1901. Its major publications, including the monumental *Administrative Laws of the Ch'ing Dynasty* and the *Private Laws of Taiwan* are still considered essential sources by students of Ch'ing dynasty and Formosan history.

Goto found the land system in near chaos. Concepts of land ownership were vague and remedial, for traditionally distinctions were made only between big and small proprietary rights. The big proprietor, whose rights were similar to the ancient German *dominium directum*, was primarily a squatter who held vast tracts of land which he " lent " to small proprietors. The small proprietors in turn rented their land to cultivators. The rights attached to these categories were transferred separately, and thus the rights on any given tract of land were extremely complicated. Goto established the Temporary Bureau of Land Survey in his office in 1898 which embarked on an extensive land survey as the basis for a thorough-going land reform. The Bureau was successful in three vital policies: the effective elimination of " hidden fields " (land that had long gone unregistered and hence untaxed) and a resultant enormous increase in government revenues; the forcible application of a modern concept of land ownership which saw the big proprietary right purchased by the government and the small proprietor made a land owner and tax payer; the determination of forest land ownership, 6 per cent. of the total area being alloted to private owners, the rest to the government.

SOCIAL DEVELOPMENT

The most pressing social problems facing the Japanese as colonisers lay in the areas of transport and communications, opium control, population growth, education and indoctrination, and aborigine pacification.

The Ch'ing government had done little to improve the road and rail system on Formosa, and modern communications networks were almost non-existent. What roads did exist were the products of local donations, not official financing. Under the Japanese there was impressive progress in all these fields. One of the first tasks undertaken after the occupation

51

was the construction by Japanese military engineers of an axial north-south highway which linked the major population centres for the first time. The extent of road development can be seen in the following figures:

Year	Major Roads (Total in kilometres)
1899	164
1909	325
1914	381
1923	801
1927	1,301
1935	4,456

When the Japanese arrived in Formosa only one railway line existed, between Keelung and Hsin-chu, and it was too poorly maintained to work. By 1908 it had been repaired and extended to Takao. And by 1933 Formosa had a total of 881·7 kilometres of railway line. Government-owned telegraph, telephone and postal services also grew rapidly and in time rivalled those in Japan.

The attack on opium addiction was a slower process. The Ch'ing had been notably unsuccessful in curbing the habit in Formosa and during much of the nineteenth century opium had been the island's major import. The Japanese Government-General acted quickly to control the supply and abate the demand. In 1896 it placed the import of opium under strict government monopoly but allowed the addicted to register with the authorities and purchase limited amounts from licensed retailers. In this way it hoped to minimise the number of crimes likely to occur as a result of the withdrawal syndrome. Over the long run the policy seems to have been successful and by 1935 only ·3 per cent. of the population could be counted as addicts. The following figures (representing, to be sure, only *registered* addicts), suggest the gradual decline in addiction:

Year	No. of Addicts	% of Addicts to Total Population
1905	130,476	4·2
1915	71,715	2·1
1920	48,011	1·3
1925	33,755	0·9
1930	23,237	0·5
1935	14,644	0·3

Under the impact of economic development, improved public health measures and other social reforms, Formosa's population increased rapidly. Estimates of this growth may be tabulated as follows:

Year	Aborigines	Taiwanese (Chinese-descended)	Japanese	Foreigners [1]	Total
1661 [2]		100,000			
1683 [3]		150,000			
1795		1,300,000			
1881		2,003,861			
1893 [4]		2,545,731			
1905 [5]		2,979,018	59,618	8,223	3,046,859
1914		3,307,302	141,835	19,582	3,468,719
1926		3,923,752	195,769	35,505	4,155,026
1930	89,321	4,224,601	232,299	46,691	4,592,912
1935	91,407	4,898,724	271,402 [6]	54,109	5,315,642

If the Japanese were quick to respond to the economic and social challenges in Formosa they were noticeably tardy in answering the educational needs of the Formosans. Until the 1920s, when economic development finally suggested the need for skilled and literate personnel, little was done to foster any native education except in the obvious fields of public health and hygiene. Primitive sanitary conditions had dictated the early imposition and teaching of basic public health regulations, and in 1900 a medical school for Formosan youth was established. In general, however, educational policy was dilatory and discriminatory. Japanese youth on the island enjoyed an unrestricted universal education; Formosan youth on the other hand was subject to restrictive quotas at all levels on the educational scale. As late as the 1930s, when the system had been considerably liberalised, there was still a sizeable discrepancy in the opportunities open to Japanese and Formosan pupils, even in the elementary grades:

Elementary School Attendance (% *of Qualified Age Group*)

Year	Japanese		Formosan	
	Male	Female	Male	Female
1932	99·15	98·97	51·00	19·70
1935	99·30	99·22	56·83	25·13
1943	99·00	99·00	95·00	90·00

A similar graph for the higher grades would reveal an even wider gulf, for there was a strong suspicion that education—especially in the humanities—would breed political, anti-colonial discontent. Hence discriminatory quotas were much smaller for secondary and (when finally permitted) higher education.

1 Including new immigrant Chinese nationals.
2 Year of the Dutch departure from Formosa.
3 Year in which Ch'ing rule over Formosa began.
4 Census undertaken by Liu Ming-chuan.
5 First Japanese census.   6 Including 1,604 Koreans.

Educational and social discrimination was somewhat softened in the 1930s and early 1940s with the introduction of a policy of assimilation. Called *Kominka undo* or " Movement to transform the people into imperial subjects," the policy sought to win the cultural and emotional allegiance of the Formosans. Intermarriage with the Japanese was permitted in 1932; the Imperial University in Taihoku (Taipei), founded in 1928, was opened to Formosan students; Formosan language broadcasts were banned in 1937 and replaced by all-Japanese programmes; three Formosans (along with seven Koreans) were appointed to Japan's House of Peers in 1939 and three years later all Formosans were permitted to take Japanese names. Finally in March 1945 universal manhood suffrage was declared for the island. It was to prove a hollow gesture, however, since the Pacific War came to an end and the Japanese surrender was accepted before a general election could be held. The Formosans were thus at war's end left culturally adrift. Long cut off from Chinese influence, they had been subjected to a programme of acculturation which alienated them even further from their past. For fifteen years they had been promised a new identification which could only be realised fully with the continued presence of Japan in Formosa. In this history failed them, and they were left between imperfect alienation and imperfect assimilation, more " Japanese " than " Chinese " perhaps, but seemingly neither.

Pacification of the Formosan population was one thing; pacification of the aborigines was quite another, and a more difficult task at that. As early as 1912, 761 Japanese had already been killed by aborigines. Military suppression had failed and pacification had yet to be tried. Finally the fifth governor, Samata Sakuma, proposed a five-year plan of pacification which would employ essentially persuasive means but which would also, if necessary, allow for large-scale military actions. It was successful, and by the time Sakuma resigned in 1915 the problem was under control. Thereafter the work of " civilising " the aborigines continued, and those who gave themselves up were taught to farm, grow sugar-cane, graze cattle, and raise silkworms. By 1936 71 per cent. of the aborigine children of school age were in elementary school.

The last tribal uprising against the Japanese took place in 1930 at Musha in central Formosa. On October 27 during an athletic meet held at the village school the Japanese in attendance were surprised and attacked by a band of local aborigines. 145 were killed. The government mobilised two thousand police and troops to ferret out the culprits and quell the uprising. It took more than a month and 685 aborigine lives before peace was restored. Another 551 surrendered to the Japanese but the chieftain responsible for the attack escaped capture by committing suicide. The cause of the uprising most likely lay in the Japanese imposition of involuntary servitude on the aborigines, wage discrimination against them and maltreatment of them by the officials.

ECONOMIC DEVELOPMENT

Goto Shimpei was quick to recognise the potential of Formosa's sugar crop and urged Japan's leaders to back the development of a sugar industry in the new colony. He was successful and in 1900 the Formosa Sugar Refining Company was founded. Its promise of assured profits attracted considerable Japanese capital, and by 1921 a sugar cartel was organised. Meanwhile the Government-General in Formosa made continuous efforts to improve plant strains and irrigation networks. The result was a rapid and impressive increase in production, which expressed itself in the 1920s in a surplus over and above the sugar requirements of the Japanese empire. The figures bear out the claim of rapid growth:

Increases in Sugar Production for Japan and Formosa (in long tons)

1902–3	1913–14	1919–20	1925–26
45,391	157,050	283,482	498,460

Sugar has remained Formosa's chief agricultural product down to the present day. Rice, sweet potatoes and bananas rank second, third and fourth respectively. During the fifty years of Japanese rule rice and yam production quintupled while their field acreages doubled. More noteworthy still is the story of banana production which grew twenty-six-fold between 1912 and 1935.

Prior to China's cession of the island to Japan, Formosa's trade had been conducted almost exclusively with or via China and Hong Kong and had been handled chiefly by Chinese and Western merchants. The pattern of trade changed drastically after 1895. At home the Japanese were breaking down the restrictions imposed by the unequal treaties and by 1899 had gained a threefold increase in her tariff rates and by 1911 full tariff autonomy. Formosan merchandise entered the Japanese home market duty-free and Japanese goods did likewise in the colony. The final restriction on Formosan goods, a clearance tax levied on export commodities in Formosan ports, was abolished in 1910, and thereafter an untrammelled colonial trade developed. As the figures show, Formosa's colonial trade far outstripped the development of her foreign trade:

Value of Total Imports and Exports

	1897	1926	1935
	yen	yen	yen
Foreign Trade ...	25,411,000	111,323,000	81,523,100
Colonial Trade			
(Formosa and Japan)	5,828,000	323,514,000	532,341,320

Formosa's economic development followed the classical colonial pattern: production was geared to the needs of the mother country. This accounts for the significant increases in rice, sugar, banana, and sweet potato production; all were in constant demand in Japan. In the 1930s, in fact, nearly half of Formosa's rice crop and more than three-quarters of the banana crop were shipped to Japan. For the same reason tea production languished. Formerly Formosa's chief export commodity, it was simply not needed for the Japanese home market.

Efforts were made to exploit the other natural resources of the colony, too, notably mining and fishing. In general, however, Formosa was earmarked as a market for Japanese manufactures, not as a supplier of them. Hence native industry was slow to develop and, with the major exception of the sugar industry, lagged behind the agricultural sector of the economy.

GOVERNMENT AND POLITICS

The Japanese Government-General in Formosa functioned not unlike the British East India Company in India. The governor-general was vested with the sole right of enacting ordinances, which, to quote *Law 63* of 1896, "had force in the territory under his jurisdiction equal to the laws legislated by the Imperial Diet." *Law 63* was first made operative for a period of three years; later the time limit was extended; and finally a new ordinance, *Law 41* of 1906 gave the governor-general these powers without restriction in time. The governor-general was also the source of special criminal ordinances, the most notorious of which stated that "those who assembled for any purpose the accomplishment of which suggested an intent to use violence or intimidation would be considered banditti" and punished severely.

As the economy developed and social progress was made, and as the political sensitivities of the Formosans grew, there was an increasing pressure to modernise and liberalise the laws. This began gradually in the 1920s with the wholesale introduction to Formosa of large parts of the Japanese legal system. Japan's education laws were extended to the colony in 1922; the main body of the Japanese Civil Code was recognised to be effective in Formosa in 1923; the Japanese Criminal Code was enforced there in the same year; and the legislative power of the governor-general was gradually circumscribed.

Again like the British East India Company, the Government-General relied heavily on the income from its monopolies for much of its revenue. Opium, salt, natural camphor, tobacco, and spirits were monopolised by the government as were the rail, telephone, telegraph and postal services, and the management of most of the forests. Income from all these sources, represented as a percentage of annual total government revenue, appears thus: 1897: 22 per cent.; 1912: 41 per cent.; 1926: 54 per cent.; 1932: 60·9 per cent.; 1935: 60·8 per cent. and 1941: 44 per cent. The government-processed opium had a world-wide reputation for its excellence, was often smuggled to China, and brought in huge profits. And since Formosa produced 70 per cent. of the world's camphor in the 1930s (before the advent of the synthetic camphor industry) the government reaped enormous profits from that source too.

The similarity with British India ends when we compare their approaches to local government administration. The British relied heavily on native administrators; the Japanese on their own police. The police system was strong and all-pervasive. At least one or two policemen were stationed in every village and their functions far transcended the usual task of keeping the peace. They exercised strict control over the *pao-chia* system, enforced sanitary regulations, tried criminal cases and saw to the supervision of undesirable persons, oversaw household and census registrations, superintended road and irrigation improvements, introduced new plant specimens to the farmers and encouraged education and the development of local industries. They also instructed the Formosans in the complexities of land registration and the purchase and sale of government bonds and stocks, and preached the gospel of frugality. Their political power was felt in most native organisations and their persuasive power in educational circles, where they often went so far as to discourage Formosan youths from going to Japan for their higher education.

The arbitrary nature of this kind of rule obviously bred contempt and discontent. So did the inevitable break-down of the old rural-community before the pressures of modernisation and social change. The antagonism, however, was rarely well organised, and the uprisings which did occur remained sporadic, localised and generally impotent. Nevertheless the beginnings of a Formosan " nationalist " or " nativist " movement can be traced back as early as 1914. To be sure, it was a Japanese peer, Count Taisuke Itagaki, once a prominent leader of the *Jiyuminken undo* or " Movement for civil liberty and popular rights," who started it all when he went to Formosa and organised the Association for the Assimilation of the Formosans. Much to the displeasure of the Government-General he argued that the Formosan people deserved to enjoy the same rights held by the Japanese people at home. Needless to say, the Association was disbanded the next year, shortly after Itagaki's departure.

In 1918 a group of Formosan students in Tokyo organised the Alliance to Accomplish the Abolition of *Law 63*. They published a periodical entitled *Taiwan Chinglian* (Young Formosan) and subtitled in English, *Formosan Civil Press*. In 1923, two years after 178 Formosan intellectuals had submitted a petition to the Imperial Diet calling for the creation of a Diet in Formosa, several of the movement's leaders were arrested and imprisoned in Formosa. Nevertheless the movement continued to grow and its members kept up a flow of petitions to the Diet in Tokyo. The ninth petition, submitted in 1928, was signed by more than two thousand Formosans.

Meanwhile the leaders of the movement created another organisation, the Association of Formosan Culture, whose aim was to enlighten and lead the mass of Formosans on the island. A group of Marxist youths joined the Association and after a bitter struggle, finally managed to take it over. The non-Marxist members retaliated in 1927 by forming a new party, the People's Party of Formosa. The left group, made up of social democrats, anarchists and communists, gradually came under the control of the Comintern and at one point succeeded in penetrating the Formosan peasant movement. In 1928 and 1929, however, they were effectively crushed by the Government-General and never again appeared on the Formosan political scene.

The People's Party, on the other hand, was caught between the Marxist left and a suspicious government on the right. For a while it managed to control and lead the nascent urban workers movement but was finally suppressed by the Government-General in 1935. Thereafter the colonial government prohibited all further native political activity and concentrated its energies and those of the people on a large-scale, rapid assimilation movement. It ended only with the end of the war and the end of Japanese rule in Formosa.

Politics on Formosa

By JOHN ISRAEL

THOUGH Chiang Kai-shek may vow to " sleep on faggots and drink gall " until the mainland is liberated, he has some reason to rest more easily today than at any time in his long career as Nationalist leader. On the mainland his government never clearly controlled more than one of China's three " key economic areas " (the Yellow River plain, the Yangtze valley, and the Szechuan basin). At least he can effectively control Formosa, a realm 1/260th the size of the mainland. Nationalist cells permeate schools, factories and government bureaux. Local police organisations, semi-autonomous in mainland days, are now under the central control of loyal mainlanders. The powerful security force, the Formosa Garrison Command (FGC), operates under martial law. The two minority parties are as impotent as their mainland counterparts. There are no treaty ports to harbour leftist critics and the mountainous half of the island is effectively patrolled by government forces painfully aware of the dangers of banditry and rebellion.

Chiang's tight rein on the countryside presents a dramatic contrast to his mainland days. Then the government generally shied away from reducing rent, redistributing land or other measures which would have alienated sympathetic landowners. The Nationalists, however, had no ties with Formosa's local gentry. On the contrary the large landlords, well-endowed and deeply entrenched, were a likely rallying point for opposition. For the Nationalists enlightened self-interest called for sweeping reform. Through the now famous programme which set an upper limit on rents, sold public land to the peasants, deprived landlords of most of their holdings, Formosa became largely an island of freeholders. This gained enough goodwill to compensate for the post war misrule, the bloody suppression of the February 1947 uprising, the universal conscription, government manipulation of the rice-fertiliser exchange, political domination, etc.

SUN YAT-SENISM ON FORMOSA

Some aspects of Sun Yat-sen's Three People's Principles can be read into Nationalist rule on Formosa. Rural reform may be considered to spring from the " People's Livelihood." Local elections have given an air of democracy at the grass roots level, which is closer to the spirit of " People's Rule " than the sudden resort to national elections just before the Nationalists fled the mainland. The principle of " Nationalism," which Sun himself reinterpreted to suit changing circumstances, has been enshrined in the " National Polity "—to liberate the mainland from the agents of international communism and reunify it under Nationalist rule. This is used to rationalise the Nationalists' control of Formosa.

Sun's three stages of national political development—military dictatorship, tutelage, and democracy are, however, hopelessly confused on Formosa. All of China, including Formosa, supposedly entered the period of democracy under the Constitution of 1947. But since 1948 martial law has prevailed with the government simultaneously fostering the extension of communications and education and the understanding of party principles—which Sun thought appropriate for the period of tutelage. The Nationalists may, therefore, be said to rule by martial law under a democratic constitution while practising local tutelage.

The difficulties of moving from party tutelage to democracy are evident in Formosa's local elections for mayors, *hsien* (county) councils, provincial assemblymen, etc. Sometimes, non-Nationalists are given a fighting chance of victory (*e.g.*, Kao Yü-shu [Henry Kao] was elected mayor of Taipei in 1954), but the ruling party never allows a real challenge to its supremacy. It is not always necessary for the Nationalists to buy votes and stuff ballot boxes. After all, theirs is the only well-organised and adequately financed political party on the island. The party label is camouflaged and ambitious local politicians absorbed into its organisation. This helps, at least on the local level, to avoid the stigma attached to Formosa being ruled by mainlanders.

Election regulations favour the Nationalists. Candidates are criminally liable for their speeches, which must not raise such issues as Formosan-mainlander relations, the policy of counter-attack, and the leadership of Chiang Kai-shek. The Ministry of Interior recently prohibited all campaign speeches outside of government-controlled meetings, where indiscreet remarks may be tape-recorded. Democracy has been debased to a contest for the spoils of office and elections fail to arouse popular enthusiasm.

Numerous anomalies mar the ostensibly democratic system. The provincial government in Taichung is eclipsed by the national régime in Taipei. Executive authorities make the legislatures public debating clubs rather than important law-making bodies. The Nationalist controlled Provincial Assembly is popularly elected, but the Governor of Formosa is an appointee of the central authorities. The National Assembly and Legislative Yüan, which were chosen in manipulated nationwide elections in 1947 and 1948, have continued in power on

Formosa due to the obvious impossibility of holding new elections on the mainland. Their membership, halved by attrition (many did not flee to Formosa; others have died), includes but a handful of Formosans. The prestige of these impotent bodies, which may remain until the last aged member has passed away, lends valuable moral support to the government.

THE POLICE STATE

Formosa is ruled by what might properly be called a *party*-military dictatorship. The chief of state, Chiang Kai-shek, is both the leader of the Nationalist party and commander-in-chief of the armed forces, while the Nationalists' apparatus permeates military as well as civil branches of government.

The military has exercised its unlimited powers sporadically. The most oppressive period followed the abortive Formosan uprising of February 28, 1947. Besides the estimated 10,000 killed outright by government troops, untold thousands were executed or imprisoned in subsequent years. Many were arrested on anonymous accusations and held for months or years while their cases were " under investigation."

A loosening of control was apparent by 1954—the year that the Sino-American Mutual Defence Treaty was signed—as Formosa began to develop into a " showcase " of American aid. Kao Yü-shu who opposed the Nationalists became mayor of Taipei; Li Wan-chü, another Formosan, called for greater power for the " native-born " through his newspaper, the *Kung-lun Pao*. Bold criticisms of the party state were voiced in the *Free China* (*Tzu-yu Chung-Kuo*) fortnightly, edited by the former Nationalist official Lei Chen. At National Formosa University, Yin Hai-kuang, a free-thinking admirer of Bertrand Russell and one of *Free China's* most impassioned writers, spoke before appreciative audiences of young liberals.

Faced with mounting criticism the Nationalist party reminded its critics of the limits of freedom. In the spring of 1956, the Peace Preservation Command threatened the English-language *China Post* for reporting a conciliatory statement from Chou En-lai to Nationalist officials. In December 1957, the *Kung-lun Pao's* chief editorial writer, Ni Shih-t'an, was arrested on charges of failing to register his past Communist affiliations. Since Yin Hai-kuang's speech on " Hu Shih and the National Destiny " in December 1958, he has been unable to give extracurricular speeches and his articles have been deleted from student publications. In the offending address before a large student crowd, Yin had discussed Ch'en Tu-hsiu (an outstanding figure of the May Fourth Movement and early leader of the Chinese Communist Party) as one of the four most influential modern Chinese thinkers and had suggested that Sun Yat-sen's Three Principles of the People were more suitable for historical study than as guides for contemporary China.[1]

The crippling blow to free speech came on September 4, 1960, with the arrest of Lei Chen and three of his *Free China* colleagues on charges of sedition. The Nationalists had long been irked by the publication's bold criticisms of party dictatorship, its accusations that anti-Communist slogans were being used to justify internal coercion, and its suggestion that the United States use its influence to encourage democratic reforms in Formosa. The authorities took no action, however, until Lei joined with Li Wan-chü, Kao Yü-shu, and other Formosan politicians to organise the China Democratic Party.

Three days after the arrests, one of the four, Liu Tzu-ying, was accused of being a Communist secret agent. In a subsequent " confession " Liu said that seven years before he had asked Lei to co-operate with him in subversive activities. He had dropped his plans after a stern warning from Lei. Nonetheless, Lei's failure to turn in a known Communist agent was a serious offence. Lei's outspoken articles, coupled with his alleged Communist associations, led to the indictment that " his ultimate purpose " was " to overthrow the government by means of writings favourable to the Communist rebels." On the basis of Liu's confession, which neither Lei nor his attorney was allowed to challenge by cross-examination, Lei was sentenced to ten years in prison. Liu was given twelve years (a light sentence for a Communist agent), and the other two were sent away for shorter terms of " reformatory training."

With Lei behind bars, the China Democratic Party was not inaugurated. The official press speeded its end by placing " red hats " (Communist labels) on the heads of Formosan leaders Li Wan-chü and Kao Yü-shu when these men protested that Lei's arrest was really aimed at destroying their new party. Li Wan-chü lost control of his newspaper to a group less critical of the government, leaving Formosa with no opposition press. *The Humanist*, Formosa's only magazine of political satire, was suspended for a year on vague charges. Most recently the respectable weekly news magazine, *Time and Tide*, also received a year's suspension for printing a poem by Lei Chen and an interview with his wife.

WEAKNESS OF PUBLIC OPINION

The government's handling of the Lei case raised a storm of protest abroad. In Formosa, however, only a bare handful of people sprang to Lei's defence. Hu Shih's temperate and ironic criticism of the government

[1] See *Tzu-yu Chung-kuo*, May 1, 16, 1960.

received little backing from Formosa's academic community. Of the nearly 500 members of the Legislative Yüan on Formosa, only two signed a manifesto defending the cause of free speech. Besides the *Kung-lun Pao* only one local paper, the normally pro-government *China Post*, gave Lei strong support.

Nationalist coercion does not explain away the public's silence. Before the Nationalists fled the mainland, where critics stood in danger of assassination, non-Communist intellectuals were staunch defenders of civil liberty.

The local Formosans, for their part, are politically quiescent. Fifty years of Japanese colonial rule, which denied them political opportunities, was followed by the slaughter of their dynamic leadership by the Nationalists in 1947. The local people are unwilling to fight for their own political advantage, let alone for that of the mainlanders.

The mainlanders on Formosa are a well-educated, politically conscious group representing a wide range of opinions. Many agreed with Lei's critique of party dictatorship, but not his forthright approach. However, they all want to go home and hope is kept alive by the Nationalists' myth of retaking the mainland. Lei Chen's arrest aroused the common reaction: We are now at war with the Communists; the overriding goal is to defeat the enemy and return to our homes; if our leaders want us to sacrifice free speech for this end, so be it.

The effectiveness of Nationalist control is evident to all would-be dissidents. Once Lei was arrested, it seemed obvious that his cause was doomed. There was nothing to gain by speaking out, and everything to be risked—the loss of a job, the persecution of a son in the army, police harassment, or worse. There were few candidates for martyrdom.

The party press, which enjoys a near monopoly on Formosa argued that the Lei affair was a " legal " and not a " political " case. It was civic duty to accept the verdict on this issue which involved questions of national security. The last card was to attack Lei's moral character in the press and through a whispering campaign. This was highly effective in a country where a man's personal character is considered more important than abstract principles.

Chiang Kai-shek seldom steps down from his imperial dais to mix in the less noble realm of politics, which his subordinates control. He had no wish to be publicly involved in the Lei affair. The crime of *lèse majesté*, of which Lei was conspicuously guilty, was not included in the government's indictment. Chiang's only statement came nine days after Lei's arrest. He told persistent American correspondents that Lei would be proved guilty of abetting the Communists. Once the oracle had spoken any defence of Lei would have been an attack on the President.

Subsidies to *Free China* from the United States Information Service and the Asia Foundation finished some time before Lei's arrest. In the case of USIS it is not clear whether this was related to *Free China's* increasingly controversial views. USIS subsidies are only to help new publications get established. But the withdrawal of American aid in this case suggested that the Americans were dissociating themselves from an embarrassing project. America was silent following Lei's arrest. American policy was to interfere only in Nationalist economic and military questions, where American dollars and power interests were directly affected, but to avoid imposing American political ideals on the Nationalist government.

THE CASE OF SU TUNG-CH'I

With Lei Chen in jail, *Free China* closed down, and the island's first and only opposition movement including both mainlanders and Formosans destroyed, a pall of silence fell over Formosa. Apparently the imprisonment of four men had coerced all others into acquiescence. It came as a surprise, therefore, when the Garrison Command seized more than 100 Formosans including Su Tung-ch'i (a popular political leader in the southern part of the island) in September 1961, a year after Lei's arrest. Su was little known outside of southern Formosa and completely unknown abroad. The FGC was therefore spared the unfavourable publicity of the Lei case, though its methods were even more objectionable.

Su was dragged from his bed in the little town of Peikang at 2 a.m. on September 19 and whisked off to the prison in Taipei where political suspects are interrogated and tortured. Unable to completely conceal the disappearance of the local notable, the FGC announced that he had been caught *flagrante delicto* in the act of rebellion. His house was searched and numerous publications (including old copies of *Free China*) confiscated. His wife was interrogated ceaselessly for two days and nights, although she fainted several times from fatigue, menstrual sickness and worry about her husband and six untended children. She was released and assured that she would be allowed to visit her husband only after signing an " interrogation record." She was arrested on two more occasions and then released. But, apparently alarmed by the persistence of Su's wife in telling about her persecution, the Garrison Command seized her for a fourth time—not to be released.

Rumours spread like wildfire—Su Tung-ch'i had plotted a *coup d'état*; he had planned to kidnap the Generalissimo; he was in league with the Free Formosa movement in Japan—but the FGC neither confirmed nor denied. Meanwhile, more than a hundred (perhaps several

64

hundred) Formosans were quietly rounded up. Some were charged with no crime, but they were put through marathon interrogations, asked to write about their own thinking and that of their associates, and released as suddenly and inexplicably as they had been arrested. Others were broken by torture. At least one attempted suicide. Not until mid-January did the Garrison Command announce the indictments against twenty suspects of armed rebellion. No trial was announced. On May 27, 1962, the *New York Times* reported that a military court had sentenced Su and two associates to death and 42 others, including Mrs. Su, to prison sentences ranging from one year to life. There has been no announcement of Su's execution sentence, if indeed it has been carried out.

THE FUTURE

The Su case marks a return to the police state of 1947–54. It would, therefore, be unrealistic to see Formosa's immediate future in democratic terms. We must look instead to the evolving movements within the Nationalist Party. Chiang Kai-shek is still, at 75, a combination of the emperor—aloof, austere, and sacrosanct—and the political juggler—manipulating and co-ordinating the complex network of cliques that constitute the Nationalist party. The cliques of the mid-1940s have gone. The Ch'en Brothers faction has disintegrated. Kuo-fu is dead, Li-fu raises chickens in New Jersey—though many of their followers still hold office on Formosa. Mme. Chiang influences both her husband and Americans, but the " Soong dynasty " has fallen. Of the old alignments, only the Whampoa group remains, dedicated to the Leader and for ever hoping that the military will vitalise the party. While Chiang lives, it will continue to be a major power. Both Provincial Governor Huang Chieh and FGC commander Ch'en Ta-ch'ing (the post Huang occupied until November 1962), are graduates of the first Whampoa class.

New groupings centre around 66-year-old Ch'en Ch'eng, Vice-President, Premier and legitimate successor to the presidency, and Chiang Kai-shek's 53-year-old son, Ching-kuo, who heads the secret police, the youth corps, the veterans association and army political department. Ch'en is supported by the old party figures, high-ranking army officers and economic and technical modernisers. The core of Ching-kuo's strength lies in the security system and in the middle and lower rank officers, but in recent years his influence has extended to every branch of the army, the Party and the government. The present chiefs-of-staff of the army, the air force and the navy support him. Of the two contenders for the Generalissimo's mantle, the young, vigorous Ching-kuo has the upper hand, and is continually strengthening it.

As Chiang Kai-shek grows older, he may play an increasingly passive role. Even now, the process of deification—the transformation of the Leader into the Sage—has begun. Celebrating Chiang's seventy-fifth birthday, the October 31, 1962 editorial of the *Central Daily News* said that:

> People generally admire the President from the view-point of his exploits as a great military man, a great revolutionist, and a great political leader, but the President's true point of greatness cannot adequately be portrayed in these laudatory terms. The President has often said, " The basic responsibility of the revolution is to carry out principles of humanity." We deeply feel that the [greatest] exploit of the President is here, in the revelation and propagation of his sincere humanity. . . .

Chiang's successor can never occupy the same position as the Nationalists' leader of nearly four decades. The next ruler will be *a* leader, not *the* Leader. Both the elder son and the Vice-President are much too deeply immersed in political mire to take on Chiang Kai-shek's transcendent image. Ching-kuo, moreover, in spite of his real power, is still regarded as an upstart by many Whampoa alumni who refuse to kow-tow to any one but their old commandant.

Chiang's successor, whoever he may be, cannot rule without military support. Formosan conscripts, who constitute a majority of enlisted men, have demonstrated no potential for independent political action and are unlikely to attach themselves to any clique of their mainlander officers. Irredentist sentiments of the mainlanders may be sufficient to compel Chiang's successor to continue a national policy aimed at military reconquest, if not to reach an agreement with Peking. However, the cost of maintaining a huge military establishment in the face of a growing population and likely cuts in American aid would create serious economic and political problems. If, on the other hand, the army is reduced to a Formosa defence force, the economy and society will have to absorb a large number of ageing, maladjusted mainlanders. Even now, homesick non-commissioned officers from the mainland who have not shared in the island's prosperity, are a restive element. Any sign of political instability will frighten away the foreign investment on which Formosa depends for economic progress. There is no easy solution.

Educated youth is also alienated. The cream of Formosa's college graduates now study in the United States; a bare 7 per cent. return. Chiang's government faced a similar problem on the mainland, where China's most talented and dedicated students drifted into the Communist camp. The voluntary exiles in the United States will go back to Formosa only if the island offers incentives untrammelled by ideological claptrap and party coercion. At present, there is no room for them in the already overstaffed bureaucracy, and teaching offers neither economic security nor intellectual freedom.

The police state now seems unassailable, but for how long? Beneficiaries of universal education—even party education—cannot be expected to remain blind for ever to the contradictions of government propaganda and policy. The rising middle class may be expected to demand a political voice as well as economic advantages. As the welding of mainlanders and Formosans slowly but inexorably proceeds, some political contender may once again try to form a coalition of discontented elements. The last echoes of Lei Chen have not yet been heard.

Some Aspects of Formosa's Economic Growth

By SHEPPARD GLASS

FOURTEEN years have elapsed since a shattered Nationalist Government fled to Formosa with the hope of reorganising and revitalising its forces and of building an effective base for a counter-attack against the Chinese Communists. At that time it appeared to have little chance of survival. However, because of changing international conditions and Formosa's impressive domestic economic performance, the Nationalist Government has been able to re-establish itself as an effective political force. Formosa's economic achievements have given the Government a certain international prestige and, combined with military assistance from the United States, have allowed it to maintain a large, well-equipped military establishment.

Formosa's economic achievements have been outstanding for any under-developed country: continuing high rates of growth, increasing per capita income and consumption levels, and the building of a considerable infra-structure of electric power, communications, transport and educational facilities. The record is all the more impressive when one remembers that a large portion of the island's resources (estimated at as much as 12–15 per cent. of gross national product) [1] has been poured annually into the armed forces. Economic considerations have been subordinated to military requirements in the determination of policy. Moreover, Formosa has pushed up the standards of living in the face of a wave of 1·4 million immigrants (who fled after the Communist victories on the mainland) and a subsequent rate of population increase of 3–3·5 per cent. annually—and it has achieved this despite a limited supply of arable land.

In this context American assistance has been, and continues to be, essential to Formosa's robust economy. More than U.S.$3,000 million of military and economic aid has provided the armed forces with their hardware and the island with much of its capital formation. The aid has released local resources for other military purposes and for the increases in consumption deemed necessary to preserve political stability. It has also permitted the Nationalists to duck unpleasant choices between

---

[1] Excluding dollar assistance under the U.S. Military Assistance Programme (MAP).

the often conflicting requirements of their political objectives and Formosa's economic development.

This article will first review in broad outline Formosa's economic growth and use of resources. Following this I will describe American assistance and discuss some of the problems involved in trying to satisfy the needs both of the military and of the economy. Finally, I will consider the effort now under way to overcome, or compensate for, obstacles to growth.

DIMENSIONS OF GROWTH

Recent economic development on Formosa is indebted to the considerable development carried out by the Japanese during their fifty-year dominion over the island (1895–1945). The Japanese devoted attention primarily to the agricultural sector, in order to provide Japan with most of its imports of sugar and rice. An extensive irrigation network was constructed, biological improvements introduced and farmers' organisations established. Of equal importance were the Japanese efforts to raise the literacy of the farm population and to make the Formosan farmers generally receptive to technological change. A good network of communication and transportation facilities was constructed. Industrial investment was centred initially on sugar refining, but as the Second World War approached, electric power capacity was sharply increased to allow for expansion in the chemical, oil refining and aluminium industries. Almost all managerial and technical positions were held by Japanese.

When Formosa was returned to China at the end of the war the economy was nearly in ruins. American bombing had destroyed many basic facilities. The more than 20,000 Japanese technicians who had supported the economy had gone. The early phase of Nationalist rule was marked by a run-down of the economy and, until 1949, by the export of capital to the mainland. Agricultural production declined precipitously because of reductions in fertiliser imports and the deterioration of irrigation facilities. Widespread shortages led to astronomical price rises and the economy reverted to a near barter state.

The period 1949–53 was essentially one of reconstruction—of stabilising the economy and restoring output to the pre-war level. The process quickened as the Nationalist Government became more firmly established. Basic electric power and transportation facilities were repaired. Most important, large-scale agricultural reconstruction was carried out, including an extensive programme of rent reduction and land redistribution which contributed significantly to political stability. By 1952 rice production had reached its pre-war peak. The gains in other areas of production during this period also were tremendous—reflecting the low state to which the economy had deteriorated and the relatively large and quick returns from reconstruction work. By 1953 the economy was again working at a fairly normal capacity and in assessing growth under the Nationalists we should probably take that year as the base year.

During the post-reconstruction period Formosa's rate of growth has been one of the highest in the world. From 1953–61 gross national production in real terms, according to official statistics, increased 72·7 per cent. or an average of 7·1 per cent. per year (compounded), and real national income increased 62·9 per cent. or an annual average of 6·3 per cent.[2] The highest annual rate of growth in gross national production was 8·4 per cent. (1954); the lowest, 4·0 per cent. (1956). Real income per capita during the period increased steadily, but less dramatically because of the high rate of population growth. The total increase was 25·1 per cent. or an annual average of 2·9 per cent. (compounded). Despite the continued growth, per capita income was still very low (U.S.$115 in 1961). However, as is the case in under-developed countries, the official figures probably understate the standard of living in terms of local currency, and the different price levels of Formosan consumption goods no doubt further exaggerate this tendency.

Formosa remains unquestionably an agricultural country but is making rapid strides towards industrialisation, primarily in the processing of agricultural products. While agricultural production rose 36 per cent. from 1953 to 1961, industrial production increased 120 per cent. and industry's share (including mining and electric power) of the net national product rose from 16·7 to 21·9 per cent.[3] Even in the agricultural sector, a considerable portion of farmers' income now comes from non-agricultural pursuits. A recent survey shows that between 1952 and 1957 farmers' income from non-farm sources increased from 13 to 22 per cent. of their total income.[4] Moreover, agricultural employment increased less than 6 per cent. during 1953–61 and dropped from 61 per cent. of total

[2] Preliminary figures available for 1962 show a fall-off in the rate of growth; gross national product increased 6·5 per cent. and national income 6·8 per cent. Until 1962 two series of national income statistics were available, one published by the Government's Director-General of Budgets, Accounts and Statistics (DGBAS) and the other by the AID Mission in Taipei. The AID series, now discontinued, was based on primary data supplied by the Chinese, and the major difference was in the treatment of inventories. National income statistics used here are all derived from the DGBAS publication in both Chinese and English—*National Income of the Republic of China, National Accounts in Taiwan for 1952–61, Preliminary Estimates of National Income in Taiwan for 1962* (Taipei: 1963), hereafter *DGBAS*. Formosa's statistics, while not reaching the standards of the more developed countries, are considered to be quite good. The most serious deficiencies are in employment and labour statistics.
[3] Ministry of Economic Affairs and Central Bank of China, The Republic of China, *Taiwan Production Statistics Monthly* (Taipei), September 1962, pp. 4 and 53, and *DGBAS*, p. 19.
[4] Su I-shih, " Taiwan chih nung-chia so-te " (" The Income of Taiwan's Farm Households "), in Bank of Taiwan, *Taiwan chih nung-yeh ching-chi* (Taipei: 1962), p. 123.

employment to 56 per cent.[5] At the same time industrial employment increased by 116,000 or 43 per cent. and rose from 9 to 11 per cent. of total employment.

By almost any of the usual measurements of welfare Formosa progress is impressive. Private consumption has risen at an annual rate of 6·6 per cent., while the proportion of food in private consumption expenditure has steadily declined.[6] Daily consumption of calories per person increased from a pre-war (1935–39) average of 1,865 to 2,390 in 1960, and the daily protein content of *per capita* food supplies for the same period increased from 44·9 grammes to 57·17 grammes.[7] Although Formosa is still beset by basic sanitation problems, such diseases as plague and malaria have been virtually eradicated. Life expectancy increased by about fifteen years between 1941 and 1958.[8] Strides have also been made—even in rural areas—to meet the great need of the people for education. The number of schools rose from 2,325 in 1953–54 to 3,801 in 1961–62, and the number of students enrolled increased even faster—from 1·3 million to 2·6 million.

In the 1961–62 school year, 96 per cent. of the school-age population was in primary schools (this is based on enrolment and not attendance figures, which would be considerably lower).[9]

Perhaps the biggest single change that development has wrought has been in foreign trade. Imports of capital goods have almost tripled since 1953, rising from 18 per cent. of total imports to 30 per cent. in 1961. More significant is the change in the structure of exports. Until 1959 sugar and rice dominated Formosa's exports. In 1953 these two commodities accounted for 78 per cent. of total exports and as late as 1959 still represented 56 per cent. However, reductions in the world price of sugar and in the amounts shipped under Formosa's quota laid down by the International Sugar Convention, greater domestic consumption of rice, and rapid increases in other exports reduced the proportion of rice and sugar to 33 per cent. of total exports in 1961. Reaping the benefits of

---

[5] The increase of agricultural employment during the period would appear to be understated. Labour force data runs into serious problems of definition, particularly in handling unemployment. Except for the industrial sector, employment statistics are derived from household registration data. For employment statistics, see Economic Research Centre, Council for U.S. Aid, *Taiwan Statistical Data Book* (Taipei: 1962), p. 7, hereafter, *Data Book*.

[6] Consumption data is found in *DGBAS*, pp. 16–21, and United Nations, *Yearbook of National Account Statistics, 1960* (New York: 1961), p. 50.

[7] Chow, Senyung, editor, *12th General Report of the Joint Commission on Rural Reconstruction* (Taipei: 1962), p. 131, hereafter, *JCRR XII*. Statistics are from production data and are probably understated.

[8] *Op. cit.*, p. 51. In 1958 the life expectancy on Formosa for males was 60·5 years and for females, 65·0 years.

[9] *Data Book*, pp. 133 and 140. For a discussion of some of the educational problems of Taiwan, see Henry F. McCusker and Harry J. Robinson, *Education and Development—the Role of Educational Planning in the Economic Development of the Republic of China* (Stanford: Stanford Un. Research Institute, 1962).

past investment and the devaluation of 1958 (a fundamental reform of an overvalued exchange rate), industrial exports soared from U.S.$18·8 million in 1958 to U.S.$85·1 million in 1961, or from 11·4 per cent. of total exports to 39·7 per cent. (Exports of textiles, which were non-existent in 1953, reached U.S.$38 million in 1962.) This growth more than made up the loss of exchange from reduced exports of sugar and rice. Total exports in 1962 reached U.S. $238·6 million, an increase of 84 per cent. over 1953, and almost equalled the original goal set for 1963 in the Government's third four-year plan.[10] However, the jump in exports has not been completely healthy. Some industries—notably paper, iron and steel, and textiles—have built up capacity in excess of current domestic needs and foreign orders, and are attempting to increase exports by lowering export prices far below domestic market prices—that is, by " dumping " goods.

Furthermore, despite the change in its foreign trade, Formosa's balance on goods and services remains in chronic deficit and is covered almost entirely by American aid—indeed the size of the current deficit would certainly be less if American aid were not available. From 1957–61 this deficit increased from U.S.$96 million to U.S.$134 million. Of course the widening gap reflects in part the spilling over of greater consumption into imports. However, it must be viewed primarily as a result of the needs generated by industrialisation, as well as the considerable worsening in the terms of trade that was caused by the slump in world sugar prices. The recent recovery in sugar prices should contribute to a significant reduction in the deficit in 1963.

THE USE OF RESOURCES

Formosa is a high consumption economy; although living standards are not high, a large proportion of income is spent on consumption. Total consumption during 1953–61 was as high as 91·8 per cent. of gross national product, and never less than 85·5 per cent. However, the trend since 1956 has been generally downward. Although continually increasing in absolute terms, private consumption has steadily decreased as a percentage of gross national product. Private savings have fluctuated, but have shown an upward trend since 1957. Government consumption rose fairly steadily during most of the period, reaching 20·1 per cent. of gross national production in 1959, but its relative share has since decreased. The sharp changes that occur in the relative figures

[10] Statistics on foreign trade are derived from exchange settlements of the Bank of Taiwan and are widely published. One easily available reference is the *Data Book*, pp. 109–120. Figures for 1962 are from Council for U.S. Aid, *Industry of Free China* (Taipei: February 1963), pp. 86–92.

largely represent savings in military activities—especially the expensive hostilities over the offshore islands.

Table I provides a breakdown of GNP according to major uses for the period 1953-61 (based on official statistics).[11]

TABLE I. *Expenditure on Gross National Product*, 1953-1961
(as percentage of GNP)

	1953	1954	1955	1956	1957	1958	1959	1960	1961
Total consumption expenditure	89·2	91·8	88·5	90·3	89·8	89·1	88·8	86·0	85·5
Private	74·4	74·8	71·3	71·3	71·1	69·2	68·7	67·9	67·5
Public	14·8	17·0	17·2	19·0	18·7	19·9	20·1	18·1	18·0
Gross capital formation	16·6	16·9	15·3	15·0	16·5	18·2	20·0	21·7	22·0
Depreciation	4·3	5·0	5·0	5·5	6·3	6·3	6·4	6·7	7·0
Net investment	12·3	11·9	10·3	9·5	10·2	11·9	13·6	15·0	15·0
Gross domestic savings	10·8	8·2	11·5	9·7	10·2	10·9	11·2	14·0	14·5
Net domestic savings	6·5	3·2	6·5	4·2	3·9	4·6	4·8	7·3	7·5
Private	4·7	1·7	4·4	2·6	1·6	3·1	4·0	5·7	6·6
Public	1·8	1·5	2·1	1·6	2·3	1·5	0·8	1·6	0·9
Net import surplus	5·8	8·7	3·8	5·3	6·3	7·3	8·8	7·7	7·5
Ration of net import surplus to net investment	47·1	73·2	36·9	55·8	61·4	61·2	64·9	51·4	50·2

The rate of gross capital formation has risen steadily (except for two years) and in 1961 reached a high of 22 per cent. of gross national product —a ratio which compares favourably with that of most developing countries. In terms of constant prices, gross capital formation during 1953-59 advanced at an average rate (compounded) of 7·6 per cent. At the same time the share devoted to depreciation increased from approximately 26 to 32 per cent. in response to the increasing tempo of industrialisation and the need for greater savings to foster further growth. Net domestic savings have been low. They have shown an upward trend since 1957, reaching a high of 7·5 per cent. of gross national product in 1961, but remain insufficient to maintain growth without outside assistance.

By any standards the role of the import surplus—financed mostly by aid—has been crucial in promoting growth. As a percentage of the gross national product, the import surplus reached a high of 8·8 per cent. in 1959. As part of gross capital formation, the import surplus has loomed even larger, ranging from 25 to 52 per cent. during 1953-61. As a proportion of net investment, the weight of the import surplus has been

---

[11] The table is derived from data in *DGBAS*. Figures for gross domestic savings are residuals.

tremendous; during this eight-year period it ranged between 37 and 73 per cent. and averaged about 56 per cent. The island's dependence on American economic aid is obvious.

THE GOVERNMENT AND ECONOMIC POLICY

The Political Framework. The Nationalist Government considers itself in a state of civil war: its foremost aim is to return to the Chinese mainland. Everything else is subordinate to this objective. The economic development of Formosa is viewed primarily as a means of providing support for, and increasing the effectiveness of, a large military machine, and of maintaining a stable political base. This is an improvement over the attitude of the Government while on the mainland, when the relationship between effective military power and a healthy economic base was not given due weight.

Important economic consequences flow from this basic attitude. Most important in the use of resources is the great volume of direct government consumption. Huge military outlays are deemed essential, and their magnitude is limited only by the paucity of resources, the fear of inflation, and the urgings of responsible Chinese economic officials and the United States Government (see below).

Two governmental structures are maintained, one for Formosa province and one for the whole of China. Although an effort has been made to demarcate the scope of the two bodies, a great amount of overlapping has occurred. Red tape, inefficiency, and lack of co-ordination have arisen as well as entrenched interest groups—all of which discourage the expansion of private industry and make central planning difficult. The number of government personnel is further increased because of the commitment the Government feels to provide in some way for those who followed it from the mainland. Since employment opportunities in the private sector are limited, government payrolls have swollen. There is a particularly large number of superfluous advisors to government corporations.[12] Not too surprisingly, financial resources are inadequate to provide for all these employees in an acceptable fashion. Government personnel, especially at the lower and middle levels, have not shared in Formosa's prosperity. The administration is generally free from large-scale corruption, in sharp contrast to the conditions on the mainland during the forties. Petty corruption, however, is prevalent and is recognised as an important problem by leading government officials. Prosecutions of corruption in the courts receive wide publicity

---

[12] The " old faithful " who must be retained in the armed forces is simply a drag on military modernisation.

in newspapers, indicating that the society possesses, in the judiciary and in the organs of public opinion, mechanisms of self-correction.[13]

The primacy of the goal of retaking the mainland has also put a premium on stability—both political and economic. One economic aspect of the search for political stability has been the Government's solicitude for the farm population (which is almost completely Formosan) and its unwillingness to employ stiff measures to siphon off the agricultural surplus for other sectors of the economy. Most noteworthy of the government agricultural measures was the land reform programme, largely carried out between 1949 and 1953. The impetus to this reform arose partially from the Government's determination to make amends for its neglect of this area. At the same time, land reform was a basic means of conciliating the Formosans and of reducing potential political opposition. Few mainlanders owned land on Formosa while the Formosan leadership was largely centred in the landlord class. As a result of the land reform, annual rents were slashed to a maximum of 37·5 per cent. of the annual crop and tenantry reduced from 300,000 families in 1949 to 140,000 in 1961.[14] The incentives of private ownership have doubtless contributed to increases in agricultural production. However, it is also true that the redistribution of income to a large number of poorer farm families has increased national consumption and has made it difficult to mobilise rural savings.

Unlike most developing countries, where governments have obtained the main amount of capital for development from the agricultural sector, the Nationalist government has taxed the rural sector relatively lightly, and largely in an indirect fashion. Any efforts further to tax the farmer draws considerable political criticism, and from 1952 to 1961 agricultural taxation remained relatively unchanged. The main direct tax on the farmer has been the land tax, which in recent years has produced 5–8 per cent. of total government tax revenue. More money has been pulled into the government's coffers through less offensive, indirect devices which are not measurable—food prices have been kept low and the ratio at which the government barters fertiliser for rice (discussed below) has been rigged against the farmer. Nevertheless the Formosan farmer is relatively prosperous, and farm income and consumption have generally increased.[15]

Equally important for maintaining morale and preventing unrest has been the emphasis on price stability. This also has been partly a heritage of the past—a reaction to the great inflation on the mainland. In periods

---

[13] The Government apparently tolerates the abundant publicity given to corruption in the hope that corrupt practices will be discouraged.
[14] *JCRR, XII*, p. 68.
[15] For a discussion of conditions in the countryside, see E. Stuart Kirby, *Rural Progress on Taiwan* (Taipei: JCRR, 1960).

of inflationary pressure the Government has restricted capital expenditures and clamped down on credit expansion to the private sector. It has attempted to keep food prices relatively low and rice payments in kind have been provided to civil servants and military personnel. The government has frequently released stores of rice to stabilise market conditions and in times of shortage, such as in 1960, the government has used scarce foreign exchange to import large amounts of rice. Heavy imports of wheat, financed by American aid (which releases rice for export), have occurred continually since 1949. Until 1961 price controls were maintained, although indifferently enforced, and the Government at times used police to patrol the markets and prevent price rises. The policy has extended beyond food policy to rates charged by public utility and public transport corporations—in fact rates have been held so low that these enterprises have been unable to earn enough to finance their needed expansion. (They have expanded largely through American aid.) In some ways the policy of holding down food and raw material prices has contributed to industrial development, but it has also helped raise the level of consumption. Government action has not managed to prevent a high rate of inflation (as will be discussed below).

Economic development is essentially a long-term activity. However, the priority in Formosa to the huge military establishment has engendered a short-term view toward the island's economic problems and detracted from effective planning. Subsidies permeate the economy so it is often difficult to weigh up the cost of one course of action against another. Once granted, subsidies are difficult to remove. More important, major problems are often shelved or solved in an *ad hoc* fashion. And the longer crucial economic decisions are put off, the greater becomes the difficulty of eventually solving the problems—especially in view of the population increase. Indeed, the government lacks even an effective population policy. The issue has been ducked in belief that the problem would cease to exist once the mainland was recovered.

Another reflection of the government's shortsightedness is the inadequacy of its revenue system. At present the revenue system is largely a carry-over from the mainland. Indirect taxes account for roughly 75 per cent. of all tax revenue and generally fall on the modern sector of the economy in the form of custom and commodity taxes.[16] Income taxes provide less than 10 per cent. of tax revenues. The nature and administration of the present system puts a premium on tax avoidance with the curious result that firms continually report that they have ended up in

---

[16] Statistics on public finance are found in the *Data Book*, pp. 89–94. The statistics, however, are not comprehensive, especially as to expenditure data. For a brief discussion of the Chinese tax system and some recommendations for reform, see Joseph P. Crocket, *Taxation in China* (Taipei: 1960), mimeographed.

the red and yet go on doing business. (The easiest way of doing this is by having stockholders lend money to the firm at very high rates of interest.) Moreover, the system has been unable to expand to cover rising expenditures. The total tax burden has remained relatively light, averaging about 17 per cent. of gross national product. From 1957 to 1961, gross national product at current prices increased 75 per cent. and government expenditures even more, but total tax revenues (including tobacco and wine monopoly profits, but excluding the profits of government corporations) increased only 37 per cent. Nevertheless, because of its great military outlays and the inadequacy of its tax administration, the government has been reluctant to institute large-scale reforms for fear that revenues might be reduced in the short run. Lately, however, there has been an increasing awareness of the deficiencies of the tax system and a recognition that soundly conceived tax measures can foster growth as well as produce increased revenues.

A third example of the economic effects of the short-term view is the system under which the government distributes fertiliser and collects rice. This was introduced in 1948 to enable the authorities to obtain rice easily during a chaotic period for military personnel and civil servants and for purposes of stabilisation and export. Fertiliser, which is completely under central control, is traded to the farmer in exchange for paddy rice at a set ratio determined by the government. The major part of the government's supply of rice—at present approximately 400,000 tons, or 20 per cent. of annual production—is obtained this way. The terms of exchange—at present 1·1 tons of fertiliser for 1 ton of rice—of course directly affect the farmers' application of fertiliser. And, although the ratio has been adjusted downward six times since the inception of the system, it has generally favoured the government and discouraged the maximum use of fertilisers. Both the application of fertiliser and its use for particular crops has been far from optimal and has directly affected production.[17] The government has not moved to a free market both because of budget considerations and because of a somewhat irrational fear that it cannot employ any other effective means to get the rice it requires for military and civilian personnel.

Military Expenditures. Although the detailed military budget is not published, information is available from government publications (and from press reports) to provide a reasonably good overall picture of the military's direct claim on resources. Table II shows military expenditures

---

[17] This is a simplified discussion of a very complex problem involving many types of fertilisers, the establishment of a local fertiliser industry, administrative difficulties and rivalries, and other factors.

from 1953 to 1961 and their relation to the gross national product and government expenditures.[18]

TABLE II. *Total Government, Central Government, and Military Consumption Expenditures, 1953-1961*

Year	Total Government Consumption	Central Government Consumption	Defence Consumption	Defence Consumption as per cent of:		
				Total Government Consumption	Central Government Consumption	GNP
	New Formosa Dollars (in thousands)					
1953	3,145	1,790	1,524	48·5	85·1	7·2
1954	3,935	2,750	2,315	58·8	84·2	10·2
1955	4,792	3,106	2,793	58·3	89·9	10·0
1956	6,132	3,803	3,186	52·0	83·8	9·9
1957	7,125	4,631	3,838	53·9	82·9	10·1
1958	8,296	5,660	4,790	57·7	84·6	11·5
1959	9,798	6,619	5,637	57·5	85·2	11·6
1960	10,856	7,549	6,254	57·6	82·8	10·4
1961	11,976	8,275	6,693	55·9	80·9	10·1

The impact of the military is overwhelming. Total expenditures on the Chinese armed forces (including United States military dollar assistance) far exceed net capital formation. From a budgetary point of view the central government's concern is almost exclusively military, and military expenditures during the period covered have ranged from 48 to 58 per cent. of the direct consumption of all levels of government. Through 1960 the lowest rate of annual increase of military expenditures was 10·9 per cent., but in 1961 it dropped sharply to 6·9 per cent. The military's claim out of the total resources of the economy appears to have tapered off after 1959. The bulges in 1954, 1955, 1958 and 1959 generally reflect fighting over the off-shore islands and show the economy's vulnerability to external events.

The tables show the direct costs of the military—that is, the amounts on which there exists budgetary and other official data. However, the military also enjoys significant subsidies. Each year the forces consume about 200,000 tons of rice. This rice is sold to them by the Formosan Food Bureau, not only below market prices but below the cost of rice to the Bureau—which just writes off the loss. Military personnel ride the railroads at half price, and military freight gets preferential rates. For that matter, freight bills, electric power bills and other utility charges

[18] *DGBAS*, p. 39. The table includes expenditures of U.S. aid-generated local currency provided in support of the military budget but not dollar assistance under the Military Assistance Programme. The table also does not include the approximately U.S.$50 million (from U.S. aid) which was used to remove from the Chinese armed forces a large number of the aged, sick and other ineffectives during this period. The present exchange rate is N.T.$40 to U.S.$1.

are frequently unpaid. Military factories produce items for the civilian economy and the profits are used strictly for military purposes, especially to support welfare funds. These funds are also fed by the proceeds from the sales of the bran which the forces extract from wheat provided under American military aid. All servicemen also get a premium rate on savings deposits.

Aside from their effects on the use of resources, the huge military expenditures confront the economy with constant inflation. The government borrows heavily from the banking system. At the same time because they must contribute, under various guises, large amounts to the Treasury, government enterprises find it necessary to go to the banking system to finance a significant part of their working capital and fixed capital needs. (And this expansion of credit to the public sector is largely at the expense of the private sector.) From 1953 to 1961, the money supply rose from New Taiwan (NT)$1,683 million to NT$7,335 million, an increase of 336 per cent.[19] The growth of government indebtedness and a large rise in bank claims on private enterprises have been only partially offset even by a phenomenal increase in time and savings deposits.[20]

Inflationary pressures as a result were severe—and would have been even more so but for the economy's great increases in productivity and the supplies of food and other commodities provided under American aid. Before 1949 inflation was extreme and public confidence in the currency collapsed; it was ended only when the New Taiwan dollar was issued. Under the new currency inflation resumed but at a much slower rate, and by 1954 relative stability was achieved: prices rose by less than 3 per cent. in that year.[21] From 1954 to 1958, however, the price level again increased rapidly, rising 40 per cent. In 1958, the year of the Quemoy crisis, the price level advanced only one per cent. but the delayed effects of the Quemoy crisis and the aftermath of a disastrous flood in 1959 boosted prices 26 per cent. between 1958 and 1960. In 1960 a strong anti-inflationary programme was adopted, and in 1961 the price level rose about 3 per cent. A trend toward stability is reflected in the fall in Taipei market interest rates for secured loans from 9 per cent. per month in 1951 to 2·4 per cent. in 1962; official rates are even lower.[22] The relentless strain of inflationary pressure nevertheless adversely affects both the level and the direction of investment. And the tendency of the

19 Financial statistics are found in Economic Research Department, Central Bank of China, Republic of China, *Taiwan Financial Statistics Monthly* (Taipei) January 1963.
20 Savings and time deposits rose from NT$822 million in 1953 to NT$9,500 million in 1961.
21 The wholesale price index for Taipei. For price statistics, see Bureau of Accounting and Statistics, Provincial Government for Formosa, *Taiwan Monthly of Commodity Price Statistics* (Taipei), No. 48, December 1962.
22 *Taiwan Financial Statistics Monthly*, pp. 56–60.

authorities to rely almost entirely on monetary policy—the restriction of credit to the private sector—to combat inflation has hardly helped matters.

Population. The Formosans are amazingly fertile. Japanese rule did little to change the economic structure or social system of the island while rapid increases in food production and simple public health measures resulted in a doubling of the population between 1905 and 1945. Under Nationalist rule, population has increased even faster—from 8,438,000 in 1953 to 11,149,000 in 1961, an annual rate of 3·5 per cent. (compounded) —even discounting most of the 1·4 million immigrants from the mainland.[23] The main factor in this increase has been the continuing decline in the death rate. Further public health measures have lowered the death rate from 9·4 per thousand in 1953 to 6·7 in 1961. The birth rate has declined but remains at a high level, 38·3 per thousand.[24] The annual rate of net increase appears to have dropped now to about 3·2 per cent.

As a result of the population increase, Formosa's density of population rose from 608 per square mile in 1953 to 803 in 1961. The pressure on the land is enormous despite a continual migration from the countryside to the city. The number of farm families increased from 702,000 in 1953 to 786,000 in 1960, while average acreage per farm family decreased from 1·24 to 1·11 hectare.[25] In 1959, 60 per cent. of all farms were under one hectare. The structure of the population is such that 46 per cent. of the people are under fifteen years of age. The labour force participation rate has been steadily falling, from 35·0 per cent. in 1953 to 30·9 per cent. in 1961.[26]

Government population policy has for the most part been notable for its absence, and few leading Nationalists have publicly admitted the problem. Indeed, in 1959, in an interview with a western correspondent, Chou Chih-jou, then Governor of Formosa (province), complained that population growth was " his most serious problem " but his administration was hamstrung by the stand taken against artificial birth control by the central government in Taipei and the ruling Nationalist party.[27] The reasons for the government's attitude are mainly political. Both Sun Yat-sen and Chiang Kai-shek are on record against birth control. In the government's early days on Formosa, to admit of a population

---

23 Population statistics exclude persons in the armed forces. In 1961, armed forces personnel were about 600,000. For population statistics, see Director-General of Budgets, Accounts and Statistics, the *Taiwan Economic Indicators, Republic of China* (Taipei), No. 28, June 1962.

24 *Data Book*, p. 5.

25 *Op. cit.*, p. 24.

26 *Op. cit.*, pp. 7–10.

27 *New York Times* (International edition), December 22, 1959, News of the Week in Review, p. 3.

problem on Formosa was considered defeatist since the recovery of the mainland was supposedly imminent. Indeed, it was often publicly argued that more population was needed to increase the armed forces—actually an even more defeatist argument since it would take a generation before the baby crop came of age for military duty. The psychological unwillingness to admit of a population problem is still strong and shows up in the caution with which normally forthright economic officials approach it.[28] Inertia is also a factor, in addition to the plain unwillingness of the government to antagonise anyone on this important question. Catholic influence is strong, particularly in the Legislative Yuan, and Catholic legislators are quick to attack what they detect as government efforts in this direction. Doubtless, sociological reasons, such as traditional Chinese attachment to a large family, also help to prevent action.

Nevertheless, the relentless pressure of growing numbers is moving the country, including the government, toward positive action. The press is devoting increasing attention to the problem. A family planning association was inaugurated in 1954, and many private physicians are, on their own responsibility, recommending and providing birth control devices to their patients. The birth control movement has found an important voice and leader in Dr. Chiang Mon-lin, an elder statesman and the Chairman of the Joint Commission on Rural Reconstruction (JCRR). Since 1960 the government, without publicity, and largely because of Dr. Chiang's urgings, has been providing a very small amount of funds for the propagation of birth control information and the provision of birth control devices to the rural population through the medium of the island's 330 health stations. The programme seems to be well received and the Provincial Health Administration which administers it is currently receiving some assistance from private American foundations. While still far from the effort required, it is at least a beginning. The question of timing, however, is vital.

The economic consequences of this rate of population growth, especially its effect on capital accumulation and the great demand for such services as education, need little elaboration.[29] The economy must grow at over 3 per cent. annually simply to stand still. One aspect of this whole phenomenon may worsen (and it has only recently begun to attract the attention it deserves)—the problem of under-employment and outright unemployment. The economy is presently plagued with both, particularly in the agricultural sector. One recent study estimates agricultural under-employment at over one million.[30] Moreover, the economy

[28] For example, see K. Y. Yin, *Economic Development in Taiwan, 1950–1960, Record and Prospects* (Taipei: 1961), pp. 38-39.
[29] For one study in relation to Taiwan, see JCRR, *A Study on the Effects of the Population Trend on Economic Development in Taiwan* (Taipei: 1961), English abridgment, preliminary and mimeographed.　　　　　　[30] *Op. cit.*, p. 16.

will have to absorb an increasing number of people when the post-war crop of babies begins to appear in the labour market. Especially important in this regard is the island's present inability to use its expanding number of college graduates, a situation which has only been partially relieved by the migration of nearly 1,000 students a year to the United States.[31] The employment problem will become acute in a period when the Nationalist Government may already be under severe political strains.

The Government has somewhat belatedly recognised the importance of the employment problem and made increased employment one of the chief goals of its third four-year plan. The plan envisages an increase of 400,000 jobs between 1961 and 1964, 326,000 of these outside of agriculture.[32] The realism of these estimates is open to question. Under the first two four-year plans (1953–60) the total growth in employment, according to official statstics, was only 390,000. (Even if the planning estimates are achieved, they may not meet the problem.) The difficulty of this is illustrated by a recent survey on investment opportunities. The survey recommended establishing a transistor industry. The total increase in employment was estimated at 102.[33] Of course, as long as large-scale capital inflow is maintained and there is no disruption in demand, the big labour supply should contribute to development.

General Economic Policy. Despite the overwhelming predominance of the military and its effect on the economy, the development of an economically independent Formosa is a major goal of national policy, and leading officials from the President down have stressed its importance. Much publicity has been given to the importance of development and thrift.

Nationalist economic policy has always been vague. Prevailing policy appears to be an amalgam of Sun Yat-sen's socialist and welfare principles and those of free enterprise. The latter are being increasingly emphasised. The keystone of policy is pragmatism. There are virtually no legal or theoretical limitations on the government's power in the economic sphere, and it has used its power flexibly to stimulate the economy and to direct the use of resources. Economic activity has been conducted under numerous direct and indirect controls over foreign

31 Director-General of Budgets, Accounts and Statistics, *Statistical Abstract of the Republic of China, 1961* (Taipei: 1961), pp. 390–393. This source lists 3,750 students going abroad for study from 1955–60. This is considerably underestimated, since it covers only those who had permission to leave the country as students. However, many young people go abroad for study who are not able to qualify under the government's strict regulations for study abroad. This source also states that during the same period 367 students returned to Formosa.

32 Executive Yuan, *Ti-san ch'i Taiwan ching-chi chien-she szu-nien chi-hua (Taiwan's Third Four-year Economic Development Plan)* (Taipei: 1961), p. 38. An abridged English version is available.

33 William T. Kopp and Ned D. Osborn, *The Feasibility of a Transistor Radio Plant in Taiwan* (Stanford: Stanford Un. Research Institute, 1962).

exchange, prices, production, the establishment of businesses, the acqui-sition of land, etc., which stemmed largely from a period of shortages and chaos. To help development there has been a gradual lifting of such controls, the most prominent measures so far being the great liberalisation of imports and the move from a system of multiple exchange rates to a unitary rate (1958–61). The government is also an important entrepreneur and producer of goods and services, having taken over all the industries, utilities and banks owned by the Japanese Govern-ment, including a number of direct manufacturing activities.[34] After repeated urging by American aid officials, the Government had promised it would get rid of its holdings of non-basic industries (*i.e.*, those industries other than sugar, petroleum, electric power, railways, etc.). However, except for four enterprises transferred to landlords in partial payment for land taken under the land reform progamme, and a travel agency in 1960, the Government has not divested itself of its holdings—although it has generally avoided branching out into new areas of activity. Opposition to the sale of enterprises has stemmed largely from interest groups within the Government and the distrust in important Nationalist circles of private capitalists.

National economic planning on a systematic basis has been expressed in a series of four-year plans which began in 1953. Instituted largely as a response to American aid programmes, planning has developed a momentum of its own. Planning consists mainly of determining target goals (revised each year), calculating the resources required to reach these goals, allocating resources by sectors, and putting forward possible projects for both the public and private sectors. There is no compulsion on the private sector, but considerable control is effected through mone-tary policy, low interest rate loans and other subsidies, and through the ability to control foreign exchange and important raw materials. The greatest deficiencies in planning have been in the lack of consideration given to alternative uses of resources and the lack of checks on consis-tency and feasibility. Another defect has been that the plans have consistently under-estimated both the imports required and the time and money needed to complete major projects. Perhaps the greatest pitfall in implementing has been the lack of co-ordination in the public sector, especially in the control of the capital expenditures of public enterprises. There is no centralised planning agency. Planning is done by various groups for major sectors (*e.g.*, agriculture), with co-ordination the responsibility of the Ministry of Economic Affairs and the Council for

---

[34] There are 65 government enterprises, the majority of which are owned by the Central Government. For a description of the financial activities of the enterprises owned by the Central Government, see *Statistical Abstract*, pp. 466–504.

United States Aid (CUSA).[35] Formosa has been especially fortunate in having as its architects and managers of economic policy a remarkable group of energetic, sophisticated, and able officials, centred mostly in the agencies that handle American aid, the Joint Commission on Rural Reconstruction and the Council for United States Aid. Although the plans have resulted in considerable achievements, the original goal of self-sufficiency has not been reached.

Industrialisation has been a primary aim, but the government has always stressed the importance of agriculture and the need for balanced development. Industrial planning has emphasised three sectors: electric power, fertiliser, and light industries such as glass, cement, textiles, etc., which require little capital, generate quick returns, and replace imports. The emphasis on electric power was particularly wise since power has been the key to the development of other industries, and in 1961, for the first time, electric power was sufficient to satisfy all domestic demands.[36] Planning has also stressed the importance of encouraging private enterprise and establishing a suitable investment climate. The third four-year plan declares that " the main force for success must come from the private sector."[37] Indicative of the growth of private enterprise is the rise in the share of the private sector in total industrial production from 42 per cent. in 1953 to 61 per cent. in 1961.[38]

AMERICAN ASSISTANCE

The American investment in Formosa is massive—over U.S. $3 billion since 1951. Large-scale assistance to the Nationalist Government began in 1951, following the decision after the outbreak of the Korean War that the defence of Formosa was vital to United States security. The main purpose of the aid has been to create the necessary economic and military conditions to keep Formosa out of Chinese Communist hands. Military assistance has consisted largely of the provision of military hardware items and has been directed towards modernising the Nationalist armed forces. From the fiscal year 1951 through to the fiscal year 1962, over U.S. $2 billion was provided for the armed forces.[39] For the same period, all forms of programmed American economic assistance totalled

---

[35] For a description of the planning process and some recommendations for improvement, see Ralph J. Watkins, *Economic Development Planning in Taiwan* (Washington: 1961), mimeographed.
[36] Electric power generation increased from 1·6 billion KWH in 1953 to 4·1 billion KWH in 1961.
[37] *Third Four-Year Plan*, p. 29.
[38] *Data Book*, p. 46.
[39] AID Statistics and Reports Division, *U.S. Foreign Assistance July 1, 1945–June 30, 1961* (Washington: 1961).

U.S.$1·155 billion.[40]   The lowest annual aid figure was U.S.$81 million in the fiscal year 1952; the highest, U.S.$138 million in the fiscal year 1955.   Formosan dollars generated from the local sale of aid commodities have been used to finance investment and to defray a portion of the Nationalists' military budget.

The economic assistance programme has gone through many vicissitudes and structural changes, responding to the changes in the economy and to American bureaucratic and legislative regulations.   Until 1961 most economic aid was generally known as defence support.[41]   The purpose of this type of aid was to promote stability in order to permit the economy to withstand the burden of military expenditures and to prevent political developments that might impede the defence build-up. Consumer items (wheat, soybeans, pharmaceuticals, etc.) accounted for approximately 35–40 per cent. of all aid shipments until the end of 1961.[42] At the same time considerable investment funds and technical assistance were provided to ensure against any fall in income levels.   This was viewed as the only basis for hopes of any reduction in future levels of assistance.

Because of ease of handling and the immediate needs of the economy, the greatest amount of investment assistance has gone to the public sector for social overhead purposes.   Two sectors, electric power and transport, had received through the financial year 1961 U.S. $219 million, or 59 per cent. of the authorised total, for investment purposes.[43]   Much attention has been devoted to fostering private enterprise both through continual prodding of the Nationalist Government and through direct assistance— notably by establishing a development bank for private industry. (Implicit in this effort is the hope that the quick development of a strong business class would have beneficial political effects.)   Because of the subsidised rates of interest on American aid loans and a Chinese penchant for the newest and most expensive machinery, there is reason to believe that capital intensity has been fostered at the expense of employment.   Until 1961 virtually all economic aid was in the form of grants or " soft "

---

[40] *Data Book*, p. 122.   Programme figures are amounts authorised, not actual expenditures, which would be slightly less.   Chinese aid figures differ slightly from those of AID.

[41] The various categories of aid and authorised amounts from fiscal year 1951 to fiscal year 1961 are as follows: defence support, U.S.$797·5 million; technical co-operation, U.S.$20·8 million; direct forces support, U.S.$152·3 million; Public Law 480 surplus agriculture commodities, U.S.$64·9 million; Development Loan Fund, U.S.$119·7 million.   Not included are relief goods supplied under a separate section of P.L. 480. These aid categories differ primarily in the manner that aid commodities generate local currency and in the uses of aid commodities as to consumption and investment.

[42] *Data Book*, p. 129.   Basic commodity imports under defence support aid were known as non-project aid, that is, they were commodities not directed towards a defined capital project.

[43] *Data Book*, p. 126, and AID Mission to China, *Project Funding Status* (Taipei: 1962), mimeographed.

loans repayable in local currency. Since a serious drain on the economy would occur if local currency loan repayments were in fact called in, these soft currency loans may be considered as grants.

Measured by Formosa's economic achievements American aid has been successful. A critic might question the price of this success but, in view of the difficulties of generating growth in other parts of Asia, a generous appraisal seems warranted. Nevertheless, because the economic programme has had to bridge the military-economic dichotomy of the island and to follow in large measure the priorities of the Chinese— especially the emphasis on stability—it has been beset with the same difficulties which hamper the development efforts of the Chinese themselves. The effectiveness of investment aid depends on the recipient nation's use of its own resources. In so far as increasing military and civilian consumption eat up the increments of national production, investment aid mainly underwrites the country's unwillingness to save. At the same time, inflationary pressures have often been sufficiently strong to induce the authorities to slow the pace of investment. Thus American aid local currency deposits (whose use must be mutually agreed upon), which are a main source for financing capital formation, were allowed to increase from NT$2·6 billion in December 1960 to NT$4·0 billion in April 1962.[44] While some of this increase reflected increased dollar aid and soft loan repayments, it also reflected much stricter standards in approving investment. Thus American control over resources is limited.

Since 1960 the Formosan economic aid programme has undergone substantial change. This has been intensified by the overhaul of America's aid efforts and concepts. Although the support of Formosa's defence is still an important goal, major emphasis is now laid on economic development, and the objective is a significant reduction of, or a complete end to, economic assistance in a relatively short time. All grant assistance has been terminated, except for the sales of agricultural products for local currency under United States Public Law 480 and a small amount of technical assistance.[45] Loans are repayable in (U.S.) dollars, though at very low interest rates (under 1 per cent.) and extended repayment periods (as much as forty years). The loan programme is not expected to create a significant problem of debt repayment. The new approach is tied in with the Nationalists' accelerated economic development programme described below, and is geared to inducing the Government to take the necessary measures to stimulate growth.

---

[44] *Taiwan Financial Statistics Monthly*, p. 6.
[45] In actuality, 10–20 per cent. of the currency generated from the sales of U.S. surplus agricultural commodities are used for U.S. Government purposes, and this portion would constitute a genuine sale.

NEW DIRECTIONS—ACCELERATED DEVELOPMENT

In planning for the third four-year plan it became increasingly clear to leading Nationalist economic officials that while economic development had proceeded in a generally satisfactory manner, further economic gains would be harder to come by. It was also clear that an intensive effort was needed both to increase the rate of growth and to reduce Formosa's dependence on the United States, especially in view of what appeared to be future reductions in the economic aid programme and a change in its nature. Late in 1959 the Government announced that it would undertake a programme of accelerated development (statistically embodied in the third four-year plan) designed to increase significantly Formosa's capacity for self-support. To give substance to the programme and to win greater American support, the Government in January 1960 announced a potentially far-ranging reform programme of nineteen measures and set a time limit for its implementation.

The accelerated development programme recognises that to increase growth it is essential to direct increases in income into investment. The nineteen points, as the reforms are popularly called, are an expression of the costs—the need for policies to be changed, institutions modified, and attitudes to be revised or abandoned—as well as the hope that the productive forces unleashed would be sufficient to overcome the problems posed by the island's military effort and by population growth.[46] Under the reforms, savings are to be encouraged and consumption discouraged through mass publicity. Savings institutions are to be developed and expanded, utility charges will be raised, and a progressive tax policy introduced. Defence budgets will be fixed at the 1960 level in terms of constant prices. A capital market is to be established and the banking system revamped. Budgetary as well as monetary reforms are to be enacted to guard against inflation. Private enterprise and private foreign investment are to be encouraged through a reduction in government controls, preferential treatment, the transfer of many government enterprises to private hands, and in general by the creation of a suitable business climate. The nineteen-point programme is not a full-scale reform. All the measures to be taken under the programme are economic. Nevertheless, implementation of the programme should go far towards setting in motion basic economic forces leading to a rapid change both in the economy and in the society.

Although execution of the programme has been uneven, solid achievements have been made. Most notable, perhaps, is the promulgation of a very liberal foreign investment law which gives guarantees

---

46 A description of the Nineteen Points may be found in the *Third Four-Year Plan*, pp. 30–31.

against expropriation, and includes tax holidays, freedom to repatriate capital, etc. An intensive effort is being made to attract foreign investment, and an effective investment assistance organisation has been set up to help domestic and foreign enterprises create and operate firms. These efforts have borne some fruit with a number of investments by prominent American and Japanese firms.[47] The movement of visitors both for business and for pleasure has been encouraged by a 72-hour, visa-free visit—no mean achievement in a country where security considerations are so deeply ingrained. The Central Bank of China has been reactivated, the first step in sorting out banking operations and establishing a sound financial system. Preferential tax laws and tax inducements have been directed towards export-producing industries, and some controls have been eliminated. Utility charges have been raised. Perhaps most important, the mass publicising of the development programme has gained increased public acceptance for the concept of accelerated development.

The reform programme, however, also faces many obstacles. In important Government and Nationalist circles, emphasis on accelerated development is viewed as drawing attention away from the overriding goal of a return to the mainland. Sun Yat-sen conservatives contemplate with distaste the increasing emphasis on private enterprise, and foreign investment revives memories of Western imperialism. A large portion of the bureaucracy sees the reform programme as a threat to their interests, while the sheer size of the bureaucracy in itself poses a formidable barrier to progress. Almost no government enterprises have yet been sold to private citizens. The execution of the development programme is largely in the hands of a small segment of officialdom centred in the agencies handling American aid, who are divorced from the present sources of power in Formosa.

The most damaging blow to the reform programme came in May 1960 with the announcement of a new military programme. The widely publicised economic deterioration on the mainland had raised the hopes of the Government for an early return to the mainland. For the first five months of 1962, the Chinese press on the island, taking its cue from a New Year's speech by President Chiang proclaiming an impending attack on the mainland, indulged itself in a great campaign on the urgency of an immediate counter-attack. As if to give substance to its repeated declarations of impending counter-attack, the Government on

---

[47] The largest foreign investment is a joint venture by Mobil Chemical Co. and Allied Chemical Co. with a government enterprise to build a urea fertiliser plant. The share of the U.S. Companies is U.S.$16 million. Also noteworthy is the penetration of Formosa by Japanese firms. Most Japanese investment has taken the form of technical assistance and licensing agreements.

May 1, 1962, announced a special defence budget totalling NT $2·4 billion to run through to June 30, 1963.[48]

The Government did recognise the potential inflationary effects of such expenditures and moved to offset them. It did this not through exploring new sources of taxation but by raising wine and tobacco prices an average of 20 per cent. and instituting a series of defence surtaxes on most existing taxes and utility charges. The Government announced that the surtaxes would be lifted on June 30, 1963. In recognition of its development programme, the Government, through its levy, attempted to hit consumption and to minimise the effect of the taxes on industry by such devices as exempting industrial activity from the surtaxes on power and transportation, and by not taxing capital goods imports.

Nevertheless, from the standpoint of economic development, the new expenditures were most discouraging. A vital item of the nineteen-point reform had been ignored. The rate of increase of military expenditures had been far greater than the increase in gross national product; roughly another 2 per cent. of gross national product was further diverted to government consumption. Moreover, the taxes and the build-up of war psychology could only adversely affect the Government's efforts to attract foreign investment. Most unfavourable to the cause of development was the probability that this process, given the President's age and determination, would continue. On Formosa the conflict between the short-run and the long-run has never been more stark.

Because of limitations of space this article has not examined in detail Formosa's economic achievements, particularly in agriculture, or the more purely economic questions that face the island—the shortage of capital, the lack of entrepreneurship, the difficulties in finding and developing investment opportunities, the problems of expanding export markets, and the like.[49] It has rather concentrated on the role of the Government in the economy, since many of the immediate impediments to growth are related to government action or inaction.

Upon their arrival in Formosa the Nationalists were fortunate in having a combination of factors favourable to a rapid rate of development: the small size of the country, a good base left by the Japanese, a fairly literate farm population, and a considerable number of technicians. With a minimum investment in research, extension and irrigation, the Government was able to compensate for the limitations on arable land. At the same time, immediate opportunities for rapid increases in

---

[48] This information is from assorted Taipei press reports.
[49] For a discussion of some of these problems, see Edward A. Tenenbaum, *Taiwan's Turning Point* (Washington: 1960).

production existed in import-replacing industries. Because production gains were relatively easy to come by and because of American assistance, the Nationalists were able to pursue the build-up of their military forces at the expense of a higher level of development. Economic independence still has not been achieved. With limited natural resources and with the almost full exploitation of the favourable factors of the earlier period, further economic growth would appear to be increasingly costly.

Concerted effort is required by the Government to mobilise savings and remove bottlenecks to growth if economic independence is to be approached, and, because of population pressures, necessary measures cannot be long delayed. The Government recognises this need and has initiated a programme of reform and accelerated development. This programme, however, does not involve a change in the priorities of the Government. It is based on the hope, that, through the deepening and extension of productive forces, sufficient increases in national production will be generated to satisfy both the needs of the military and of investment and to create social change that will lead to a significant decline in birth rates. Such an assumption has little basis in past history and is largely dependent upon events in the Formosa Straits. Nevertheless, unless hostilities occur, the accelerated development programme should at least serve to put off the day of reckoning. Given the present political situation, there seems to be no satisfactory alternative to the current development effort or to the United States' underwriting it.

Nationalist China's Armed Forces

FORMOSA has the unenviable distinction of having proportionally more
men under arms than any other country. With resources and manpower
being poured into keeping approximately 600,000 men [1] in readiness
for an eventual return to the mainland the military presence inevitably
pervades Formosan life. Military needs conflict with personal freedom
and restrain economic growth. Yet for all the efforts of the Nationalist
government—sustained by huge amounts of American aid—the changing
international scene and difficulties within the Nationalist forces make a
return to the mainland less likely as time goes by.

ORGANISATION

The Nationalists have never given the size of their forces but authoritative
British and American sources [1] have estimated the total at about 600,000
men since the mid-1950s.

According to Article 36 of the Constitution the President is the
Supreme Commander of the armed forces. Defence policy is carried out
through the Ministry of Defence, set up in 1946, which has been headed
by Dr. Yu Ta-wei since 1954. The Ministry controls the manpower,
budget, materials, law and legal procedures, and the stockpiling of
supplies for the armed forces. Under the Minister of Defence is the
Chief of the General Staff who, at present, is General Peng Meng-chi.
Both the President and the Minister of Defence issue orders to the
armed forces through the Chief of the General Staff. In turn, instructions
are carried out by the departments of the Office of the Chief of the
General Staff. Following reorganisation in 1958 the Office includes
departments for personnel, intelligence, operations, logistics and planning,
as well as a special staff to cover such matters as personnel administration, liaison and press relations.

Each service [Army, Navy (including Marines), Air Force and
Combined Service Force] has a commander in chief and a general
headquarters. Besides the structure of the political staff of the general

---

[1] The Chinese Nationalists exercise rigorous security on military information. Nevertheless independent estimates show surprising consistency.

headquarters, which is the same in all the services, the rest of the staff are organised to suit the special needs of each service.[2]

The Nationalists have given much more attention to the political education of the armed forces since they regrouped on Formosa. During the civil war there were massive defections from the Nationalist forces. The political department of the Ministry of Defence is responsible for the political education of both officers and men, as well as the promotion of certain cultural and recreational activities. Political officers are active throughout the armed forces.[3]

Defence policy is co-ordinated at the policy making level through the Supreme National Defence Council, set up by the President in 1954, and its subordinate organisations—the National Security Bureau, the National Defence Planning Bureau, and the Military Science and Research Committee. Among the Council's members are the President and the Vice-President, the Chief of the General Staff, and the Ministers of Defence, Interior, Finance and Foreign Affairs, as well as the Secretary-General and a Deputy Secretary-General.[4] Because the Council is intimately involved in defence matters its budget is secret and there is very little public information about its activities.

THE ATTEMPT TO MODERNISE

Without American equipment and training it would have been impossible for the Nationalist forces to have achieved the high degree of combat readiness which has characterised them in recent years. On the other hand, however, no amount of equipment or advice could have resulted in an effective military organisation, had there not been vast changes in personnel policies. The American military aid programme has considerably influenced the reorganisation and re-equipment of the Nationalist forces. With the outbreak of the Korean War (which crystallised American reappraisals towards Nationalist China) the United States in 1951 lifted the ban on military aid imposed in January 1950. An exchange of notes between the United States and the Nationalist government in January 1951 provided that American military aid was to be

---

[2] *China Yearbook 1961–62* (Taipei: China Publishing Company), p. 221, hereafter cited as *CY*.

[3] U.S. Congress, House of Representatives' Commitee on Foreign Affairs, Walter Judd, *Report on a Special Study Mission to Southeast Asia and the Pacific* (Washington: U.S. Government Printing Office, 1954), p. 9. There are reported to be a number of quasi-legal institutions for political indoctrination that are presumed to receive financial support in the classified military budget. "Wo-men te chün-shih" ("Our Military") in *Tzu-yu Chung-kuo (Free China)* XVII, No. 4 (1957) 3–4.

[4] There is considerable discussion about the existence of personal cliques in the armed forces, centred on General Chiang Ching-kuo. For an alleged description of this problem see Sun Chia-ch'i, *Chiang Ching-kuo Chien-kuo Nei-mu (The Inside Story of Chiang Ching-kuo's Seizure of Power)* (Hong Kong: Tzu-li Chu-pan-she, 1961).

used only for defensive purposes. Furthermore, the Nationalist government was not to transfer aid nor to use it for other purposes without consulting the American government.[5]

America gives the Nationalist government military aid to defend Formosa, the Penghus, and the off-shore islands against attack and or in more general terms contribute to the collective strength of the non-Communist world in Asia.[6] The Nationalists pursue their avowed goal, of returning to the mainland, which falls outside the purpose of the aid programme, through units which are not supported by the provisions of the military aid programme.

The Nationalist force evacuated to Formosa in 1949 was made up of a variety of units, many fragmented, understrength and with low morale. Generally, the troops were poorly trained and equipped with a hybrid mixture of Chinese, American, German and Japanese materials. Moreover, there was an acute shortage of ammunition and spare parts. The Navy was very short of combat ships. The Air Force had some well trained pilots, but only a few obsolete P-51 and B-24 planes from the Second World War. The process of modernising these forces can best be understood by discussing the development of each service separately against the background of the figures given below:

Military Forces of Nationalist China (Estimated)

	Total	Army	Navy (including Marines)	Air Force	Combined Service Force
Estimate A[7]	600,000	400,000	50,000	80,000	70,000
Estimate B[8]	600,000		85,000	80,000	
Estimate C[9]		400,000	50,000	100,000	
Estimate D[10]	580,000	400,000	62,000	110,000	

In 1955, four years after the first Military Assistance Advisory Group (MAAG) staff arrived, the Army was estimated at 380,000 men divided into 10 armies, or 21 divisions [11] and various other units.

---

[5] Joseph W. Ballantine, *Formosa: A Problem for U.S. Foreign Policy* (Washington: Brookings Institution, 1952), 218 pp., for a discussion of the early phases of this programme.

[6] U.S. Congress, Senate Committee on Appropriations, Dennis Chavez, *Report on United States Military Operations and Mutual Security Programs Overseas* (86th Congress, Second Session), Committee print (hereafter referred to as the *Chavez Report*), p. 45.

[7] *Chavez Report*, p. 46. This estimate was for 1959.

[8] Barnett, A. Doak, *Communist China and Asia* (New York: Harper Brothers, 1960), p. 403.

[9] *Boei Nenkan 1962 (Defence Yearbook 1962)* (Tokyo: Boei Nenkan Kankokai, 1962), pp. 431–433. Hereafter cited as *BN*.

[10] London Institute for Strategic Studies, *The Communist Bloc and the Western Alliance* (London: Institute for Strategic Studies, 1962, p. 23).

[11] *BN*, 1955, p. 417. *BN* gives a figure of 12,000 for a Chinese Nationalist division. The *New York Times* for the same year (August 29, 1955, p. 3) gives the figure as 11,200.

Although considerable American equipment was available, only 120,000 troops were considered well organised and equipped. The rest of the troops were part of obsolete commands with inferior training and equipment. Many of these commands were considered as units beyond the scope of the military aid programme. Nevertheless it appears that aid was diverted to them. The MAAG pressed, with support from some Nationalist military officers, to eliminate the obsolete units. Figures about the success in dissolving such organisations are classified, but apparently the number of such units has steadily decreased.[12]

A major reorganisation of the army, known as the " Forward Look " plan began in 1958. It was designed to increase the firepower, the mobility, and the logistic support of the ground forces. The Nationalist government stresses that this reorganisation is intended to make the army an effective fighting force in a nuclear war. Each division has been divided into five smaller groups of approximately 2,500 men capable of operating independently.[13] In re-equipping the Army, the infantry divisions were given priority. It is interesting to note that, in general, equipment provided for " force improvement " has been newer tanks and guns but not what would be classified as advanced weapons and equipment. Moreover, only one-third of the military assistance funds requested of Congress in 1959 for the Far East[14] were for " force improvement." The changes implied in the " Forward Look " plan have extended over five years.

The Nationalist Army, in 1961, was believed to consist of 21 infantry, 1 paratroop and 2 armoured divisions.[15] There is also a large training headquarters, which is part of the Army headquarters, and a missile battalion, as well as miscellaneous units.[16] Although the missile battalion is under the direct command of the Army General Headquarters, it receives orders from the Air Force Headquarters. The missiles (Nike-Hercules) were originally manned by American troops until their Chinese counterparts received the necessary training. The Nationalists are very proud at having these missiles, manned by Nationalist troops, on Formosa.

[12] *BN*, 1955, refers to these units as remnants of warlord forces. Their existence is confirmed in the U.S. Senate *Hearings Before the Committee on Foreign Relations on the Mutual Security Act of 1959*, p. 141. The precise figures are deleted.

[13] For an official description of the plan see *CY* 1960–61, pp. 225–226. See also Ting K'uang-hua, " Tzu-yu Chung-kuo te chin-pu yu fan-yung " (" Progress and Prosperity of Free China ") in *Tzu-yu Tai-p'ing-yang (Free Pacific)*, VI, No. 1 (January 1962), pp. 9–14.

[14] U.S. Senate, *Hearings Before the Committee on Foreign Relations on the Mutual Security Act of 1959*, p. 359.

[15] *BN*, 1962, p. 433.

[16] Besides the Army field commands there is the Formosa Garrison Command whose major task is to deal with subversion. This was set up in 1958 to replace the Formosa Defence Command, the Taipei Garrison Command, the Provincial Peace and Preservation Command and the Civil Defence Command. China News Service, *Free China Weekly* (May 20, 1958), p. 3; hereafter cited as *CNS*.

Quemoy and Matsu are governed by the military rather than civil authorities and serve as training facilities for military government officers in the Army. In the mid-fifties it was estimated that six divisions, about 72,000 men,[17] were stationed on the off-shore islands. By the late 1950s the number was thought to have increased to about 100,000 [18] It is clear that many of the well-trained combat troops are garrisoned on the islands.

Naval reorganisation has emphasised training crews for mine sweeping, anti-submarine operations, night engagements, and to transport supplies under fire.[19] A number of vessels have been provided through American aid. Published estimates of tonnage have varied considerably, partly because of the lack of standardisation and partly because of the difference between total number of vessels and the number ready for operation. For example, in 1955 the Navy was estimated to have 80 vessels with a total tonnage of 170,000 tons. The estimate noted that many vessels were undergoing repairs and hence were not on active duty. By 1962 the total number of vessels was estimated at 180 with a tonnage of 140,000 tons. These are believed to include 12 destroyers, 26 escort ships, plus a variety of other vessels including some landing craft.[20]

A significant addition to the Navy is the Marines. In 1955 Marines, including some armoured units, were in training. By 1962 the total force was estimated at 25,000 men. Contemporary estimates generally refer to one Marine division, or one division and a brigade,[21] but the total forces are sufficient for two divisions. Although there is a separate faculty for training Marine officers, the Marines have used a number of specialised army facilities and participated in numerous combined service manoeuvres and training exercises. Nationalist reports stress the offensive training and capabilities of the Marines

The Air Force has been regarded as the best trained of the services. It is estimated to have 500 planes, the vast majority of them fighters, and a total manpower of 100,000 men. In the last few years the total number of planes appears to have declined slightly, but there has been a marked increase in the number of modern aircraft.[22] The introduction of jet planes has placed prime importance on a high level of training for effective operation and maintenance. Training has been given in

17 *BN, 1955*, p. 417.
18 *NYT* (August 28, 1958), p. 1. Barnett, *op. cit.* p. 403.
19 *Tang-ch'ien fei wo ch'ing-shih fen-hsi (An Analysis of the Rebels and Our Present Situation)* (Taipei: Hsing-cheng yuan, hsin-wen chü, 1962), p. 27.
20 *BN, 1955*, p. 417. *BN, 1958*, p. 486. *BN, 1962*, p. 432.
21 *Chavez Report*, p. 46. *BN, 1962*, p. 432.
22 Compare *BN, 1955*, p. 417; *BN, 1957*, p. 464; *1962*, p. 432.

Formosa, the United States and at United States Air Force bases in the Far East.

The Air Force has had continuously to adapt to new innovations. For example, in 1955 there were reported to have been five fighter groups, of which two were flying F-86 Sabrejets and two F-84 Thunderjets. In addition, there were reported to be one bomber group, two transport groups, and a number of reconnaissance planes.[23] A major problem was the lack of trained maintenance crews. Since then, the F-84 Thunderjets have been officially retired and the F-86 fighters have been supplemented by the " century " series of aircraft.[24] Continual re-equipment has called for constant retraining and a need to improve Formosa's airbases.

The Combined Service Force is interesting and important. Its primary concern is to produce and procure military supplies, plus the handling of "military science, technical research and development, together with survey and map-making." Pensions for survivors of the dead and care of military dependants are also part of its work.[25] There are few estimates of the manpower of this service, probably because its members are classified as non-combatant. The scope of the Combined Service Force has broadened in recent years to include arsenals, producing, for example, 30-calibre ammunition and artillery shells, clothing and battery plants. Some landing craft are built on the island, but the parts come from the United States. The Nationalist forces note that the Combined Service Force often produces military goods cheaper than the United States.[26] Furthermore, the more such production develops, the more self-sufficient the Nationalists will be. At present, production is only for eight hours a day, but the Nationalist government has noted that the output of military supplies could be boosted rapidly at an appropriate time.

REJUVENATING THE ARMED FORCES

The problems of keeping a steady flow of recruits to the armed forces and providing for the retirement of aged and disabled troops, has been of crucial importance to the Nationalist government in its military reorganisation. In 1950 more than 150,000 men were cut from the military payroll. This step involved 89 separate units. The next year another 43 units were abolished, with the release of 14,000 more men.[27]

[23] *NYT* (July 6, 1955), p. 7. *BN, 1955*, p. 417.
[24] *An Analysis of the Rebels and Our Present Situation*, p. 28. The London Institute for Strategic Studies reports the presence of Sidewinder missiles on Nationalist jet aircraft.
[25] *Cy 1961-62*, p. 226.
[26] *CNS* (April 29, 1958), p. 3 ; (December 12, 1960), p. 2 ; (May 2, 1963), p. 3.
[27] *CNS* (April 15, 1952), p. 3.

The Nationalists, like the Communists on the mainland, have provided for the security of retired personnel.

Legislation in 1958 was designed to supersede the temporary retirement programmes started in 1952. Under the 1958 legislation officers with more than two and less than twenty years' service receive a lump sum payment; those with more than twenty years' service or those who reach the age of sixty having completed fifteen years' service can choose between a pension and a lump sum payment. The value of pension depends upon rank and duration of service. The lump sum payment is based on the length of service, with a set maximum. Additional benefits to field and company grade officers (but not to generals) for food and housing depend upon rank and there are provisions for hospital treatment and subsequent retirement, as well as training for new work.[28]

Non-commissioned officers receive similar treatment. An NCO is eligible for retirement after ten years' service with compulsory retirement at age fifty (except for master sergeants, who must retire at 58). NCOs have the right to request extension of service if they have not reached retiring age, and the government may also extend enlistment under specified conditions. The government also insures NCOs, soldiers, and cadets against death and disability. Officers have had similar treatment since 1950.

Legislation providing for the retirement of members of the armed forces was accompanied by the establishment in 1954 of the Vocational Assistance Commission for Retired Servicemen (VACRS) which was designed to help resettle the aged and the disabled who were retired from the armed forces. Over the years VACRS has expanded to include a variety of agricultural establishments, mining and industrial projects, hospitals, homes for aged veterans, and vocational training schools. Its programmes reflect the government's interest in providing land to eligible veterans as well as developing certain parts of Formosa. However, VACRS and the retirement programmes are unduly restricted by a lack of funds.

Through the policies mentioned above the government has been able to prune its armed forces of many over-age soldiers. However, since the government was unwilling to accept a reduction in its total armed forces the gaps have been filled by conscription and a reserve.

Although universal conscription was instituted in the early 1950s, the government recognised in 1954 that " the bulk of the men in active service today are mainland professional soldiers and conscripts who withdrew to Taiwan with the government." [29] A revised military service law was, therefore, passed. All youths were subject to two years military

28 *CNS* (June 17, 1958), p. 2.
29 *CNS* (August 17, 1954), p. 1.

service and remain in the reserves until the age of forty-five. At the same time, special incentives were to be arranged for volunteers. A year later the China News Service claimed that two-thirds of the men in the services were Formosans.[30] The average age of servicemen is estimated to be twenty-five.

In 1956, however, the government recognised that most conscripts were serving only twelve to fourteen months. The law was revised to enforce the full two-year period and provided for a more even flow of conscripts into the army. In this way more men could get experience with modern weapons. A one-month refresher training course was begun which initially drew on the pool of men who had received some military training.

Before 1956 American aid was not used in training reserve divisions. After extensive discussions the Ministry of Defence and MAAG announced a plan to create eventually nine reserve divisions.[31] Equipment for one reserve division would be provided by the United States with which one division would be trained at a time. Individuals covered by this plan would receive four months training before being transferred to regular army units and subsequently into reserve divisions, with the requirement of one month's service each year for five years.

To back up the general reorganisation of the armed forces many more military training schools were set up. A large number of the military training schools, particularly the academies and the command staff schools of the three services, have been raised to the level of colleges with opportunities for post-graduate training and research. A National Defence College was created to train officers to direct and plan national defence matters in a total war. At lower levels, service schools for ordnance and communication, etc., have been established along American lines. Some specialised training is given in the United States.[32]

The Nationalists, well aware of the criticisms made against them when they were on the mainland, have now tried to improve the treatment of the individual serviceman. Pay scales have been raised and food allowances provided for soldier's dependants. In 1952 a programme to verify that soldiers were properly paid was instituted to guard against the frequent charges of financial corruption which had previously plagued the Nationalist forces. It is reported to be successful.[33] In

---

[30] *CNS* (March 29, 1955), p. 2.

[31] *CNS* (January 10, 1956), p. 3.

[32] The development of facilities and programmes for advanced training and research are a particularly noticeable feature of the Nationalists' military education programme. See comments in the *People's Daily (Jen-min Jih-pao)* (July 3, 1962), p. 3, and *An Analysis of the Rebels and Our Present Situation*, p. 28.

[33] Chiang Yun-t'ien, " Shih-nien lai tzu-yu Chung kuo te chu-shih tsai-cheng chiao-yü yü wai-chiao " (" Military Affairs, Finance, Education, and Foreign Relations of Free China in the Past Ten Years ") *Tsu-kuo (China Weekly)*, XL, No. 2, p. 27.

an attempt to ensure opportunities for promotion in the services, limits were set on the number of years an officer could remain at any given rank. Officers who are not promoted within the given period of time must retire. Two-year terms of office are specified for the Chief of the General Staff, and Commander-in-Chief of each service, unless specifically requested by the government to remain in office for an additional term.

CONTEMPORARY PROBLEMS

There can be no doubt that the Nationalist government has made great strides in modernising and rejuvenating its armed forces. However, there are certain problems inherent in the Nationalist position which they may well be unable to overcome. One problem is the discrepancy between Nationalist goals and the aims of the American aid programme. As a constant renewal of equipment is indispensable to modernisation and Formosa has a limited industrial base, this discrepancy is important. Probably the potential of the Nationalist forces for offensive action will always be limited. For example, the Nationalist Air Force has mainly fighter planes, and only a few bombers and transports. The Navy has been, and continues to be, developed with very limited offensive capabilities. Although some landing craft are built on the island, there are not enough support ships for an invasion of the mainland. Even in the Army, where the discrepancy may have the least effect, the problem of transport vehicles,[34] as well as limited armoured forces, is recognised.

Secondly, although the government has been willing to risk Formosa's economic development for what it believes to be military priorities, there are economic realities to be faced. For example, the government saw the reserve system as a possible way of maintaining a large force ready for mobilisation. Consequently it asked America to equip three training divisions. But the Americans equipped only one division; it is unlikely that the Nationalists can provide or acquire the balance themselves. Although the government has recognised the need to increase military pay it has not been able to afford more than token increases.

Thirdly, the government must pay a price for continuing with political indoctrination. Apparently the Nationalist government is more concerned with political reliability than with military efficiency. The disgrace of General Sun Li-jen in 1955 is said to have resulted from his opposition to the political department and his alleged interest in a politically neutral officer corps. At all levels in the armed forces, there are intelligence and counter-espionage organisations. Such

---

[34] Meng Che, " Fan-kung fu-kuo wen-t'i " (" Problems of the Recovery of the Mainland "), *Tzu-yu Tai-ping-yang* (*Free Pacific*) (March 1962), pp. 9–10.

activities, which are expensive, almost inevitably interfere with military efficiency.

Fourthly, the government now finds itself in an interesting dilemma over leadership in the armed forces. It will be recalled that large numbers of men were retired after the mainland evacuation to meet the need for a younger military force. As a result the present generation of commanders, most of whom have had limited mainland experience, achieved high command posts at a relatively early age. Therefore the two-year limitation for certain commands has resulted in rotation among a small group of men too young to retire. This has repercussions on the middle level commanders. With the present retiring age for generals at seventy, an early solution to the lack of promotional opportunities is not in sight. If, however, the government revises regulations to enforce early retirement, it stands to lose men who have had mainland experience —a commodity that cannot be replaced—and who presumably share the strong belief in returning to the mainland.

There is a similar difficulty with senior NCOs. Here the government has tried to enhance the professional aspects of military life and to use the soldiers from the mainland in the more technical aspects of the services. Nevertheless, at present the government depends on a hard core of NCOs whose family ties remain for the most part with the mainland. Undoubtedly this poses problems of morale and discipline which will tend to be aggravated as time goes by.

Formosa's Diplomatic World

By DONALD KLEIN

NATIONALIST China's diplomatic relations were in shambles as the disastrous year of 1949 came to a close. Major cities in southern China were falling rapidly to the Communists, Mao Tse-tung had arrived in Moscow on his triumphal trip and Chiang Kai-shek had fled to Formosa in bitter defeat. Only seven nations had established permanent missions in Formosa. Meanwhile, on the mainland a diplomatic never-never land existed; there were diplomats accredited to Peking, " negotiating representatives," and ex-diplomats (in Chinese Communist eyes) whose countries had not recognised Peking.[1]

Few countries thought it worthwhile to have their diplomats follow the Nationalist government to Formosa after it had pulled out of Nanking in April, Canton in October and Chungking in December 1949. In rapid succession during the winter of 1949–50, Burma, India, Pakistan, Great Britain, Norway, Ceylon, Denmark, Israel, Afghanistan, Finland, Sweden and Switzerland—plus, of course, the Communist states—recognised Peking. This was a humiliation for the Nationalists who had enjoyed formal diplomatic ties with almost all these states.

Abroad, the diplomatic scene was only slightly brighter. In late 1949 Formosa still maintained diplomatic missions in thirty-seven states. This, however, was a somewhat padded figure, as several of the missions shared ambassadors. (One notes with wonderment that as late as 1955 Dr. Kidding Wang was concurrently the Minister to Honduras, El Salvador and Lebanon![2]) Two other yardsticks illustrate the difference between early and late 1949. Early in the year the Nationalists had 135 separate missions abroad with nearly 1,100 men.[3] Late in the year there were fifty-three missions (but only 19 embassies) with about 450 diplomats.[4]

Taipei's diplomatic horizon brightened with the outbreak of the Korean War. No nation recognised Peking from the spring of 1950 (Indonesia) until mid-1955 (Nepal). Formal diplomatic relations are

---

1 For an interesting description of this situation, see K. M. Panikkar, *In Two Chinas* (London: George Allen & Unwin, 1955), especially Chaps. IV and VIII.
2 *China Handbook 1955–56* (Taipei: China Publishing Co., 1955), p. 839.
3 " Taipei's Conduct of Diplomacy," Richard L. Walker, unpublished, 12 pp., p. 3. " Missions " include embassies, legations, consulates-general, consulates, delegations, and liaison offices.
4 *China News Service*, New York, September 20, 1960.

a costly business; it is not, therefore, surprising that the Nationalists did little to bolster their formal diplomatic ties in the early 1950s. The prolonged Korean War served as a built-in protective device for Nationalist diplomacy. Until the newly-independent nations began to pour into the United Nations in 1955, Formosa was not really pressed to push hard on a broad diplomatic front. (No nation gained entry into the United Nations from Indonesia's admission in 1950 until 16 nations, several of them newly independent, were admitted in 1955.) The case of Libya illustrates the point. In late 1951, just a few days before Libyan independence, Formosa extended recognition. But over seven years passed before Formosa tried to, and succeeded, in establishing diplomatic relations—including consent to a Nationalist embassy being set up in Libya.

In 1956 a storm burst into this diplomatic lull. In rapid succession, Egypt, Syria and Yemen recognised Peking. That autumn, the sixteen nations admitted to the U.N. in 1955 cast their first votes on the " two China's " issue. Formosa picked up only four of the 16 votes. Peking, on the other hand, gained seven votes which helped to double the number of votes in its favour from twelve to twenty-four. Faced with the growing " Bandung spirit " as well, the Nationalists had to re-evaluate their diplomatic activities.

The result was that 1957 was the most active diplomatic year for the Nationalists since their retreat from the mainland. In Latin America, the Dominican Republic, El Salvador and Ecuador agreed to elevate legations to embassies. The Nationalists were recognised by Uruguay, and opened diplomatic relations with Paraguay. The Argentine was persuaded to re-open its embassy in Formosa. In the Middle East and Africa, diplomatic relations were established with Jordan and Liberia, the first resident Turkish Ambassador arrived in Taipei, the Nationalist legation in Lebanon and their consulate in Jidda, Saudi Arabia, were raised to embassy status. The move in Jidda well illustrates the change in Formosa's approach to diplomatic relations from 1950 to 1957. The Nationalists closed the consulate in 1950, reopened it in 1956 and a year later raised this to embassy level.

The years 1958 and 1959 were ones of almost equal activity. The first Nationalist envoys arrived in Libya and Liberia. The first envoys from Jordan, Lebanon, Saudi Arabia and Thailand arrived in Taipei in 1958. Three Nationalist legations were raised to embassies, and three consulates or consulates-general were established or reopened in Sao Paulo, Songkhla (Thailand) and Mexicali (Mexico). Also another two legations in Formosa were raised to embassies. This trend has continued. Seven more embassies or legations were opened in Taipei. The

Nationalists, for their part, raised six missions abroad to embassies, and the consulate in Cebu, the Philippines, was reopened.

Under no circumstances can Taipei afford to ignore the newer countries, for however insignificant they may be individually, collectively they could deprive Formosa of its seat in the U.N. It will be recalled that in 1955–56, Peking formalised its relations with Nepal, Egypt, Syria and Yemen. From then until the flood of new nations (mostly African) in 1960, formal ties were established with Cambodia, Iraq, Morocco, the Sudan, Guinea, Ghana and Cuba. Each autumn during this period the Nationalists saw Peking closing the gap in the " China vote " at the United Nations. The stage was clearly set for the struggle for recognition in Africa.

Communist China is a much more newsworthy subject than Nationalist China.[5] Nevertheless, Formosa has done exceptionally well in the contest in Africa. Since 1960, twenty-three African nations have gained independence, and all have become U.N. members. Thirteen of them recognised Formosa, five recognised Peking, and five recognise neither. Formosa also gained recognition from newly independent Cyprus[6] and Jamaica. On the other hand Peking gained a bonus U.N. vote when Syria split off from the United Arab Republic and another when Mongolia was admitted to the U.N.

Formosa, however, fared much less well in the United Nations. There were a record number of twenty-two abstentions in the 1960 " China vote." More important, it was the closest vote to date with Peking falling only eight votes behind Formosa. The Nationalists quickly strengthened their diplomatic ties in Africa and elsewhere, invited many African leaders to Formosa, and concluded a long series of economic and technical assistance agreements which sent large numbers of Nationalist technicians to Africa and brought many groups of Africans to Formosa for training.

It would be a distortion of history, however, to give credit solely to Formosa and its diplomats.[7] The United States, for one thing, actively

---

[5] A suggestive illustration of this situation occurred in the autumn of 1961 when Mr. Cyrus Eaton wrote to the editor of the *New York Times* that 71 nations had diplomatic relations with Peking. Though he was 30-odd countries over the mark, the *Times* did not see fit to add an editorial note. See the *New York Times Sunday Magazine*, October 8, 1961.

[6] Despite the opening of diplomatic relations, Cyprus did not support Formosa in the 1960–63 U.N. votes, but abstained each time.

[7] The writer is not in a position to remark on the day-to-day efficiency of Formosa's present ambassadors abroad. Based on somewhat incomplete information, however, two facts stand out. First, almost every man has had a long background in diplomatic work, ranging up to about 30 years. Secondly, the level of education is extraordinary. The overwhelming majority are college trained (more often than not abroad), many have done graduate work, and about a third hold Ph.D. degrees. In terms of education and diplomatic experience, Formosa's diplomats appear to be considerably more suited for their tasks than their counterparts from Peking. (For a discussion

bolstered Formosa on all fronts. Nor should it be forgotten that many of the ex-French colonies maintain close ties with France, which recognises Formosa. But the greatest assistance came from Peking itself. For example, Peking managed to anger Nasser in 1959 by undue (in Nasser's view) attention to a Syrian Communist visiting Peking.[8] Similar revolutionary gestures have been made toward virtually any leftist group in Africa. While such revolutionary support may have appealed to many African leaders before 1960, they apparently adopted a different view once in office.

Whatever the causes, Formosa has clearly bolstered its position in the United Nations since 1960. This is most easily illustrated by the vote of the twenty-seven members admitted to the United Nations since 1960 (seventeen in 1960, four more in 1961, and another six in 1962).[9]

	Supported Taipei	Supported Peking	Abstained
1960 [10]	0	3	13
1961	5	4	12
1962	15	8	4

Moreover, by early 1963 Formosa could take considerable comfort from the state of its diplomatic missions abroad, as well as foreign missions in Taipei. The reader will recall that in late 1949 Formosa had missions in thirty-seven different nations. This figure has now grown to fifty-eight.[11] Of this number, 52 are embassies (as opposed to only nineteen in late 1949), and almost all are manned by a full-time (rather

of Peking's diplomats, see my " Peking's Evolving Ministry of Foreign Affairs," *The China Quarterly*, No. 4, October–December 1960).

The only real diplomatic fiasco known to the writer occurred in 1961 when ex-warlord Ma Pu-fang was involved in a scandal in Saudi Arabia, where he was serving as Ambassador. He was quickly whisked away by the Nationalists. Another relatively minor incident in Australia in 1962 evoked harsh comment from a San Francisco Chinese-American newspaper not particularly friendly to the Nationalists. Though the charges were rather vague, the *Chinese World* (April 18, 1962) editorially alluded to the " . . . inefficiency of many of the Kuomintang diplomatic officials now being assigned . . . " abroad.

8 On the eve of Peking's 10th anniversary (October 1, 1959), a Syrian Communist visiting Communist China delivered a speech denouncing Nasser. Cairo objected violently and there were rumours of a pending diplomatic break. After a month of hesitation, the Chinese came forth with the lame excuse that the speech was delivered at the invitation of the Party rather than the Chinese government. Cairo accepted this, and relations gradually improved. See the *New York Times*, October 1, 2, 4, 5, 10, 13 and 26, 1959.

9 On the grounds that Syria was actually readmitted to the U.N. in 1961, it is not included in this calculation.

10 Although the Congo (Leopoldville) was among the 17 nations newly admitted to the United Nations in 1960, it abstained from the " China vote " of that year.

11 In addition to the embassies and legations in national capitals, Formosa has about 25 consulates-general or consulates in the U.S., Brazil, Canada, the Philippines, Thailand, Vietnam, Australia, Tahiti, Japan, Mexico and Timor, plus its U.N. mission and a special liaison office in Macao.

than concurrent) ambassador.[12]   Plans are reportedly under way to
establish a mission in at least one other country.[13]   In contrast to
Formosa's missions in fifty-eight nations, Peking has forty-two, all but
two of them embassies.[14]

The Communists, on the other hand, have the edge in the number of
missions accredited to Peking or Taipei. Thirty nations have missions
accredited to Taipei (plus two honorary consulates), all but two of them
are embassies. However, about a third of the heads of missions are
concurrently accredited (usually to Japan) and do not reside in Taipei.
Another third of the missions have, as the ranking resident official, a man
of less than ambassadorial rank (ministers, counsellors, etc.).[15]   In
contrast there are thirty-seven missions in Peking, all but two of which
are embassies.[16]   (Given the state of relations with India and Yugoslavia,
it might be more realistic to reduce this figure to thirty-five.)

*   *   *   *   *

Both Chinas have nearly run out of countries with which they could
have diplomatic relations. Aside from West Germany and pocket-sized
countries such as Monaco, Andorra, West Samoa (none of which belongs
to the United Nations), ten members of the United Nations recognise
neither China: Austria,[17] Central African Republic, Ethiopia, Iceland,

---

12 Latin America provides a good area case study of this growth. In 1952 Formosa had
   five embassies, seven legations, and two consulates-general; by early 1963, 16 embassies
   and three legations.
13 The intention to establish an embassy in Chad " soon " was reported in the official
   Chinese News Service, New York, January 23, 1962.
14 Peking has only two concurrent heads of mission; Ch'en Chia-k'ang is ambassador
   to the U.A.R. and the Yemen, and Ho Ying is ambassador to both Tanganyika and
   Uganda. In addition, Peking (aside from missions in national capitals) has eight
   consulates-general or consulates in Burma, Indonesia, Laos, Poland, Switzerland and
   Vietnam.
15 Toward the end of 1962, eight heads of missions resided outside of Taipei. The writer
   has not been able to determine whether two recently arrived ambassadors will reside
   in Taipei or elsewhere. It should also be noted that Great Britain has a Consulate,
   technically accredited to the province of Formosa, but which can more realistically be
   considered the British " embassy " in Nationalist China.
16 Technically, Algeria has a " diplomatic mission " in Peking, but apparently at the
   ambassadorial level—the same level at which the Chinese envoy is accredited in
   Algiers. All of the heads of missions in Peking reside, although a small number
   are concurrently accredited to Mongolia. In addition to the missions in Peking, the
   following nations have one or more consulates-general or consulates in various cities
   (mainly Shanghai and Canton): Burma, Czechoslovakia, Denmark, East Germany,
   Indonesia, Korea, Laos, Nepal, Norway, Poland, Switzerland and Great Britain. (The
   British office in Shanghai is actually a branch office of the Office of the Chargé
   d'Affaires in Peking.) Although it has not been mentioned in the Chinese Communist
   press, apparently reliable reports claim that the four Soviet consulates-general and
   consulates in Shanghai, Harbin, Urumchi and Ining were closed in the autumn of 1962.
   See the *New York Times* (international edition), November 30, 1962.
17 Although *official* Nationalist sources continue to list Austria as a country recognising
   neither China, the writer has in his possession a letter dated April 15, 1961, from the
   Austrian Embassy in Washington stating that diplomatic relations " do exist in the
   form of co-accreditation of Austria's Ambassador to Japan " with the Nationalist
   Chinese regime.

Ireland, the Ivory Coast,[18] Malaya, Niger,[18] Sierra Leone and Tunisia. Using the 1962 U.N. vote as a guide, four lean toward Formosa, three toward Peking and three abstain. Certainly a more active role by any or all of these nations will not swing the " two Chinas " issue.

If the Nationalist victory in the struggle for diplomatic relations and support in the U.N. was slow in coming, it has clearly been decisive at least for the immediate future. It will take notable changes in Formosa and Communist China, or possibly in the African states or United States policy, to upset this substantial, if not overwhelming victory for Nationalist diplomacy.

[18] The Hong Kong *Tiger Standard*, July 17, 1963, reported that the Nationalists will " soon establish " diplomatic relations with the Ivory Coast and Niger.

Dilemmas of American Policy towards Formosa

By AKIRA IRIYE

AMERICA'S policy towards Formosa has come under fire in recent months from all three groups of Chinese. The Nationalists and the Communists alike share the heritage that China is one state; some of the facts of international life, however, have given American policy a preference for accepting two Chinas in the world. The apparent American support for the Formosan independence movement is favoured neither by Peking nor Taipei. On the other hand the native Formosans criticise the contradictions and indecisions of American policy which, they say, encourages their democratic liberal movements, but at the same time helps Chiang Kai-shek to stay in office.

The question of Formosa's legal status, with its far ranging implications, has long bedevilled American policy. Before the Korean War, Formosa was regarded as lying beyond America's " defence perimeter "; but legally Formosa was thought of as part of China. The Cairo and Potsdam Declarations together with the Japanese instrument of surrender had made this point amply clear, and the incorporation of Formosa as a Chinese province, soon after the Japanese surrender, created no legal or political problems. President Truman explicitly recognised China's title to the island in January, 1950. By this time mainland China had fallen to the communists and Sino-American relations had been exacerbated. However, the consensus of American officials was that no counter-offensive against China was feasible, in view of the more urgent need to concentrate American resources on the defence of freedom in Europe. The political future of Formosa was essentially irrelevant. Whether Chiang Kai-shek held it as the stronghold of anti-communist China, or whether it was joined to Communist China, the outcome was the same—Formosa was part of China.

With the outbreak of the Korean War, American policy departed from this simple and complacent stand to become militarily well defined but legally ambiguous. Formosa was now incorporated into the American security system in the Far East. The mutual defence treaty of 1954 between the Nationalist government and the United States was an integral part of the recently evolved defence strategy based on the " island chain in the Western Pacific." Thus Formosa joined the extensive network of American alliances, which included Japan, South Korea, the Philippines, Australia, New Zealand, Thailand and Pakistan, designed to " contain " Communist aggression. Communist territories were not, however, to be attacked by force. Both Truman and Eisenhower, except briefly between 1953 and 1954, restrained Chiang Kai-shek from staging a counter-offensive against the mainland. The United States continued to regard Formosa as Chinese territory; the mutual defence treaty implicitly recognised this in stating that the terms " territory " and " territorial " in the treaty " shall mean in respect of the Republic of China, Taiwan and the Pescadores." Also the United States persisted in refusing to recognise Communist China as the representative government of the Chinese people, thereby continuing to regard Chiang Kai-shek's régime as the government of China.

This logic has, of course, led to a dilemma for American policy. If there is only one China and one Chinese government, conflict between Chiang Kai-shek and Mao Tse-tung must be regarded as civil war, not as a war between two countries. How could the United States, then, sign a mutual defence treaty with a government against its rebels, not against its external enemies, while restraining that government from subjugating the rebels? As long as the Nationalist government was regarded as the government of China, the defence treaty was a legal anomaly which prevented a legitimate government from being overthrown by its internal enemies but tacitly assured the latter that they would not be subjugated by this legitimate government. This logical dilemma led the United States government, almost immediately following the outbreak of the Korean War, to issue statements to the effect that the status of Formosa remained undefined and would have to be determined by the United Nations. This was not the same as saying that Formosa was not Chinese territory, for to do so would have been tantamount to regarding the Nationalist government as a government in exile. Nevertheless, the San Francisco peace treaty between Japan and some of its former enemies took pains to omit explicit mention of Formosa's status except that Japan renounced its title. This technical ambiguity remains.

Such a shift in American attitude gave a long-awaited opportunity to some Formosan leaders to assert their people's independence from China. They believed that Formosa's independent legal status had been recognised by America's policy of separating the island from mainland China and treating it as part of the American alliance structure. They expected that ultimately the native Formosan leaders, supported by the United States, would replace the Chinese in exile as the true government of Formosa. By the same token, American policy encouraged Peking officials to extend overtures to Chinese in Formosa to effect rapprochement, rather than see Formosa go to the Formosans.

Moreover, there was some reason to believe in the machinations of the " anti-American group " within the Nationalist government to bring about a truce with the Communists.

Granted that the defence of Formosa was essential for defending freedom and containing aggression in Asia, how could the United States ignore the principles of national self-determination or democracy? If Formosa was Chinese, could the United States really erect a wall around it, in effect preventing Formosa truly becoming Chinese? If Formosa was not Chinese, how could the United States justify its continued assistance to a government which was predominantly Chinese and which discouraged free political expression by the native Formosans? If Formosa was neither Chinese nor Formosan, could a way out be found to transcend legal niceties and regard Formosa as a separate Sino-Formosan state? How could such a state be administered to assure freedom and economic benefits to the Chinese and Formosans alike?

These problems were bequeathed to President Kennedy in 1961. Certain nuances in policy statements by the President and the State Department hint that the United States is now more aware of these problems and more interested in solving them. There seems to be a more definite trend toward a two Chinas policy. During the 1961 debate in the United Nations on the question of Chinese representation, Ambassador Stevenson took pains to point out that Formosa was a big country by any standard and therefore a very respectable member of the United Nations. The Japanese delegate, supporting the American stand against unseating the representative of the Nationalist government, stressed how Formosa was different from mainland China and should not, therefore, be swallowed up by the Communists. All this was indicative of America's determination to uphold Formosa's identity and autonomy. The United States has since continued to discourage Chiang Kai-shek's counter-offensive against the mainland while accusing Communist China of being the most aggressive of all Communist countries.

It is difficult to gauge the importance of the State Department's publication of *Foreign Relations of the United States 1943: China*, which contained unfavourable reports on the Chungking government in wartime, and Formosa's cool reception of Admiral Kirk as United States ambassador to replace an ambassador who openly supported Chiang Kai-shek. Evidence suggests, however, that American officials had become acutely aware of Formosa's critical political condition and were considering what moves to take should Chiang Kai-shek pass away or retire. This does not necessarily imply that the United States would recognise the Formosans as sovereign people on the island and the

Chinese merely as exiles. Neither would it mean perpetuating Nationalist rule. Whether a workable compromise can be worked out remains to be seen. Secretary of State Dean Rusk has spoken of " the emergence of a new, modern generation of men and women " in Formosa as well as in other countries in Asia, who would carry forward the task of promoting economic development and political freedom. It is far from clear, however, that Chinese and Formosan youths would actually work together for these common ends.

Formosa alone seems unimportant to the United States except as a symbol; it is believed that surrendering the island to the Chinese communists could be a severe blow to those in Asia who stand for freedom. Formosa is more important as a part of what is emerging as a political and economic community in Asia. Conceived with the blessings and military support of the United States, such a community would integrate Japan's industrial potential with India's man-power and natural resources of other regions. America's military assistance to India, encouragement of rapprochement between Japan and South Korea, and pressure for political reforms in certain South-east Asian countries are all part of the same effort. It is not accident that Japanese trade and investment activities have recently gained momentum in Korea and Formosa; Japan is an essential part of the new American vision of free Asia.

All these trends in American policy are disturbing from the Chinese point of view. The People's Republic of China has consistently maintained that there can be no compromise with the United States unless its forces are withdrawn from Formosa. For the Chinese communists, the autonomy of Formosa connotes the return of Japanese imperialism to the island. The Nationalists refuse to accept " two Chinas " let alone " one China and one Formosa " which would imply the perpetual separation of Formosa from China proper. Formosan leaders, on the other hand, seem confident that the United States will eventually support them as governors of Formosa. Meanwhile, they criticise America's support of Chiang Kai-shek, which financially amounts to nearly $100 million a year.

Both China and the United States have grown up as empires and confront each other in the Far East which has traditionally been ruled by empires, not by nation-states. Communist China's vow to liberate Formosa, and America's vow to stop them may, therefore, be considered another round in the history of the rise and fall of empires in Asia. Yet America's security system in Asia is more than an empire of the conventional type, made up of conquered territories. If successfully developed in the light of basic American axioms, this empire could be a new Pacific community made up of democratic, free, and peace-loving peoples. There are, at present, many difficulties. Few of America's allies in Asia are democratic; political conditions are unstable in so many of them; there is latent hostility between Japan and some of its former colonies; and there is no cultural unity nor economic integration among Asian countries as there is in Europe. But unless this emerging unity is retained and improved through political and economic reforms and American policy towards Formosa transcends the exclusively military association between the United States and the Nationalist government, the Far East can easily fall prey to the domination of another empire.

Peking and Taipei

By LEWIS GILBERT

UNTIL recent events so rudely contradicted them, the Nationalists officially regarded Mao Tse-tung *et al.* as a puppet government whose strings were pulled from Moscow; the Communists, for their part, have found it equally convenient to look at the Nationalists as a rebellious local government suffering under American " occupation." However, in spite of the often renewed vows of one side to eliminate the other a sporadic dialogue has gone on between Peking and Taipei. This is not so surprising when one remembers the many short honeymoons which have occurred during the oft-renewed marriage of political convenience between the Nationalists and the Communists.

With China divided as it is, Peking has much to gain if it can talk the " misguided " Nationalists back into the fold. Perhaps the Nationalists have judged their position correctly in never having let the Communist leaders talk them into retirement. Chiang Kai-shek believes that he will return to the mainland in the wake of an invasion from Formosa which will spark off a mass rising against the Communists, or that the Chinese people—to whom the Nationalists have so endeared themselves—will cast down the gods with feet of Russian clay who now rule in Peking and welcome back the Nationalists with open arms. But, whenever Chiang Kai-shek is at odds with Washington he has a vested interest in rumours that he has come to terms with Peking. After all, Washington has its Rapallo complexes about Far Eastern politics and the Generalissimo doubtless feels that these are fair diplomatic game.

FAMILY TIES AND OTHER LINKS

The civil war split many of China's politically influential families between the Nationalists and the Communists. Perhaps the Soong sisters are the most notable example. Madame Sun Yat-sen (Soong Ching-ling), one of two Deputy Chairmen of the Chinese People's Republic, is the elder sister of Madame Chiang Kai-shek (Soong Mei-ling). The late Huang Ching [1] (whose real name was Yu Chi-wei), Central Committee member of the Chinese Communist Party, former Mayor of Tientsin and later Minister of the First Ministry of Mechanical Engineering, was

---

[1] *Dictionary of Modern Chinese Names*, or *Who's Who in Modern China*, compiled under supervision of Japanese Foreign Office (Tokyo: Konan Shogan, 1957), p. 188.

the nephew of David Yu Ta-wei, the Nationalist Defence Minister. Yu Ta-ying, the sister of David Yu Ta-wei, now teaches in Peking.

The Chinese Communists conducted a " letter offensive " in 1955. Using their overseas newspapers and powerful transmitters, the Communists released letters from family members, friends, teachers or students of the Nationalist leaders. The letters had a standard theme of a motherland greatly changed: only under Communist rule could China undergo such a tremendous transformation; it is advisable to return to the motherland to participate in the " great Socialist construction " at the earliest date.

In 1957 Yeh Kung-chuo, wrote from Communist China to his nephew (George) Yeh Kung-chao, then Foreign Minister and later Nationalist Ambassador to Washington, and presently Minister without portfolio, urging him to " realise the present situation and find some feasible ways and means to contribute to the motherland."

One article in the *Wen Wei Pao*, a pro-Communist newspaper in Hong Kong, stated that Ch'en Chin-hua, the elder sister of the Nationalist Vice President and Premier Ch'en Ch'eng, thought longingly of him and wished her friends and relatives in Formosa a peaceful and lucky New Year. The article also said that the life of Nationalist army dependants left behind in Ch'en's native place was getting better and better.

The " letter offensive," which relaxed somewhat between 1960–62 when Peking had little to boast about, seems to have started up again early in 1963. In March, Hong Kong's pro-Communist *Ta Kung Pao* published a story, with pictures, about the life of Yeh Kung-shao, a Delegate to the Peking Municipal People's Congress and head of the Public Health Department of the Peking Medical Academy. Even without the title " Yeh Kung-chao's Aunt," most Chinese readers would immediately know that Yeh Kung-shao is an aunt of the Minister without portfolio in Taipei. The motive of the " letter offensive " is to convince all Chinese outside China that they would be safe and well treated, no matter who their relations, as long as they worked sincerely for the Peking Government.

The " letter offensive," criticised by the Nationalist leaders as absurd and ridiculous, exploits all kinds of social relations. There are Communist military leaders who graduated from the Whampoa Military Academy, which Chiang Kai-shek helped found and over which he presided. For instance, the Communist military genius Marshal Lin Piao, Minister of Defence, is a graduate of this Academy—China's West Point of the middle 'twenties. Large numbers of old students of the Whampoa Academy remained in China and many of them wrote this spring to " advise " their former comrades on Formosa to make " wise choices."

During the early coalition, between the Nationalists and the Communists, personal relations were sometimes good. Mao Tse-tung served as head of the Nationalist Agitprop Department in Canton. Chou En-lai worked as Chiang Kai-shek's political aide at the Whampoa Military Academy. Some Communists later changed into Nationalists; and some Nationalists into Communists. Wu Yu-chang, a former member of the Nationalist party, became a member of the Central Committee of the Communist Party during the coalition in the middle 1920s.

DAY-BY-DAY CONTACT

Through their subsidised newspapers in Hong Kong, one side addresses the other. The Nationalists in the past twelve months have repeatedly urged Communist cadres to choose freedom. The Communists have intensified their " advice " to the Nationalist leaders urging them to do something good for the motherland. These appeals have met very little response from either side.

The Nationalist and Communist editors in overseas communities have common ground on which to meet. For instance, in Hong Kong they see each other regularly at the meetings of the Hong Kong Newspaper Society as fellow members. Though they seldom talk to each other, the opportunity is there for them to do so. At birthday or other parties given by " neutralists," they may meet again. After all, they have known each other since the old days on the mainland. In Singapore, leftists and rightists sometimes belong to the same clubs.

Battles on the radio waves are frequent. From Formosa, thirteen radio stations, two of medium wave length and eleven short wave, broadcast to the mainland using nine different dialects. One special programme advises Communist cadres on ways and means of overthrowing the Peking régime in cooperation with the masses. From the mainland, Communist medium wave broadcasts can and do reach every corner of Formosa.

There is no postal agreement between Formosa and the mainland, but letters do get through via private individuals in Hong Kong and Macao. Taipei's " Voice of Free China " has claimed that it receives a monthly average of 100 letters from its audience on the mainland. A majority of the letters were posted via Hong Kong and Macao; three were supposedly posted directly from the mainland. The Nationalists in Formosa also join Hong Kong people in sending money and food parcels to their relatives on the mainland.

Hong Kong also acts as a transfer station for people moving from the mainland to Formosa and vice versa. Again, relatives and friends are the intermediaries. The small numbers of travellers who make trips do so mostly for family reunions, or to return to their native place to die—not as an expression of political loyalty.

There is also trade between Formosa and the mainland via Hong Kong. Total trade turnover in 1962 was about U.S. $1·1 million. The Chinese Communists had a favourable trade balance of about U.S. $1 million. The Communists mainly export Chinese medical herbs which Formosa does not produce. But shrewd merchants also include large amounts of dates, lotus seeds and other items under the name of herbs. In November 1962 fresh water crabs, a great Chinese delicacy, appeared for the first time on the Formosa market. Newspaper editorials asked with indignation why Free China should import these crabs and so " provide " precious foreign exchange for the Communist " bandits." Nothing was done except that the crabs were consumed with customary delight. The major Formosan export to the mainland was crude sugar, which was not included in the international sugar agreement.

Nationalist and Communist business men meet in Hong Kong on a highly competitive basis. Mainland hog merchants frequently hold their animals at the Communist border town of Sumchun until just before a shipment of hogs arrives from Formosa by sea. Then the Communists send in their hogs, driving down the market price in an attempt to monopolise the market.

In Southeast Asian countries, consumer goods made in Communist China find their way into some anti-Communist countries at competitive prices. Several pro-Nationalist overseas Chinese businessmen handle Communist exports. Communists offer better terms to their agents than Formosa, and overseas Chinese businessmen have no reasons other than political to reject Communist deals.

One large drug company on Formosa, packing antibiotics for shipment to Southeast Asia, regularly purchased bulk supplies of a Czech drug through a Hong Kong wholesaler who got his supply through Communist China.

Buying " enemy " publications has been a special Hong Kong trade for several years. Researchers and intelligence groups have been willing to pay high prices for Communist provincial newspapers and trade magazines to use as source material. These publications are difficult to obtain because the Communists ban their export. One copy of a 4-page daily newspaper can be sold at from U.S. $0·40 to U.S. $35·00 depending upon supply and demand. Even a photostat copy of *People's Hand Book, 1961*, 250 pages, supplied by Hong Kong dealers, was priced at U.S. $45–55. An original copy in Peking's bookstores sold at U.S. $1·50. The Communists buy Nationalist publications regularly. Special cadres in Canton can read Taipei's official organ, the *Central Daily News*, the day after it is published. Many of the Communist New China News Agency's stories datelined Taipei are based upon Formosan papers.

Quemoy and Matsu remain symbols of the unended Chinese civil war. With these islands in Nationalist hands, the Communists can, by artillery barrage, protest to the world against the "two Chinas plot." To take these two strongly fortified islands would indeed be expensive for Peking. It may well be that Peking, after its fiasco of 1958, does not now particularly want to take the islands. One Communist confided to a Hong Kong journalist: "Even if Chiang Kai-shek would agree to withdraw his army from Quemoy and Matsu under American pressure, our shore guns would not allow him to do so."

THE DEALERS?

Peking's attitude towards Formosa has changed several times since 1949. Until 1954, Mao Tse-tung's plan for taking Formosa was primarily a military one. But, with the outbreak of the Korean war and Peking's participation, America abandoned its position on the sidelines of the Chinese civil war and took Formosa within the American defence perimeter. From 1955 to 1958 political offensives coupled with military pressure were used alternately to test America's determination to defend Formosa. However, in 1958, Mr. Khrushchev apparently made it clear to the Chinese Communists that he would not go along with their forward policy of trying to blockade the offshore islands. On October 5, 1958, the day before Peking announced its cease fire on the offshore islands, Mr. Khrushchev told a Tass correspondent that "The Soviet Union will come to the help of the CPR . . . if the United States attacks the CPR. . . . But we have not interfered in and do not intend to interfere in the (Chinese) civil war." It is not surprising, therefore, that Peking, restrained by Moscow, while still confronted by the American Seventh Fleet in the Formosan straits and economic calamities at home, should have played a passive role from 1959 to the present. In 1961, one Communist spokesman stressed that Peking could wait for many years to see the Formosan problem settled.

Rumours of dealings between Peking and Taipei started spreading after Premier Chou En-lai had proclaimed Peking's willingness, at Bandung in April 1955, to open talks with the United States to ease and eliminate tension in the Formosa Straits. In July, at the National People's Congress, Chou announced that "Provided that the United States does not interfere with China's internal affairs, the possibility of the peaceful liberation of Formosa will continue to increase. If possible, the Chinese government is willing to enter into negotiation with the *responsible local authorities* of Formosa to map out concrete steps for Formosa's peaceful liberation."

Peking's political position towards Formosa in this period can be summarised by quoting Chou En-lai's address in the National Congress in 1956. " There are two possible ways for the Chinese people to liberate Formosa, that is, by war or by peaceful means, so far as it is possible. . . . At present the possibility of peacefully liberating Formosa is increasing."

According to one well informed leftist in Hong Kong, this Formosa policy was decided upon at an unannounced top level meeting at Peitaiho preceding the Fifth Plenary Session of the Seventh Central Committee of the Chinese Communist Party in March 1955. This meeting had been preceded by two separate shows of military force. The first was a large scale bombardment of Quemoy in September 1954. The second was a move against the northernmost offshore islands then held by the Nationalists. In January 1955 the Communists assaulted and took the island of I Kiang Shan, 270 miles north of Formosa, forcing the evacuation of the nearby Ta Chen Islands a few weeks later. Having demonstrated their military power, the Communists were in a position to speak of the " peaceful liberation " of Formosa.

Stories of " peace talk " in late 1955 were leaked by the Communists to the Hong Kong press. These in turn were taken up by the international press. Documentary evidence suggests that the Communists took the initiative in trying to arrange talks.

It is known that Shao Li-tzu, a member of Peking's KMT Revolutionary Committee did write to an intermediary, resident in Hong Kong, regarding the peace terms. This man, who had worked under Chiang Ching-kuo before the Nationalist collapse, wrote three letters to the President's son. The first went early in August 1955 and asked that a contact man be sent to Hong Kong to discuss an " urgent " matter. The second, a few weeks later, indicated that no reply had been received to the first and emphasised the urgency of sending a contact as soon as possible. The third, written at the end of December 1955, again indicated that Chiang Ching-kuo had not replied. This letter appealed to young Chiang's patriotic sentiments as a fellow Chinese and urged him to reply before the wonderful " opportunity slipped away."

As far as is known, this particular attempt to get the two sides together—even at a very low level—failed. It is hard to establish whether any other contacts have been attempted.

Had the Nationalists sent an envoy to Hong Kong in 1955 or early 1956, Chiang Kai-shek would, according to stories current among pro-Communist Hong Kong sources, have been offered a honourable retirement either in China or abroad. The Nationalists could maintain their own armed forces on Formosa. They could set up an autonomous government on Formosa. The price of this was a Nationalist pledge to sever all relations with the United States. No mention was then made of the United Nations seat. A variant of this rumour was that Chiang was to be given the governorship of Formosa provided that he recognised Peking's suzerainty.

After the futile bombardment of the offshore islands in 1958, the Chinese Communists talked less about military liberation and more about peaceful deals. Chou En-lai in his 1960 talks with Takasaki, a member of the Japanese House of Representatives, assured the Japanese visitor "China would not use force to 'liberate' Formosa." [2] In April 1961 Marshal Ch'en Yi spoke in Jakarta: "We persist in this stand; withdraw the Seventh Fleet from the Formosa Straits. This ought not to be a difficult thing for the United States to do." These two statements show China has modified her stand considerably. Chou has modified his former stand of taking "all suitable means, at a suitable time, to recover Formosa." Ch'en has retracted his former demand for the "withdrawal of all U.S. armed forces from China's territory of Formosa and the Formosa Straits area" to simply the "withdrawal of the Seventh Fleet from the Formosa Straits."

The policy line, as put forth by one CCP Central Committee member, during the 1959–61 period was that "China will get control of Formosa no matter how long it takes, ten years or twenty, but China aims at a united front with the Chiang government, not its overthrow." [3]

At present Peking's political attitude has changed to a somewhat more hostile attitude toward the Nationalists. Communist newspapers again use "Chiang bandits" instead of "Formosa local authorities" or "Chiang group." One Communist explained this change, saying: "We tried to be genial to the Nationalists for a time (implying 1959–middle of 1962), but they thought us weak and even attacked us with guerillas and saboteurs."

Peking's policy towards Formosa is limited by its military strength. If Peking had been strong enough, it would have taken Formosa long ago. However, the recent tougher attitude could mean that the Communists may again use the Straits to stage a fresh international crisis whenever such a crisis suits Peking's needs.

The Nationalist position towards the Chinese mainland is much less flexible than the Communist position toward Formosa. President Chiang Kai-shek has repeatedly asserted his determination to eliminate the "Communist bandits." Answering a question privately in June 1956 on the rumours of peace talks, Chiang Ching-kuo told a Hong Kong Chinese journalist that the Communists were the world's most shameless people

[2] Tseng Shan, April 2, 1961, to Austrian Communist Party Congress.
[3] Kyodo News Agency, January 1961.

and that the peace rumour had been fabricated with malicious intentions. Chiang Ching-kuo's political position towards the Chinese Communists is along the standard Nationalist line—the total elimination of Communism.

The Nationalists strongly denied the report by Mr. Dennis Bloodworth in the London *Observer* of August 12, 1962, that the Chiang family was trying to preserve its dynasty by negotiating with Peking. According to the agreement said to have been reached, neither side would make a serious attack on the other during General Chiang Kai-shek's lifetime; but after his death Formosa—still expected to be under Nationalist control—might be allowed an autonomous status under Peking " similar to that held by Tibet." During the subsequent decade or so, there would be a referendum to determine whether Formosa would be independent or part of China proper—as both sides, to date, have claimed it to be. Nationalist spokesman, James Shen, went on to reiterate the Nationalist determination to " uproot the Communist rule and to save hundreds of millions of peoples on the mainland . . . this dedication is immutable and not subject to compromise."

But at this time both the Nationalists and the Communists could well have wanted to put talk of such a deal in the pipeline. It would help the Nationalists play on America's Far Eastern Rapallo complex. The Communists were worried at this time that the Nationalists would invade the mainland. Although they despise the notion of Formosan Independence, they may have been willing to use talk of a deal to drive a wedge between the Formosans and the mainlanders on Formosa. Peking knows that a large proportion of the conscripts in the Nationalist forces are Formosan who are unlikely to want to ride to a mainland Valhalla.

In the past two years, at the same time as the Nationalists have been intensifying their calls for a return to the mainland, they have been modifying their tactical policy toward Chinese Communists as individuals and as members of the communist bureaucracy. Taipei has proclaimed a series of lenient measures for those officers and party members who defect from the Communists. President Chiang in 1961 promised safety to all Communist defectors. Premier Ch'en Ch'eng in 1962 promised to give substantial monetary awards to those who " actively oppose tyranny " on the mainland. He also promised to give legal recognition to all anti-Communist organisations and local anti-Communist authorities on the mainland. These Nationalist political manoeuvres indicate that they seem willing to negotiate and cooperate with all anti-Communists including Communist defectors as individuals, as groups, or even as local authorities. The Nationalists promise that, with the exception of top ranking Communist leaders, they will pardon all who have worked with the Peking régime.

Since both the Nationalists and the Communists are using nationalism to recruit support from Chinese both at home and abroad, it is possible that national ties may one day surmount political power rivalry. The longstanding political confrontation could be altered suddenly when Mao Tse-tung or Chiang Kai-shek dies. Mao will be 70 in December this year, and Chiang turns 76 in October. Thus the possibility of new leaders with new policies increases with each passing year.

If the Communist offer of peace contacts in 1955 had not been disclosed and if the over-enthusiastic and hasty intermediary had handled his job tactfully, the Nationalists and the Communists might have used that opportunity to exchange views. It is possible that other unrevealed feelers have been extended and perhaps have resulted in talks of some kind. One ranking member of the Nationalist Party in Hong Kong maintains regular social contacts with a member of the KMT Revolutionary Committee, a satellite party in Peking. It is safe to assume that the Revolutionary Committee of the KMT could and perhaps does serve as a medium for the Communists to contact the Nationalists. There is no guarantee that the known individual " social " contacts do not serve other functions as well.

The Intellectuals on Formosa

By MEI WEN-LI

*" The gestation, birth, and continuing life of the new states of Asia and Africa, through all their vicissitudes, are in large measure the work of intellectuals."**

CHIANG KAI-SHEK rebuilt his régime on Formosa not through his military might alone. Rather, he succeeded through rallying a group of intellectuals who could help him consolidate his rule on Formosa, work on propaganda, attract foreign aid and organise military control.

THE CULTURAL DESERT

These intellectuals who fled from the mainland during the civil war, and are now more than forty years old, have dominated the Formosa scene for over a decade. Only recently has their influence begun to wane. Aside from their political service, however, they have generally shown little genuine intellectual interest and creativity. In a friendly, unpublished memorandum to the educational and academic authorities on Formosa, three American professors described the island as a " cultural desert." [1] Lack of freedom, however, cannot explain this away. The narrow margin of freedom left by the tsars in nineteenth-century Russia did not stultify Russian thought. China's May Fourth Movement was not the result of official encouragement.

Poverty has played its part in sapping the energy of those intellectuals who sought refuge on Formosa. Few seem to have recovered from the miseries and frustrations of the days on the mainland during the Second World War and the Civil War in the late 1940s. In recent years foreign aid and subsidies from the American Boxer Indemnity have given them a somewhat better living. Still, the average salary of a teacher or government worker is less than US $50 a month, while the most successful of journalists may earn no more than US $100 a month. These people have to find other sources of income. College teachers often teach at more than half- a- dozen schools in one week. The more famous professors devote their time not to research or teaching but to compiling textbooks for elementary or middle schools. This brings in much more money than their university salaries. The less well-known teach at night-schools, or

---

* Edward Shils, " The Intellectual in the Political Development of the New States," *World Politics*, XII, No. 3, April 1960.
[1] The memorandum was quoted by two professors of the National Taiwan University. See Li Chi, " Cultural Desert," and Shen Kang-peh, " Education in the past fifty years," *Tzu-yu Chung-kuo*, XXI, No. 10, November 1959.

121

do clerical work as well as teaching. Few have the physical energy left for creative thinking.

Old age and disease take their toll among the older intellectuals. Lectures are often read from notes written decades ago. In writing books about the distant past they shield themselves from the hardships and disillusionment of more recently troubled times. Sometimes they simply reprint the works of their youth. When they venture to write on more modern times they rarely do more than compile dry and empty memoirs. The generation of refugee intellectuals which accompanied Chiang Kai-shek to Formosa are neither physically nor intellectually capable of keeping abreast with the latest developments in their fields and of contributing new and original research. Moreover, the Nationalists from time to time have drawn the more capable intellectuals into political service. The appeal of more security, power and prestige encourages the intellectuals to accept.

But hardships like those which have been mentioned did not make the Japanese thinkers in the post-war period intellectually impotent. The difference lies in a defeatist state of mind. With the collapse of the Nationalists most of the intellectuals who fled the mainland had lost confidence in themselves and could find no meaning in the life for which they were trained. They can do little more than cherish the myth of the return to the mainland. When the intellectuals arrived on Formosa they were not prepared for permanent exile. Many cherished the Chinese tradition of returning to die in one's hometown. " Even if a tree is as tall as 1,000 feet, its leaves fall back to the very spot where it is rooted." Quite a few see many more opportunities on the " conquered " mainland than on Formosa. Some rationalise the present unsatisfactory conditions on the island. Once back on the mainland, democracy will be realised, taxes reduced, and all will be well with the world. The Nationalists have fostered this myth which in so many ways is its *raison d'être.* To Chiang Kai-shek it must seem that to rethink the ideology of his régime could only lead into dangerous ways. Dogma is the order of the day.

THE ANGLO-AMERICANS

Despite their intellectual poverty, the political attitudes of the older intellectuals had tremendous influence on the course of events on Formosa since 1950. Their attitudes were determined mainly by two factors: the power they enjoyed, and their commitment to the broad lines of Anglo-American thought. The dominance of the " Anglo-American " attitude around 1950 was fostered by Chiang Kai-shek. He accepted the view of his " Anglo-American " advisors that some democratic usages were necessary to win the sympathy and support of the United States. He appointed K. C. Wu, an American-trained politician who had won a reputation as a "democratic mayor" in Shanghai in 1948, as governor of Formosa. Students returning from Britain and the United States dominated officialdom. The Chief of the Education Department, for instance, graduated in psychology at Columbia University, the general secretary of the provincial government was a professor of Western political thought. General Sun Li-jen, who graduated from the Virginia Military Academy and had co-operated with American officers during the Burma campaign in the Second World War, was appointed Commander of the Army. Chiang hoped that this would improve contacts with American military leaders and possibly attract American military aid. Moreover, the whole "democratic" structure of government which Chiang had built in Nanking on the eve of his total defeat on the China mainland was moved to Formosa. Perhaps Chiang's most important move was his invitation to Hu Shih and other liberal intellectuals to launch a "Free China" movement on the island. Consequently the liberals not only supplied the personnel of the bureaucracy but also were dominant in publishing and education.

The symbol of the "Free China" movement, the *Free China* fortnightly, emerged with Hu Shih as publisher, but later developed beyond the limits which Chiang had endorsed. Under its leadership, anti-Communist propaganda was based on liberal Western political theory. "Freedom" and "democracy" became popular slogans along with "Fight Communism" and "resist Russia." An exaggerated view of the power of the "free world" in general and of the United States in particular characterised their writings along with charges of the inhuman tyranny of Communism.

Liberal influence could, however, penetrate neither the Nationalist Party machine nor its secret police. Mass arrests and rampant secret-police activities were not reduced in the slightest by the toleration of liberal theories. Many intellectuals who did not share this "Anglo-American" outlook and were excluded from other sources of power, drifted into the Nationalist Party itself.

As Chiang consolidated his position on Formosa with large-scale American aid, he began to reorganise his government on a more dicta-torial track. Governor Wu was dismissed and General Sun has been subjected to house-arrest. Nationalism was substituted for liberalism as a popular rallying-point. But since concepts of political freedom had been taught so widely that they could not be suppressed overnight, the official line began to advocate "national freedom" instead of "individual free-dom." "Individual freedom" was described by the Party as a synonym for "selfishness," which would lead to anarchy or would serve as camouflage for the subversive propaganda of the "Communist bandits" on the mainland.

The Anglo-Americans were most influential in the schools. To penetrate these last bastions of liberalism on Formosa, a Youth Corps, a military training system, and school branches of the Party were set up. Many publications continued but the arrest of journalists became frequent. Those American-educated intellectuals who maintained their government positions were shunted from the main lines of policy making into administration. With the intensified manoeuvering for influence between Ch'en Ch'eng, the premier and Chiang's right-hand man, on the one hand, and Chiang Ching-kuo, Chiang's eldest son, the real boss of the Party and the secret police, on the other, the American-educated administration have regained some influence through Ch'en's support, but they could never restore their dominant position around 1950. The "Anglo-American" intellectuals gradually veered towards more radical criticism of the régime; *Free China* was soon the chief forum of the liberal critics. By the late fifties, the division of the "Anglo-Americans" into liberals and conservatives was complete.

Nevertheless, the "Anglo-American" liberals were able to debate their case against those who doubted democratic ways of life and were closely connected with the Nationalist Party. They were not only able to bolster their arguments by drawing freely from American and English political theories, but corruption and the secret police provided them with two popular targets for attacks. The Nationalists, on the other hand, were inhibited from citing either Marx or Lenin even though the Nationalist Party had its structural origins in Leninism. Paradoxically, therefore, so long as the régime formally endorsed the principle of democracy, its defeat in this debate was assured. Even in trying to replace "individual freedom" with a concept of "national freedom," the Nationalists had already paid homage to the value of freedom *per se*. Moreover, by not asserting the need for a secret police force when denying charges levied against it, they implicitly recognised the evils inherent in such a system. Throughout the Party cadres expressed a personal respect of those who were daring to challenge the Party's authority. While Party apologists often felt guilty at having to whitewash the evils of the régime and even to lie in its defence, the liberal critics felt entitled and even morally compelled to exaggerate the virtues of Western democratic institutions. These debates showed very little originality. Much of the debate was a repeat of what had been said on the mainland, thirty or forty years ago. As the régime tried harder and harder to justify itself according to traditional Chinese values, the Anglo-American educated intellectuals not unnaturally championed the ideals of the May Fourth movement. The Party repeatedly reminded the people that the May Fourth movement had been the forerunner of the Communist movement in China. Generally speaking, the debate on democracy, the only intellectual discourse on Formosa during the 1950s, was conducted between the non " Anglo-American " Party cadres and the " Anglo-American " radical critics excluded from power.

Those " Anglo-Americans," enjoying power in the government,[2] during this controversy apparently remained impartial, though they secretly welcomed the protests of the liberals. They were well aware that the louder the liberals shouted the more important the moderate " Anglo-American " politicians became in the régime.

Sometimes, however, other intellectuals, who were not hand in glove with the Nationalists, were caught up in the debates. Those who studied in Russia, but were excluded from any source of power, tended to support the liberal critics but accepted that the government should monopolise major industries. The traditionalists outside of the political machine were more vociferous. On the one hand, they opposed the use of abbreviated Chinese characters, supported the government policy which required all students to study the ancient Chinese classics, and, of course, denounced the May Fourth movement. On the other hand, they often joined in the outcry for democracy. But from the traditionalist viewpoint, a ruler exemplifies the highest moral order. Thus, Hsu Fu-kuan, a professor of Chinese classics, courageously criticised Chiang's character on the President's seventieth birthday, but he said nothing about the government's infringement of individual rights.[3] Nevertheless, during the winter of 1961–62 the traditionalists joined with ex-Marxists in an attack on " the monopoly of education and academic institutions " held by the Anglo-American returned intellectuals.

HERETICAL THOUGHTS

The first notable evidence of the deviation from the official myth of re-conquering the mainland appeared in an editorial in *Free China* fornightly on August 1, 1957. The editorial started from the premise that a healthy policy should be based on rational calculation and, therefore, on " probability." But with Formosa inferior to mainland China in manpower, natural resources and industry, the conquest of Communist China was highly improbable. In spite of the government's prediction that America would crush the Chinese Communists in a third world

[2] Such as Mei Yi-ch'i, late Minister of Education, and George Yeh, the retired diplomat who served as the Minister of Foreign Affairs in the fifties. Other more important names cannot be mentioned here, because they are still in active political service.
[3] See Hsu's article in *Tzu-yu Chung-kuo*, XV, No. 9, October 1956.

war, it was unlikely that a third world war would break out in the near future, so there was even less hope of re-conquering the mainland.

The editorial concluded that the government and people on Formosa should make the material best of living on Formosa. This, in the long run, would better serve the cause of reconquest. The editorial raised a storm of condemnation from the Party controlled press. It was pointed out that not all human history was in the realm of probability—it had shown many miracles. However, this incident marked the beginning of the collapse of the official myth in the minds of mainland refugees.

Although those intellectual mainlanders grouped around the *Free China* fortnightly did not formally abandon the myth of an eventual return to the mainland, they did, nevertheless, co-operate with native Formosan leaders advocating self-government on Formosa. It was Lei Chen, the chief editor of the *Free China* fortnightly, in his late sixties, who was arrested in September 1960, tried by court-martial and sentenced to jail for ten years. His arrest ended the debates on democracy. He had committed the double heresy of doubting the myth and wanting self-government for Formosa. The movement for self-government was suppressed along with various liberal publications, including the forthright *Free China* fortnightly, in the autumn and winter of 1960. Since then, there has been no significant stirrings among the older mainlander intellectuals.

The older Formosan intellectuals encountered peculiar problems of their own. Their first difficulty is language. With restricted imports of Japanese language publications these intellectuals, most of whom were educated in Japanese and can read neither Chinese nor English well, have been living in something of an intellectual vacuum. Moreover, they have no rich intellectual tradition from which to draw. When part of the Manchu empire Formosa was one of its acknowledged underdeveloped areas. Under the Japanese the percentage of Formosan students who received higher education was extremely low and those who did receive higher education were discouraged from developing an interest in the humanities or the social sciences. Many of the most talented intellectuals later sacrificed their lives in the cause of self-rule either in the struggle with the Japanese or in the massacre following the February 28th incident of 1947.

The older Formosans live in an even more arid intellectual climate than the older mainlanders. The articles written by Formosans in the last decade show an assimilation of various views of the mainlanders, though what they have really been thinking and wishing may not necessarily be the same as that which succeeded in passing through the hands of the censor. In the only articles that reveal some of their true yearnings, they have asked for fair elections and self-government at the local level.[4] The Nationalists, however, regard this as the cunning Formosan strategy which would inevitably lead to a Formosan government over all of the island.

THE CONFUSED OUTLOOK OF YOUTH

The younger Formosan and mainlander intellectuals, now in their twenties or thirties, have much more in common with each other than with the older intellectuals of their respective groups. These younger people have spent the formative years of their lives on Formosa. Moreover, they have neither nostalgia for Japanese rule, nor homesickness for their native towns in China.

Aware of the futility of open political discussions, the younger intellectuals take little part in the political debates of their elders, with the exception of a handful of articles on freedom of expression and education.[5] They have turned their energies more to poetry, philosophy, art and journalism, than to politics. Contrasted with the contributions of the older generation,[6] the mediocre achievements of the younger intellectuals appear promising.

There is something almost feverish in the way the young intellectuals pour out new material. Liang Shih-ch'iu, former Dean of Liberal Arts of the Provincial Normal University, estimated six years ago that there were about 15,000 poets on Formosa. The existence of so large a group of poets has been accompanied by the proliferation of literary magazines, poetry clubs and art exhibitions.

Unlike the older intellectuals, both mainlander and Formosan, most of whom are from the upper-classes, the younger poets, painters, writers, philosophy students and social scientists have a wider range of social backgrounds. For example, a female short-story writer is the daughter of a carpenter from Tainan City. The majority of the graduates from National Formosa University are from the middle-class, from the families of physicians, clerks, government workers and teachers. The social origins of the average graduates from the Normal University and normal

---

[4] See, for instance, Yang Chin-hu, " A Formosan View on the Construction of a Model Province of Formosa," *ibid*. XVIII, No. 11, June 1958; see also Yang Chi-chen, " The Lessons that I learned from an unsuccessful election campaign for the Mayorship of Taichung," *ibid*. XVII, No. 12, December 1957.

[5] A group of Formosan students wrote a series of articles but the suppression of the *Free China Fortnightly* allowed only two of them to be published; Shih Ts'ui, " The Problem of Academic Freedom in Formosa University " (see *Tzu-yu Chung-kuo* [*Free China*], XXII, 9, May 1, 1960), and P'an-hsin, " The Voice in the Heart of the Youth in Formosa University " (*ibid*. XXIII, 1, July 1, 1960).

[6] Contributions from older intellectuals to non-political matters are exceptionally few. Among the older mainlanders, I can mention only Chou Ch'i-tzu, a talented literary critic. Among the natives are Lan Yin-ting, a painter, and Chen Shao-hsing, a working sociologist.

schools are even lower. Quite a few of the college students in Formosa today are of peasant and working-class families.

While intellectual flippancy is widespread among the new generation, the opportunism and cowardice of many of their elders is absent. Su Tung-ch'i, a courageous member of a local council, who was sentenced to death by the Nationalists, was in his late thirties when arrested in 1961. Other Formosans involved in his case were much younger.

Nevertheless, there is a clearly discernible nihilist tendency among the younger intellectuals. Few young men on Formosa would label themselves as nihilists, because the translation of the word "nihilism," *hsu-wu-chu-i*, means "emptiness, lack of commitment to any principle," but it does not carry the idealistic sense of the original word.

A recent example of this tendency is the debate, which started in January 1962, on the "problem of East and West." The young intellectuals, both Formosan and mainlanders, mostly graduates or students of National Formosa University, are defying Chinese tradition as well as all the older intellectuals who have defended it. Li Ngao, a mainlander student of history, became a popular hero among the young people after he mercilessly condemned, in print, a host of older intellectuals from Liang Shou-ming to Ch'ien Mu.[7] The more serious articles written by Formosan students headed by Hung Ch'eng-wan, advocated a "wholesale Westernisation" as a substitute for the present society on Formosa. But none of them, however, attempted to clarify the concept of the West or differentiate Western civilisation into ancient, medieval and modern, or into different national or regional types. Significantly, however, no young intellectual spoke up for the Chinese tradition. The older men acknowledged their intellectual impotency when they sought legal and political means to end the debate. Since the young critics have never been to the West, nor are well versed in Western languages and learning (although they pompously cited many American books and English terms in their articles), their plea for Westernisation is at least symbolic of their disgust with the present situation.

But this was not the first outburst of such feelings. A more specific attack on the *status quo* appeared in the spring of 1956 in a journal entitled *Intellectual Trends in Formosa University*, edited by Hsieh Wen-sun, a student at the University. Advancing the ideal of liberalism, the magazine used the Statute of Liberty for its cover design. The editor not only advanced a rather naïve wish for the freedom of education on Formosa; he also categorically, though only by implication, rejected Nationalist control over college students in general and denounced the military training system in universities in particular. Aside

---

[7] The discussions on the cultural problem are mainly in the 1962 issues of *Wen Hsing* (*Literary Star*) (*Taipei*).

from its youthful optimism, the editorial gives no voice to positive political demands. Nevertheless, the Nationalists held a special Party session to study the only case of student protest on Formosa since 1949 and the magazine soon disappeared. The incident reveals the unconstructive attitudes of many young people who are discontented with the *status quo* but who can find no constructive path to follow that will give them the feeling of achievement which they seek.

ISOLATION

The development of this new generation is, however, stunted by its intellectual isolation. A teacher of literature on Formosa pointed out that " nearly all the important creative works since the May Fourth movement are inaccessible." [8] With Formosans idealising the days of Japanese rule the government is even more suspicious of Japanese works. Moreover, even anti-Communist publications in Chinese from Hong Kong are under strict control. With no significant heritage to rely on the younger intellectuals must start from the beginning. Often they are unaware that they are just repeating the discussions and debates which took place in China of thirty or forty years ago.

Fortunately the government, accepting as it does American aid, cannot entirely exclude American influence. This single overwhelming influence has been intensified by the liberals' exaggeration of the " democratic paradise" in the New World. American motion pictures and the generally superior quality of American commodities as compared to local products have also helped convince the youth of America's attractions. American publications dominate the book market. They are in such demand that the huge amount of locally " pirated " editions of American books has caused serious protests from American publishers. Most students are familiar with the speeches of Lincoln and other American leaders, which are included in their English textbooks (English is a required course for all middle-school students and college freshmen).

Thus the prevalence of Americophilia on Formosa is not surprising. The anti-American incident in Taipei on February 24, 1957, resulted basically from envy of the living conditions and the status of Americans on the island. Envy, however, is derived from admiration.

With the aspiration for the " paradise " in the New World, and with his utter disgust of the present conditions on Formosa, it is natural for these young people, Formosans and mainlanders, to seek to go to the

---

[8] See the appendix on Formosa by T. A. Hsia in C. T. Hsia's *A History of Modern Chinese Fiction* 1917–1957 (New Haven: Yale Un. Press, 1961).

United States. Once they arrive, they have little desire to return to Formosa.

The government was forced to stem the tide by limiting passports to those who planned to study abroad. Later, the government further limited the permission for going abroad to college graduates. The number of applications for passports is still striking. In recent years the government has required every college graduate to pass a " going abroad " examination before they have the right to apply for a passport. Efforts by the government to counter this American bias by trying to persuade students to study in countries other than the United States has had little success.

This American intellectual or cultural influence seems no less significant than the well-known political dominance of the United States on Formosa. Aside from the tradition exemplified by the Nationalist régime, the American model provides the only alternative for the discontented younger islanders. Some American values have already been planted in the minds of the younger generation. Judging from their writings published so far, no young intellectual, Formosan or mainlander, Party member or non-Party member, has doubted the value of democracy or human rights. Such an ideological commitment will certainly influence the future course of Formosa. The attraction of American ideals, however, also has its negative implications. Since most of the young men and women wish to live in the United States, and since the better qualified ones are the most likely to fulfil that wish, the " rush to America " tends to skim off the cream of the young intellectuals, who might otherwise contribute greatly to the development of Formosa.

Literary Formosa

By LUCY H. CHEN

FOR decades, Formosa was a frontier for those people who set out from Kwangtung and Fukien in the waning days of the Ming dynasty, during the early part of the seventeenth century. By the time Koxinga defeated the Dutch in 1661 Formosa could claim a body of literature of its own. This, however, consisted mainly of histories and reports compiled by scholar-officials leaving an account of their stewardship, chronicles telling the story of settlement, cultivation and perennial skirmishes with the local aborigines, and poetry of the sort with which the learned men of China have traditionally amused themselves. This literature followed classical forms and was written in the traditional *wen-yen*.

THE MAY FOURTH MOVEMENT AND THE JAPANESE: 1895–1945

Japan's scheme of empire provided no room at the top for any of her new colonial subjects. With higher education denied to all but a very few, the people of China's lost island province became much more acutely conscious of their national and cultural identity. As time went by, however, the Japanese relaxed their control over the islanders and some young men went abroad to Japan, China and even Europe and America. These students became exposed to European currents of liberalism and nationalism as well as to the winds of change in China and Japan. When these students returned to Formosa although they organised themselves and talked revolution, literature was a more practical outlet for their feelings. The May Fourth Movement in 1919 stirred them as it stirred young intellectuals on the Chinese mainland; some, in fact, came to believe that a cultural reformation through literature was the only way to unite Formosa with mainland China again. One of the most significant events of this time, however, was the return in 1920 from the new electrifying intellectual atmosphere of Peking of a young student named Huang Chao-ching. When Huang began to preach the use of the collo-quial *pai-hua* instead of the traditional literary language, *wen-yen*, he provoked in miniature the same kind of controversy that was dividing Chinese educators and literary men on the mainland. The elders on Formosa, overwhelmed by foreign occupation, were sentimental over traditional Chinese forms of verse, with their meaning often obscured by erudite allusion. Like the ancients they looked back to, they would gather on occasions such as the Lunar New Year and the mid-August Moon Festival, still celebrated as "Poet's Day," to drink yellow wine and compose highly mannered verses hinting in familiar and well-worn images at their regret over their loss of country. These older men regarded themselves as the rightful custodians of the national heritage and bitterly opposed the adoption of *pai-hua*, arguing that the preservation of *wen-yen* was vital to the survival of Chinese culture on Formosa.

In 1925 the battle between the innovators and the conservatives was joined in plain terms with an article entitled "How Absurd is our Formosan Literary Scene!", by a young radical named Chang Wo-chün. The same year saw the founding of a new literary magazine called *Everybody*, which made a scathing attack on Lien Ya-tung, a traditionalist poet and historian whose *History of Formosa* had been regarded as the best thing of its kind. This assault on such a respected figure created a sensation among younger intellectuals and shook the traditionalists into realising the force of the new ideas that were afloat.

Articles by Hu Shih and Ch'en Tu-hsiu proclaiming the literary revolution commanded wide attention. Young intellectuals identified themselves with radical mainland writers, and enthusiastically read and discussed Western European and Russian novels and plays. As Japanese was widely taught on Formosa, many students were able to make use of the numerous Japanese translations. Ibsen and O'Neill, for instance, first became known to Formosan intellectual circles in this way. Quite likely young Formosans were better acquainted with modern literature at this time, than their mainland contemporaries. The Formosans could read original works in both Chinese and Japanese as well as translations of foreign works.

In the twenties and the thirties the literary scene brightened as *pai-hua* became a widely-accepted means of expression. Between 1920 and 1937, at least 18 literary magazines saw the light of day and a great many novels, plays and collections of short stories and verse were published, under the eye, it might be added, of what came to be called the "iron scissors" censorship of the Japanese government. Two of the most popular novels of the time might be mentioned: *The Lovely Enemy*, by She Kuen-chien, and *Temptation*, by Chang Wo-chün. Some playwrights devoted some attention to the motion picture: a film called *Longing for Spring Wind* is remembered as a successful adaptation of a Formosan folk-song.

Also a number of literary associations took root and flourished. In May, 1935, a Formosan conference on art and literature brought a number of young writers and students hurrying back from both mainland China and Japan to attend. A Formosan Union of Art and Literature

132

was organised and the publication of a *Formosan Literary Monthly* followed in 1936. Intellectual circles looked forward to even better things. Symbolic of the optimistic climate, a talented young Formosan even managed to get to Tokyo to study with one of Japan's most distinguished playwrights and directors.

But when China and Japan formally went to war in 1937, the Japanese banned the use of Chinese in all magazines and newspapers published on Formosa. From then on intellectuals lived under close surveillance, the threat of arrest, and secret persecution by the Japanese security police.

Until Formosa was restored to China at the end of the Second World War Japanese literature dominated the island. Formosans who continued to write had to use Japanese. The one means of expression left to the people in their own language was the folk opera, a Fukienese variant of the traditional Chinese opera. Significantly, opera clubs increased by the hundreds during the Japanese war.

Lively as the literary scene was from the early twenties to 1937, the work of this period cannot be considered as notable from the critical point of view. *The Lovely Enemy*, for example, was permeated by sentimentality and owed its popularity not to literary merit but to being written in *pai-hua* by a Formosan writer. The outstanding figure of the period was Lai Ho, a physician and poet, the first writer to experiment with the use of the colloquial Formosan dialect. His short stories, collected under the title *Back from the Spring Feast*, are full of local colour and language which every reader understood.

FROM THE JAPANESE SURRENDER TILL 1955

These were years of disquiet for Formosan writers. In 1949 the Nationalists moved to Formosa, bringing with them almost two million mainland refugees, among them writers, publishers and printers. Some of the most noted mainland publishing houses were re-established in Taipei: the Commercial Press, as well as the Kai Ming and World Book Companies. These firms managed to bring with them some of their stocks of books as well as stereos of others from which new editions could be printed.

At that time, the government had little interest in literature, except in terms of security. A ban was placed on the original works and translations of all leftist writers, living and dead. The authorities were seeking to preserve the traditional virtues and to indoctrinate the population as thoroughly as possible against Communism. Popular songs became martial in spirit. Militant slogans appeared on school walls, city streets, country roads, cigarette packets, menus, bottle labels, and in public bathrooms: " Down with Chu and Mao!" and " Recover the Mainland!"

The lack of concern about literature was a considerable disappointment to Formosan intellectuals, who through the war years had looked forward to renewing their natural association with the new Chinese literature which had grown up after the May Fourth Movement. Most of the significant writers of the 30's (for example, Lu Hsun, Lao She, Pa Chin) remained only names; their works were proscribed because of their identification with the Communists. The much-admired prose of Ping Shin was at first allowed to appear in middle school textbooks but later was banned when she returned from America to the mainland. Readers had to satisfy themselves with a scanty sampling of post-1919 Chinese writing: Chu Tzu-ching's light, sentimental essays, the immature though passionate verse and diaries of the romantic Hsu Chih-mo, and the depressing sexual wanderings of Yu Ta-fu. Young Formosans who had heard at least vaguely about the strength and vigour of Chinese writing of the twenties and thirties were astonished at the sparseness of their apparent legacy. Sometimes a curious student, browsing in a small bookstand, would discover a second-hand copy of a novel by Lao She or Mao Tun, and the work would circulate privately among friends until it wore out.

Formosans who had written in Chinese before 1937 found it difficult to take up their pens again because, for one thing, they found it difficult to match mainland writers now in Formosa in the versatility of their language. The Formosa Union of Literature and the Arts, organised with such high hopes in 1936, fell into decline. One of the chief motives for the formation of the Union had been to keep writing in Chinese alive during Japanese rule. Now that the island was again part of China, the Union had lost one of its principal reasons for existence. Older Formosans retired and left the literary world to the mainlanders.

Almost all the creative writing by refugee mainland writers of this time concerned itself with the anti-Communist struggle. The setting was always the mainland. A typical plot would portray a great love; the lovers would be inhumanly separated by the arrival of the Communists, and the last chapter would provide the moral that the only hope for reunion was a fighting return to the mainland. Nostalgia was the ruling emotion: the heart of the writer remained in a Peking restaurant or drifted along the Yangtse River. Spy novels were popular. The most overworked theme was that of a handsome anti-Communist secret agent with whom one or more female Communists would fall in love and sacrifice their lives so that he could carry out his mission and return safely to Formosa. So many of these novels were published and sold that they tended to create an impression that the one thing which stood in the way of a triumphal return to the mainland was the shortage of handsome spies to prepare the way.

The only solid fare for serious readers at that time was foreign literature in translation. Best-sellers from Europe and America quickly found their way into Chinese editions, as did much great writing from the past. Formosan publishers use offset printing and can manufacture books very cheaply; since China is not a member of any international copyright agreement, they do not have to concern themselves with questions of copyright. Bookstores became plentiful and well-patronised. Every high school student could afford to buy the complete works of Shakespeare, beautifully translated by the well-known Shakespearian scholar Chu Shen-hao. Sometimes publishers even changed the translator's name if a translation had originally been done by a writer now in Communist China. A collection of Turgenev's essay's translated by Kuo Mo-jo, one of the Communist's leading literary commissars, appeared in Taipei under the name of Lin Feng. Proscribed books included some Russian works written before 1917, presumably on the theory that their nihilism or pessimism would lower morale. Recently, however, the works of Dostoevsky have been permitted to go on sale in Formosan bookstores.

Of the patriotic anti-Communist novels which dominated locally written fiction during the first five or six years after the Nanking government moved to Taipei, several writers succeeded in handling their stories quite well. *The History of Ti Village*, by one of the most politically active writers from the mainland, Chen Chi-ying, is an inventive story of a village fool, modelled on *Ah Q* in the famous story of the same name by Lu Hsun, who survives the depredations of the warlords, only to be made a puppet by the Communists. (An English translation of this story, under the title *Fool in the Reeds*, has been published in Hong Kong.) *Blue and Black*, a tale which forces the hero to choose between two women on opposite sides of the political fence, by the popular writer Wang Lan, is Formosa's all-time best seller. It has run into a dozen editions after its first appearing in a woman's magazine.

REALISM AND MODERNISM: 1956–1963

Formosan writers began to display a great deal more creativity and variety in the second half of the 1950s. I do not mean to suggest that any work has appeared in Formosa in recent years which deserves comparison with the great works of Chinese fiction or verse, but it is correct to say that there is now a substantial amount of serious work being written with some regard for critical standards. Most significant of all, in my opinion, a number of talented young people are coming up through Formosan universities with the ambition of giving Chinese writing a new character and a new vitality.

135

Measured in terms of quantity, at least, there is currently a great deal of literary activity. A wide range of periodicals, ranging from the popular and respected *Rambler* and *Apollo* to self-conscious " literary magazines " resembling American " little reviews," offer the short story writer or poet an outlet for his product. (Over the past seven years perhaps as many as 300 different periodicals have published literary work although many were as ephemeral as most of the material they published.) About 1,500 books are published in Formosa each year. Most, of course, are reprints, textbooks, and so on but a visitor to any bookstore in Taipei or one of the other four or five major cities will find an impressive stock of new fiction on display.

An important outlet for writers is the newspaper literary supplement, which publishes work of higher quality than one might expect. Three or four papers run these special sections which carry verse, light essays, short stories and serialisations of novels. The best such page, in the *United Daily News*, is edited by a leading woman writer, Lin Hai-ying.

What are the reasons for the increased vigour and creativity displayed by writers in recent years? For one thing, the basic climate has been more favourable; there has been some relaxation in official preoccupation with anti-communism. Second, educational facilities have expanded greatly since 1947. Students in the universities now (and there are over 35,000 as compared to less than 2,000 in 1946) have had their entire education in Chinese and have no sense of inferiority in their skill with the national tongue when they compare themselves with writers from the mainland. Thirdly, I believe the presence of a large colony of mainland writers has created a demand for more writing. Younger people, whether born on the mainland or in Formosa, have acquired the reading habit by reading the works of these older writers, but now they want something closer to home than spy stories or laments for lost days in Shanghai or Peking.

The publication which has contributed the most to the advancement of writing on the island is the *Literary Review*, founded in 1956 and edited by T. A. Hsia, then a professor at Formosa University. This was the first serious literary magazine with no overpowering concern with political propaganda. Most of its writers have been graduates, students and faculty members of " T'aita," the nickname of the university. Hospitable as it was to new writers, both mainlanders and Formosans, it attracted well-known writers as well, giving space to the essay as well as to fiction and poetry. The essay unfortunately no longer attracts very many skilful writers. The three most notable are Liang Shih-chiu, Liang Yung-jo, whose essays on men and women are regarded as the wittiest of their kind, and Lucian Wu Hung-tsao, whose series of wry comments on daily life published in the magazine have been collected in book form under the title of *Cocktail Party*.

There is room only for a sketchy survey of a highly complicated and controversial subject: Formosa's modern poetry. Since the early 1950s a vigorous and violent dispute has been carried on between established poets wedded to the native classical tradition and young men and women who have wanted to give new life to Chinese poetry with techniques and images borrowed from contemporary European and American verse. The classicists complain that the new poets praise beauty by addressing Helen instead of the Chinese beauty of ancient times, Hsi-shih, and write with sharp disapproval of what they describe as the young poets' use of an orgy of meaningless images from Yeats, Cubism, Arabic verse—in fact from any source as long as it is not Chinese.

This running fire of criticism has not worn down the urge to experiment. The innovators are divided into a number of groups and cliques, each with its credo and its slender magazine. Two such groups, the Blue Stars and the Genesis School, appeared as early as 1954 and the Modernists were organised two years later. Among the Blue Stars, Chou Meng-tieh manages to be both modern and Chinese. A legendary figure in Taipei who makes a modest living running a street bookstall which serves as a gathering place for poets, he has published *The Kingdom of Solitude* which expresses a personal view of life derived from Buddhism and Confucianism. One of the most talented of the younger poets is a native Formosan: Yeh Shan, a Modernist. Although Yeh did not begin to study Chinese until Formosa was returned to China in 1945, he demonstrates a sure and sensitive command of the language and a very individual style of expression in his first book of verse, *On the Water Margin*.

The struggle between the classicists and the new poets flared into heated and even malicious controversy in the spring of 1961 when an article by a newspaper columnist brutally blasted the innovators. Yu Kwang-chung, the most popular and prolific poet, fought back in print with other poets. Newspapers and magazines opened special columns to air the opinions of both sides. Teachers and scholars, including the eminent Dr. Hu Shih, took issue with the new " radicals." In the popular judgment the new poets won. The public debate not only brought the various schools of new poetry closer together but also helped to convince readers that the new verse, although so different from the classical, had now to be taken seriously. The innovators continue to flourish: over 200 volumes of verse have been published; almost 30 periodicals devoted to poetry have made their appearance. Every year new talent appears. A number of promising young poets have gone abroad for further study.

Fiction has been very much a mixed bag since 1955, but it does exhibit several trends. First, established mainland writers continue to produce the sort of work which has earned them a living for so long. Wang Lan, still Formosa's best-selling writer, repeats in his current work the kind of formula that attracted so many readers to *Blue and Black*. In *Eight Years of the Hua and Hsia Families*, Chen Chi-ying tries to give epic stature to a story of two families under communism, but his ambition is greater than his achievement. The annual official literary prizes continue to go to older writers such as these, who participate actively in political affairs.

The study of communism has produced one novel of real literary merit: *Whirlwind* (1957), by Chiang Kwei, a searching but sympathetic account of the disintegration of a north China family and the spread of communism from the hopeful times of the May Fourth Movement to the early days of the Japanese war. Popular success, unfortunately, did not bring a great reward to its author. Not long ago he was brought into court on a charge of permitting his sick wife to starve to death through neglect (poverty, in fact). However, he escaped a prison sentence after urgent appeals from men of letters all over the island.

A second trend worth noting is the more frequent appearance of Formosan writers. One of the more impressive is Chung Tsao-cheng, a middle school teacher in Taoyuan. Chung's novels and short stories exhibit conciseness and simplicity of style, coupled with close observation of the people of the countryside, rural and the small town. *Feet* is one of his best-known stories. Without a surplus word it shows objectively, but with sympathetic insight how a man who has gone to the city and has become a success is betrayed into memories of his " country wife " by the casual remark of the woman who now lives with him.

A third development is the prominence which women writers have achieved. The Women Writers Association claims 345 members, though not all of them, to be sure, qualify as anything but gifted amateurs. Most women writers are content to turn out sentimental love tales or pleasant little sketches of domestic life, but at least three have achieved equal stature with leading male writers. Lin Hai-ying, a Formosan and most popular on the island, has published two well-regarded collections of short stories, *Green Algae and Salted Eggs*, and *Anecdotes from the South City* as well as a novel entitled *Morning Cloud*. Meng Yao, a professor at the Normal University, has written at least a dozen novels. Nieh Hua-ling, Hupei born, who perhaps has a wider acquaintance with foreign writing than the others, possesses a highly individual and sensitive talent. Her most recent work, a novel about a young girl growing up in a small river town in wartime China, is *The Lost Golden Bell*.

Perhaps the most significant development in the past few years, however, is the appearance of a number of young writers in Formosan universities, impatient with their elders and anxious to explore the resources of foreign literature as well as the wealth of subjects on Formosa, yet untouched by established figures. The rallying point for these new writers has been a magazine called *Modern Literature*, started at National Formosa University in 1960 by a group of Prof. T. A. Hsia's students after he left for America and the standards of his own *Literary Review* had rapidly declined. Edited entirely by students and recent graduates, *Modern Literature* seeks to introduce systematically to young Chinese the ideas and techniques of such writers as Lawrence, Kafka, Faulkner and Sartre. Much of it, however, is given to original fiction, mostly by students in Taipei and Hong Kong. Some established writers praise their work as having freshness and vigour, but others like to attack it as crudely written, in poor taste, and " radical." It is a matter of taste, of course: they do use language simpler and more direct than that used by popular writers. What the critics mean, however, by " radical," I am not quite sure. The stories in *Modern Literature* are not radical in the political sense; in fact, they have no concern with politics at all. How can they be described as " radical " in terms of revolutionary techniques when very few are even " experimental?" Perhaps the critics mean that they are " radical " in subject matter. If so they are radical only in the sense that they try to deal with the real problems of people who live in Formosa, which is a considerable change from what most established writers have been dealing with in the past fifteen years.

Leading figures associated with this magazine include Tsung Su, previously a regular writer for *Literary Review*, Chu Shi-ning (who, some readers believe, handles the colloquial *pai-hua* better even than Lu Hsun or Lao She), Pai Hsien-yung, Wang Wen-hsing and Miss Hung Tse-hwei. Of course it is too early to tell which of these writers, or the other young writers associated with the magazine, will eventually earn mature recognition. Several have gone abroad in the hope of learning at first hand about contemporary European and American fiction and verse, and more intend to follow. They may, when they return, at least be able to do something to remedy some of the problems which impede writing on Formosa from fulfilling its potential: the lack of sound critical standards and the timidity of writers in tackling important subjects ready to hand on the island.[1]

[1] A representative sampling of recent writing in Formosa has become available in the last several years in a series of English-language books published by the Heritage Press, with assistance by the U.S. Information Service. They include *New Chinese Poetry*, edited and translated by Yu Kwang-chung, *Eight Stories by Chinese Women*, translated by Nieh Hua-ling, *New Chinese Stories* and *New Chinese Writing*, translated by Lucian Wu. For a look at what young people associated with *Modern Literature* are producing, see *New Voices*, edited by Nancy Ing, *Spirit Calling and Other Stories*, written by Lucy Hsiu-mei Chen, *The Purse*, four stories by Nieh Hua-ling. Several English-language magazines published in Taipei also print stories in translation. The best of these is *The China Review*.

139

Formosan writers are gregarious people who like to gather for *mahjong* parties or for a meal or a tea reception arranged by one of the literary associations. At these affairs they congratulate one another on the appearance of a new book and talk comfortably about literature. But they never bother to criticise a work seriously. One reason for this is politeness, a feeling that they are all members of a union engaged in a precarious and poorly-paid trade. Another, however, is the lack of any real knowledge of the theory of criticism. Established writers have some knowledge of the traditional principles of literary creation spelled out in the *Wen Hsin Tiao Lung*, a work on literary criticism written hundreds of years ago. That is about all. True, there is a course in literary criticism taught at National Formosa University, but its attention to Western critics is limited to Aristotle and Sir Philip Sidney. Book reviews in magazines either praise or simply summarise the book, and are treated by readers as advertisements. When there are feuds among literary people, and there are a few, they are based upon personalities or personal matters and political ambitions rather than upon disagreements over literary principles.

An even more important obstacle to be overcome if the talent on Formosa is going to live up to its promise is the timidity too many writers display in taking on new subjects. Some, I think, have been frightened into a feeling of inferiority by at least a vague awareness of the achievements of Western literature and are therefore afraid to strike out in a new direction. Others just feel too comfortable with the familiar themes they have been using for twenty or thirty years and are afraid to try anything fresh that might not sell as well or else injure their political standing.

Formosa is not the place it was ten years ago. But there is little sign of this in the new books that compete for readers' dollars in Formosa's bookstores. Most established literary men are afraid or too lazy to expose and analyse either their own inner selves or the changing society around them. Why do they not write about the changes in the cities with their new factories and the thousands of young men and women who come in from the farms to work in them? Or about the armies of government clerks in city and provincial governments and their numb hopelessness as the cost of living climbs further out of reach of their salaries. Or about the farmers who must still stoop to push into the mud every individual shoot of rice but who now wear blue plastic raincoats from Japan instead of the old straw cloak? Or about what happens to a farm family now when it is expected that a marrying daughter take with her as her dowry, a radio, an electric fan and a sewing machine? Or about Formosa's merchants, cursing official regulations but with enough money to support a growing number of " wine-houses " with

Hong Kong-styled furnishings and swarms of pretty "waitresses?" Or about youth, caught up in a fierce competition for places in the universities and subject to all the cross-currents of new and old ideas?

Formosa has a great many things to write about. And sooner or later Formosan writers will have to take up the challenge.

Some Impressions of Formosa

By JONATHAN MIRSKY

In Taipei a pedicab driver, living on a dollar a day, waves a cheerful greeting. When he knows you better, he will roll up his sleeve and show the scars won by 28 years in the army—with never a victory in sight. Roast Peking duck, as succulent as ever, is brought to the table by a shouting waiter. Round the corner in the police station a twelve-year-old boy is beaten with bamboo rods for pilfering. Nearby lives one of the most famous Chinese scholars of the century. He would like to go on studying the ancient documents, but at eighty-eight he finds riding the rickety bus to the Academia Sinica a little too much. He totters in with tea and talks awhile with his guests. In his quiet moments he likes to write out classical poetry in ancient calligraphy.

The small walled town built by the Manchus, near the " Goose's Nose " (the southernmost tip of Formosa), looks much the way sinophiles like Chinese towns to look. Slow creaking ox-carts pass through its narrow gates; barefoot pedestrians jog with the peculiar gait which comes from carrying two heavy loads balanced on a bamboo pole. The Nationalists have tried to keep Confucianism abreast of the times. The boldly-written characters on the town wall proclaim that " Filial piety is the corner-stone of the nation," and, perhaps more pointedly, " President Chiang, live forever! "

Only a few miles from this town Formosan aborigines slaughtered a party of Japanese soldiers less than half a century ago. The local representative of His Imperial Highness the Emperor of Japan erected a monument which said (more or less) that " This is to commemorate the death of the loyal servants of the Sun of Heaven who perished on this spot, treacherously slain. Their deaths will be remembered and avenged." When the Nationalists came to Formosa they rewrote this part of local history. The monument now commemorates " the attack by heroic aborigines on the Japanese invaders; their loyalty will always be remembered."

Some aborigines still live not far from where the deed was done. One of the elders proudly asserts that the curious tattoos on his chest record the number of Japanese heads he has taken. The aborigines maintained their head-hunting habits until not so long ago. Edgar Snow narrowly escaped a general massacre less than thirty years ago at Sun-Moon Lake, which is now Formosa's leading holiday resort. The old man's grandson, a likely lad of twenty, talks with his grandfather in an aborigine dialect or Japanese, but is just as happy in Formosan or Mandarin Chinese. He likes to show off his " Air Force American " acquired, along with a well-kept white shirt emblazoned with " New York Yankees," while working on an American base.

It is perhaps a little disconcerting to find a blue ball, ten stories high, perched on the " Goose's Nose," between the small Manchu town, the aborigines and the sea. Here two or three Americans supervise thirty or forty Chinese air force technicians manning part of the radar network which protects Formosa's southern approaches. The Americans differ little from American servicemen the world over except in their unusually high regard for the Chinese technicians. Everyone at the radar station hopes that the Communists will stay at least a hundred miles away.

Formosa is Chinese. Let there be no doubt about that. True, Taipei is not Peking. But Omaha is not Boston. About thirty million people in South-East China speak the native language of Formosa. The streets of the main towns are full of things to be seen—including oneself. Hairy arms, bridged noses, and eyes other than black seem a never-ending source of amusement and wonder to Chinese children. In the still heat of the early evening, neighbours squat down in the narrow streets between the walled houses—the men in underwear or pyjamas, the women with tight skirts hiked up, and colourful underpants. There is much fanning with bird-wings, spitting of sunflower seed husks, and laughter. Children of three carry children of two on their backs. Loudspeakers somewhere in the distance blare jazzy music heavily scored with oriental overtones. Empty bottles, shoes, comic books, aphrodisiacs are hawked at the kerbside. The cinemas are full; so are the restaurants, tiny and dirty or big and luxurious. There is little other formal entertainment for Formosa is under wartime austerity. But the Chinese like noise and crowds, and seek them out for their own sake. When night comes the eerie whistle of the blind masseur is reassuringly regular. The air is congested with the smells of noodles and dumplings from countless street stalls, " rotten " bean curd, stinging fumes from thousands of soft coal cookers and, inevitably, the overpowering stench of the night soil cart on its endless journeys about the city.

Formosans have their favourite gods and goddesses of land and water; the mainlanders have theirs. The island-born spend millions of dollars in fêteing their spiritual favourites with interminable barrages of firecrackers, parades, as fantastic as any mardi-gras, and three days of lavish open hospitality. At the Chinese New Year house after house adorns its gates with strips of red paper to beg good fortune. Servants

143

are given their only holiday of the year, and for several days little cooking is done, while families gorge on the delights laid in for the occasion. Children bow before their oldest relative and are given pennies wrapped in red paper. The streets are filled with people hurrying to present visiting cards to their friends—so hardly any of the friends can be found at home.

For all Formosa's " Chinese-ness," Japanese influence is slow to pass. Inside typically Japanese houses there still survive many of the sliding panels, the paper screens, the *tatami*, and often the vestige of a Japanese garden. Even most mainlanders, who have little love for Japanese ways, remove their shoes before entering these houses.

In the countryside Mandarin is met with scowls while the feeblest Japanese is greeted with open delight. In their day the Japanese were hardly popular in Formosa. But nearly everyone over twenty-five can speak Japanese, and people over forty prefer it to Formosan. Outside the cities Mandarin works well only on school children. In the dark recesses of a local metal-working shop it is still possible to find lurking an odd Japanese soldier, long left behind, married, and carefully introduced as a cousin.

Still, in many ways Japanese influence is little more than a veneer. Once beautiful houses are now Chinese homes. Heavy furniture, in pairs for the wealthy, an icebox or a bed, a pendulum clock or pink spittoon where once stood a bowl of flowers or hung a scroll, show all too clearly that there is more to graceful Japanese living than just sitting on the floor—which Chinese women in their tight dresses find intensely embarrassing. Eat a meal with these people and the table is circular and seats twelve according to Chinese custom; the food is unmistakably and deliciously not Japanese; nor are the shouts of joy which compel one to knock back a fiery cup of " white tiger " after losing a Chinese finger game, without which even a minor banquet would seem lifeless.

The ways of Old China—the ancient women with bound feet, water buffalo in the paddies, gangs of cheerful coolies, the courtesies of minor officials and scholars, parties of giggling schoolgirls, serious university students loudly memorising their lessons by echoing them off walls, the peaceful joy and hospitality of temple monks—linger on in their new Formosan home. Behind these " quaint " and " colourful " goings-on and Formosa's recent progress lie the injustices, the frustrations, the tragedies, major and minor, which have disfigured modern China.

One of the best-liked teachers of Mandarin in Formosa was an engaging middle-aged northerner, educated in the western tradition at a university on the mainland and from a family of considerable means. As our acquaintance deepened Mr. Chu (not his real name) tried to explain patiently what seemed to be examples of corruption. Yes, it seemed unfamiliar to the Westerner, but what was *really* happening. . . .

For several weeks conversation in Taipei speculated over a gory murder. A three-months-pregnant woman had been cut up and dumped in a large canal in the middle of the city. For days no one identified her body, although her photograph was published all over the island. But all Taipei believed that she was the mistress of an Air Force general, a national hero, and sometime personal pilot of the Generalissimo. The general's wife was supposed to have killed the unfortunate woman in a fit of jealousy, and then had her disposed of. The newspapers conjectured endlessly, the Formosan ones with some venom. But no one would make an official statement. It was hinted that the island's morale would be shattered if the general, a known wencher, were implicated, even if he was not the murderer. When I eventually asked Mr. Chu why no one would make a statement, he replied that no informer would ever emerge from the police station.

Meanwhile a grand scandal over the purchase of buses came to light. Although a few minor officials were arrested, the enormous sums involved were thought to be in the hands of people much closer to the President. All this was too much for Mr. Chu. One evening through his tears he lamented that little had changed since the old days, except that the pickings were smaller. Government and business were based on a system of personal favour and bribery, large and small, and the only reward for honesty was poverty, not even respect.

Students are given little chance to stray from the political strait and narrow of Nationalist thought. At 8 o'clock on Monday mornings every kindergarten, middle school and university on Formosa studies the writings of Sun Yat-sen. But this is no protection against heresies. A Formosan student handed me an essay purporting to be about Jefferson, but which contrived to show that the United States was maintaining a régime on Formosa which would make the American Founding Fathers turn in their graves. Then at a secret meeting with an American official, three bright and serious Formosan students asked what the Americans would do if there was another Formosan revolt. The sensible rejoinder was that it was wise to wait for the Nationalists to die and for control to come slowly into Formosan hands.

The young mainlanders are frustrated too. Many of them manage to get away from it all and study in the United States. The dignified but poignant scenes at the airport conceal an ever-present truth: the young man will not return. An uneducated cook from Peking who was a fervent Nationalist and the wife of an airman, had the secret ambition to send her son abroad to study. Her round face would shine at the prospect. What about coming back? She would become serious; if possible he should stay abroad. Another mainland university student, easily the best in his class, who had walked several thousand miles from his home in northern China to escape the Communists and had eventually made his way to Formosa, knew that because he was an orphan the Government would not allow him to study abroad. With no hostages at home, it was so "obvious" he would never return that the American Consul would not grant him a visa. Ironically, he was one of the few who sincerely wished to teach in the National University and for whom America held no special fascination. But the frustration, the lack of opportunity, the genuine embarrassment and loss of confidence in the empty promises of the government underlie much of the apathy of life on Formosa.

American officials live in splendid isolation on Formosa. Their daily encounters with servants and military inferiors breed in them a feeling of contempt for the Chinese. Yet some officials are genuinely interested in China and a few speak excellent Chinese. In many ways this adds to their frustration. In three years they were never told what American policy on Formosa really was. They see Chinese friends, but were warned officially to steer clear of Formosan "extremists," who articulate the feeling of most Formosans. The American Ambassador to Taipei, Mr. Drumright, would snort contemptuously and say that talk of corruption in Chungking during the war was leftist propaganda. He urged American students to spend their money on Chinese books— specifically the complete works of Sun Yat-sen and Chiang Kai-shek. He was pleased to know Madame Chiang, "the greatest woman in the Far East."

The American missile base on Formosa was turned over to the Chinese at an impressive ceremony. During a demonstration for an invited crowd of Chinese dignitaries and "foreign friends" Nike missiles were loosed off at a target plane which was flown out of sight. A loudspeaker jubilantly announced five hits and one "probable." All newspapers lauded the triumph of the newest weapon in the anti-Communist arsenal. The following day the American technician in charge of the target plane casually mentioned that all shots had missed completely. He was unaware of the newspaper stories and not much interested.

So Formosa continues to be China. In many ways Formosa with its misty, pine-clad gorges has the tranquil air which the Sung painters saw in the China of those troubled days. Formosa too has its recluses—from more recent troubled times.

The Development of Formosan Nationalism

By MAURICE MEISNER

EIGHTEEN years ago Formosa was liberated from half a century of Japanese colonial rule. When Kuomintang soldiers and administrators arrived to reassert Chinese sovereignty over the island province in October 1945 they were enthusiastically welcomed as liberators by the Formosans. Within a few months, however, the Kuomintang had succeeded in alienating virtually all segments of the native population by inaugurating a military régime that treated Formosa as a conquered territory rather than a liberated area. The mass pillaging, official corruption and political repression that marked the early period of Kuomintang rule in Formosa set in motion the tragic events that culminated in the revolt of February 1947 in the course of which at least 10,000 Formosans were massacred. The Kuomintang has since done little to heal the scars of 1947 and today most of the 10,000,000 Formosans look upon the nearly 2,000,000 mainlanders who fled to Formosa with the collapse of Kuomintang rule as foreign overlords and describe the Chinese Nationalist régime as a colonial tyranny far more oppressive than the former Japanese rule. That the overwhelming majority of Formosans favour the establishment of an independent Formosan state, without ties to mainland China and, preferably, without the presence of mainlanders, is a fact that can no longer be ignored in considering the present condition and future status of Formosa.

The emergence of a distinctly Formosan national consciousness in the years since the Second World War has raised the question of the origins and validity of the Formosan claim to nationhood. From the point of view of international law Formosa is generally recognised as an integral part of the Chinese state, although this view has been challenged by Formosan nationalist writers.[1] But however one may wish to interpret the legal status of Formosa the history of modern nationalist movements in both Europe and Asia has already quite clearly indicated how little legal criteria have counted in the formation of national entities. Rather than examining the legal aspects of the question the present discussion will be limited to considering how

---

[1] See, for example, Ko Kiansin, "The Legal Status of Formosa from the Viewpoint of International Law," *Formosan Quarterly*, Vol. 1, No. 2 (October 1962), pp. 37–40.

the Formosan sense of their existence as a separate nation has grown out of the peculiarities of the history of Formosa and the particular nature of the present relationship between the native Formosans and the refugee mainlanders.

For Formosan nationalists the history of Formosa has been a history of more than three centuries of colonial oppression. They argue that the settlers who began to arrive in Formosa from Fukien and Kwangtung provinces in the fifteenth and sixteenth centuries were first subjected to the rule of Dutch and the Spanish overlords (from 1624–62), and then (from 1683) to the successive tyrannies of the foreign Manchu emperors, the Japanese imperialists, and finally the " colonial tyranny " of the Kuomintang.

Like other modern nationalists, the Formosan nationalist is inclined to look as far back into the past as possible for signs of a distinctive national existence. Thus a native revolt in 1652 against the Dutch is interpreted in Formosan nationalist writings as heralding " the awakening of the national consciousness of the Formosans." [2] Since " the Formosans " in the mid-seventeenth century consisted almost entirely of peasants and numbered less than 100,000 recent migrants from the Chinese mainland, one may doubt the existence of any type of " national consciousness " at this time much less the existence of a distinctively Taiwanese consciousness.

It is also highly questionable that the Formosans felt any special sense of nationhood during the more than two centuries of Ch'ing rule. It is true that popular opposition to the Manchus was particularly intense in Formosa and the frequency of peasant rebellions became proverbial.[3] Formosa's tradition of rebellion is reflected in a conversation that is reported to have taken place in the course of the negotiations that ended the Sino-Japanese War of 1894–95. The Japanese envoy asked the chief Chinese negotiator, Li Hung-chang, the nature of the people inhabiting Formosa. " Colonists from Kwangtung," Li Hung-chang is said to have replied, " and very turbulent they are." Li went on to warn that " it is not an uncommon thing for the people of Formosa to rise and murder their officials." [4] Yet there is no evidence to suggest that these Formosan peasant revolts were significantly different in character and motivation from the local peasant rebellions (usually inspired by excessive taxation and extra-legal exactions by local officials) that were chronic throughout most of Chinese history.

---

[2] Niu Cionghai, " The Formation of the Formosan Nation," *Formosan Quarterly*, Vol. 1, No. 2 (October 1962), p. 46.

[3] " Every three years a disorder, and every five years a rebellion " is a Formosan saying that dates from the period of Ch'ing rule.

[4] James W. Davidson, *The Island of Formosa, Past and Present* (New York and London, 1903), pp. 276–277.

The relative frequency of such revolts in Formosa may in part be attributed to the frontier conditions that existed during these two centuries of migration and settlement and the unusual degree of official corruption among Ch'ing officials sent to govern Formosa, isolated as these officials were from the direct control and supervision of the central government. Another factor sometimes mentioned by Formosan nationalist writers is the tradition of anti-Manchu resistance that is said to have survived from the days of Koxinga and his sons, the Ming partisans who ruled Formosa from 1662–83. But these were differences of degree not of kind. Under the traditional political system the direct authority of the central government was rarely effectively exercised in the local areas and most Chinese peasants suffered from the extra-legal exactions of local officials. Moreover, the Chinese on the main-land, as well as those on Formosa, regarded the Manchus as foreign overlords.

In considering the development of Formosan nationalism, it is important to distinguish between the older Chinese anti-foreignism and modern nationalism. In any meaningful sense the term " nationalism " implies an overwhelming concern with the existence and power of the nation and the formation of primary loyalties to a well defined national entity rather than to family, clan and locality or to a system of cultural values. In this sense, the extent to which Formosan opposition to Manchu rule was inspired by anti-foreign sentiments rather than to particular grievances against local officials, these sentiments do not appear to have been significantly different than the similar anti-Manchu feelings prevalent on the mainland. The anti-foreignism of the Formosan was still intimately tied to the very same cultural values and the same patterns of loyalty that existed on the mainland.

While there were peculiarities in the language, social traditions and in the political and economic life of Formosa during the Ch'ing period, these were not qualitatively different from the provincial diversities that have traditionally existed in China. Perhaps the best indication that there did not exist a Formosan sense of nationalism at this time is the very events of 1895 which have sometimes been interpreted as reflecting a desire for national independence. As a result of its humiliating defeat at the hands of a modernised Japanese army in 1895, China was forced to cede Taiwan and the Pescadores to Japan. When the impending cession became known in Formosa, leaders of Formosan community joined with the Ch'ing officials in Formosa to declare a " Formosan Democratic Republic " to resist the Japanese occupation. The acting Ch'ing governor of Formosa, Tang Ching-sung, because president of the republic and the Ch'ing military commander, Liu Yung-fu, became head of its armed forces. But the purpose of those who conceived the "Formosan Democratic Republic" was not the creation of an independent Formosan nation. Rather the "republic" was intended as a temporary device to achieve international support to resist the Japanese with the view to eventually re-uniting Formosa with the mainland. The entire "republican" movement was, in fact, conceived and carried out with the active co-operation of central government officials in Peking. The famous viceroy Chang Chih-tung was reported to have been the republic's principal source of military and financial support.[5]

The character of the movement was quite accurately expressed in a memorial sent to Peking shortly before the formal declaration of independence in May 1895: "The literati and people of Formosa are determined to resist subjection to Japan. Hence they have declared themselves an independent Island Republic, at the same time recognising the suzerainty of the Sacred Tsing (Ching) dynasty."[6] In attempting to win popular support, the new government appealed not to whatever desire for an independent state that may have existed among the Formosans but rather to their feelings of Chinese patriotism. A public proclamation read: "China has been grossly insulted by the Japanese dwarfs, and we cannot be other than their enemies. Therefore, we, the literati and all the populace, must join together and oppose the barbarians if they dare to land. If anyone sympathises with the dwarfs let them be seized and killed at once."[6]

The movement to oppose the Japanese occupation acquired substantial, if not overwhelming, popular support.[7]

Yet during the stormy events of 1895 there is no evidence of the emergence of distinctly Formosan nationalist feelings. In so far as the "Formosan Democratic Republic" elicited a response from the Formosan people, it was a response that was characterised by the still racialistic Chinese antipathy to the "Japanese dwarfs" and by a general sense of loyalty to the Chinese empire. In interpreting the events of 1895 it is difficult to depart from the observation of a contemporary observer that "to the natives of the island, the opposition to the Japanese, in spite of the fact that the emperor had nominally ceded the island, appeared in no other light than an act of loyalty to their sovereign."[8]

---

[5] For a contemporary account of the formation of the "Formosan Democratic Republic" see Davidson 277–284.   [6] Davidson, p. 278.
[7] *Ibid.* p. 279. According to a Japanese account 70–80,000 native Formosans were armed and organised military resistance to the far superior Japanese forces continued for over six months, followed by several years of active guerilla warfare. It is interesting to note that a Japanese writing in 1907 attributed the difficulties of the Japanese military campaign in the latter half of 1895 to the Chinese adeptness at guerrilla warfare. Yosaburo Takekoshi, *Japanese Rule in Formosa* (London, 1907), pp. 82 & 88.   [8] Davidson, p. 279.

If the people of Formosa still felt themselves to be Chinese in 1895, it was the following fifty-year period of Japanese rule that prepared the essential social and economic preconditions for the emergence of modern Formosan nationalism. In ruling Formosa the Japanese played very much the same role that European colonial régimes played in other areas of Asia in the era before the Second World War. The period of Japanese colonial rule saw the establishment of an effective centralised administration for the first time in Formosa's history, the creation of an economic structure that was significantly different from that on the mainland, the disintegration of the older forms of communal social life and the emergence of a Formosan middle class.

The imposition of a new political structure, was in itself an important factor in the growth of Formosan nationalism. By effectively breaking off ties with mainland China and ending Chinese migration, the Japanese colonial régime fostered a sense of common identity among the Formosans and at the same time prevented Formosan opposition to Japanese rule from becoming identified with the wider currents of Chinese nationalism.

The colonial political structure was also used by the Japanese to reorganise the Formosan economy for the purposes of creating an agricultural surplus for export to Japan. During the period of Ch'ing rule, farming, which was the main source of livelihood for almost all Formosans, was operated on an entirely local basis largely for the purpose of family subsistence; the exportable surplus of agricultural products went almost entirely for the payment of rent and taxes. The basic aim of Japanese colonial policy in Formosa was to raise agricultural production and at the same time to keep internal consumption at relatively low levels, thus providing a surplus for export. This was accomplished, in part, by raising the technical efficiency of farming and by surrounding agriculture with an impressive array of capital improvements such as irrigation and flood control projects, electric power and a network of communications and transportation for the disposition of the marketable surplus. In addition to creating a large exportable rice surplus, Japanese colonial policy encouraged the growth of strictly cash crops such as tea, bananas, pineapples, and most notably, sugar.

The transformation from a subsistence to a market economy is reflected in the remarkable fact that in 1939 the per capita value of the foreign trade of Formosa was 39 times that of mainland China and one and a half times more than Japan itself.[9] This was accompanied by a steady growth in industrial production. The value of industrial output (including mining) rose from 37 per cent. of the total value of production

---

[9] George W. Barclay, *Colonial Development and Population in Taiwan* (Princeton, 1954), p. 33.

in 1914 to 48 per cent. by 1937—even though the value of agricultural output had meanwhile more than trebled.[10]

The impressive growth in production did not lead to any spectacular improvements in the economic lot of the Formosans. This was largely because much of the industry that was developed was of the food processing variety and largely under the control of Japanese capital. Also partly responsible were Japanese fiscal policies which were manipulated to insure that increases in production were accompanied by the maintenance of relatively low levels of consumption, thus providing a source of food and raw materials for export.

If the Japanese did not succeed, as they have claimed, in transforming Formosa into an industrialised area or in spreading an industrial culture among the Formosans, the economic changes that did occur had important implications for the development of Formosan nationalism. The intimate involvement of Formosan farmers in a market economy and the movement of considerable numbers of Formosans from strictly rural environments to cities and towns in order to fill positions in industrial and commercial enterprises tended to undermine traditional localistic loyalties. While the traditional Chinese family structure seems to have largely survived the economic changes that were introduced by the colonial régime, the new economic opportunities and the development of an efficient network of communications and transportation did serve to widen the perspectives of the Formosans, to create among them a feeling that they shared a common destiny, and to encourage new aspirations which made it increasingly difficult to think solely in terms of the old family and local ties. These developments were particularly apparent among the substantial number of Formosans who migrated to the newly developing cities.[11]

The development of urban areas with significant concentrations of Formosans engaged in non-traditional occupations and directly exposed to a variety of non-traditional influences not only tended to weaken the older family, clan and local loyalties, but was also associated with the rise of a small, yet significant, Formosan middle class. While the economic life of the cities was dominated by 300,000 Japanese immigrants who filled virtually all government posts and occupied the choice positions in commerce, industry and the professions, a rapidly increasing number of Formosans were engaged in commercial and

---

[10] Andrew J. Grajdanzev, *Formosa Today* (New York, 1942), p. 91.
[11] For statistics on the growth of Formosan cities see Barclay, *op. cit.*, pp. 116 *et seq.* Between 1920–40, the rate of growth of the Formosan urban population was approximately twice that of the population as a whole.

professional pursuits.[12] In addition to the Formosan middle class that developed in the cities, there was also formed a middle class of school teachers, physicians, and the business men in and around the smaller towns that had populations of perhaps ten or twenty thousand. This " small town " middle class maintained close ties with the farmers of the surrounding areas and assumed the position of local community leaders. As intermediaries between the economic and intellectual life of cities and the rural areas the members of this middle class played crucial roles in promoting a common Formosan sense of identity. Thus the two factors that have been most often associated with the rise of modern nationalisms—the weakening of the older communal and localistic loyalties and the rise of a middle class—appeared at least in embryo in Formosa during the period of Japanese rule.

Perhaps even more important in the development of Formosan nationalism were the negative effects of Japanese rule. The obviously alien character of the colonial administration, the social discrimination against Formosans in the cities and the preference given to Japanese residents in employment and professional opportunities embittered the Formosans and solidified their feelings of common interest. Equally significant is the fact that Japanese rule not only cut off immigration from the Chinese mainland but also effectively separated the Formosans from modern Chinese political and intellectual developments. The Formosans did not participate in, and were largely unaware of, the stirring events that marked the growth of Chinese nationalism. The nationalistic impulses that were generated by the Revolution of 1911, the May Fourth Movement, the campaign for national unification, the war against Japan and the Communist revolution made little impact upon the consciousness of the Formosans. Thus the internal factors that were creating the preconditions for nationalistic feelings could not be easily identified with the broader Chinese nationalistic movements.

If Formosa's fifty-year separation from the Chinese mainland had established the conditions for the emergence of a distinctly Formosan nationalism, it was not inevitable that such a nationalism would in fact develop into separatist directions. Certainly there was no widespread desire for an independent Formosan state in 1945. Even Formosan nationalist sources admit that Kuomintang troops and officials were at first welcomed as liberators.[18] But the Kuomintang was less disposed to seek unity than immediate profits. An official system of monopolies was introduced to control, and systematically exploit for the benefit

[12] In 1930 29% of the Formosans living in the seven cities of " municipal rank " were engaged in commerce and 6·4% were government workers and professionals. Barclay p. 129.
[18] *Formosan Quarterly*, Vol. I, No. 2 (October 1962), p. 52

of the new régime, all important commercial and industrial enterprises. The movable capital assets of factories and commercial enterprises were confiscated and sent to the mainland or sold to line the pockets of local Kuomintang officials. Formosan employees were summarily dismissed and replaced by mainland Chinese. A system of licensing was used to impose crippling exactions on the Formosan merchants and professional groups. Large quantities of rice were shipped to the Nationalist soldiers on the mainland, resulting in a serious food shortage.[14]

These " carpet bagging " activities of the mainlanders, coming on top of the economic dislocations caused by the war and United States bombing raids, reduced the Formosan economy to ruin, resulted in an uncontrolled inflation and severely impinged upon the life of all sections of Formosan society. The discontent of the Formosans was further aggravated by the Kuomintang refusal to recognise Formosa (even theoretically), as an equal part of the Chinese nation; instead, a military government with completely arbitrary powers was instituted.

In so far as the early policies of the Nationalists' régime in Formosa were not inspired by purely mercenary motives, these policies grew out of the belief that the Formosans had somehow been contaminated by the influences of the Japanese and that, therefore, their loyalties to China were suspect. A Kuomintang publication of 1946 spoke of the necessity of " re-educating " the Formosans, because " the invaders . . . to a great extent had succeeded in ' fooling ' the population and in stereotyping the thinking of their conquered." Moreover, " the younger Formosan generation had been ' poisoned intellectually and were forced to accept twisted notions.' " [15]

The new rulers of Formosa, although not wholly unaware of the growing popular discontent, characteristically failed to understand its causes and underestimated its importance. Shortly before the great Formosan revolt that began on February 28, 1947, it was admitted that the Formosans " feel unhappy and [were] ready to complain against their mainland brethren not long after the recovery of Formosa." The dissatisfaction of the Formosans was attributed not to the then current economic chaos and political repression but rather to a " psychic phenomenon " that causes people " to look with disfavour on the present and idealise the past." [16]

The revolt of February 28, 1947, crystallised the development of Formosan nationalist feelings. The duplicity of the Kuomintang in its

[14] For a description of the early period of Kuomintang rule in Formosa, see Joseph W. Ballantine, *Formosa* (Washington, 1952), pp. 57–62.
[15] *New Taiwan Monthly* (September 1946), pp. 1–3.
[16] *New Taiwan Monthly* (January–February 1947), p. 1.

negotiations with the revolutionaries and the brutalities that marked the suppression of the revolt cemented the differences between Formosans and mainlanders and destroyed whatever hopes the Formosans may have had that their aspirations could be realised within a Chinese political framework.[17] The term " erh-erh pa " (February 28) is not only a slogan of the exiled Formosan independence groups but it is a symbol that recalls tragic personal experiences deeply etched upon the consciousness of most adult Formosans.

The cleavage between mainlanders and Formosans widened with the mass influx of refugees from the mainland in 1949. To the Formosans the mainlanders seemed to assume the very roles and positions that the Japanese colonial rulers had so recently vacated. Like the Japanese the mainlanders congregated in the cities and, in fact, took over the very houses that had been formerly occupied by the Japanese. As during the Japanese period, Formosa was subjected to the rule of a political apparatus controlled by men whom the Formosans soon came to regard as aliens. Moreover, since the ruling Kuomintang felt obligated to provide some degree of economic support for the displaced mainlanders (most of whom were soldiers or officials when the Nationalist Government fled to Formosa) even the most menial government posts were, and still are, largely occupied by mainlanders. Thus the Formosans found themselves not only ruled by, but also forced to support through excessive taxation, a swollen bureaucracy from which they were largely excluded.

The dominance of the mainlanders became apparent even in the remotest rural areas where the local policeman is the main symbol of political authority. While the local policeman had formerly been a Japanese, he was now a mainlander. As the pro-Nationalist *China News* reported in late 1960: " the policeman remained the farmer's number one headache. For 50 years, the Japanese ruled Formosa through an autocratic police force. The Formosans feared and hated the Japanese policemen. Fifteen years after the departure of the Japanese, the dreadful spectre of a bullying policeman remained." [18]

The relatively small number of Formosans who are members of the Kuomintang and occupy official positions, or who co-operate with the government in the local areas, are generally dismissed by most Formosans as self-seeking politicians and referred to as " pan-shan "

[17] When the Nationalist " Administrator-General " of Formosa, General Chen Yi realised he did not have sufficient military forces to quell the revolt, he agreed to the major demands of the Formosans and persuaded the revolutionaries to lay down their arms. On March 8, 50,000 Nationalist troops arrived from the mainland and inaugurated a reign of terror which lasted for most of the month. The figure of 10,000 Formosan deaths was first reported by Tillman Durdin, upon the basis of the accounts of foreign observers, in the *New York Times* on March 29, 1947 (p. 6). Some Formosan sources put the number at 20,000.

[18] *China News* (Taipei), November 22, 1960.

(literally " half-mountain " people). This latter term is contemptuously applied to those Formosans who were educated on the mainland or who otherwise lived on the mainland during or shortly after the Second World War and then returned to Formosa with the Kuomintang. Most Formosans who now occupy official positions have come from this group of pan-shan-jeu, a term which implies that these people have become half-Chinese and have therefore lost their Formosan identity. The attitude of the Formosans to those of their countrymen who collaborate with the regime was quite candidly revealed in a survey published in the *China News* in 1960:

> . . . many thinking Formosans . . . dispute the government claim that native leaders thrive in high government and business levels. They would readily point out that many of these officials, business operators and bankers do not necessarily represent their interest. They even use uncomplimentary names to describe most of these " influential or wealthy native-borns." Oftentimes they simply disown them.
>
> When asked to comment on the administration, they often vented their grievances against the so-called " native " leadership. Somehow there is a missing link between these " lackeys," as these " leaders " are sometimes called, and the bulk of the native population.
>
> Many of the " lackeys " had either fled to the China mainland or collaborated with the Japanese during the Japanese domination. They stayed away on the mainland and many married mainland girls. The majority of them were often ridiculed as " men without a principle." Since the Chinese take-over of the island, many of them have returned to their native land and rejoined their " people."
>
> The lack of confidence of the native-born populace in such leadership is a cause of anxiety.[19]

The political dominance of the mainlanders impinges directly on the economic welfare of the Formosans. Most of the agricultural land and a considerable portion of urban property is owned by Formosans. (This is partly because the rootless mainlanders are unwilling to invest in land in Formosa, preferring investments that offer quicker returns or the security of foreign banks.) The Formosans also have a large share of the small and medium size business enterprises. But most of the industry and the larger commercial enterprises, the transportation system and all public utilities, are owned or controlled by the government. Formosans are discriminated against at all levels of employment in these government-dominated enterprises and have virtually no hope of rising to administrative and executive positions. A similar pattern of discrimination is maintained in the school system. University professorships are virtually all held by mainlanders (with the notable exception of medicine). The principals of middle-schools and elementary schools are almost always

---

[19] *China News* (Taipei), November 21, 1960.

mainlanders, as are most of the senior teachers, particularly in the social sciences and humanities.

The wealthier Formosans, moreover, complain bitterly that any attempt to establish industrial enterprises are frustrated at every turn by government regulations and official interference. While all commercial enterprises are subject to bureaucratic impingements, such burdens fall most heavily on Formosan entrepreneurs who have less access to government officials than do mainlanders.

Economic exploitation through political means is carried to the countryside by means of ever-increasing rates of taxation, government price controls on commodities, the arbitrary fixing of prices on the exchange of rice for fertiliser, special levies for an endless series of " campaigns " to " recover the mainland," and the necessity to satisfy local government and police officials through extra-legal payments.

The conscription of Formosans into the Nationalist army is another means through which Formosans become aware of the domination of mainlanders. Formosans now comprise somewhat more than half of the 600,000 man Nationalist army. But except for Formosan college graduates, who are obliged to serve two-year terms as lieutenants, few Formosans are willing or able to serve as officers.[20] The subordination of Formosan soldiers to mainland officers probably serves more to make the Formosan conscripts conscious of alien domination than it does to indoctrinate them with Kuomintang ideology.

Social discrimination in the cities is an additional source of discontent. As evidence of the " colonial " relationship that exists between the native population and the mainlanders, Formosans frequently point to residential segregation and the fact that while Formosans are employed as servants in the homes of mainlanders, not even the most impoverished mainlanders (and there are many very poor mainlanders in Formosa) can be found working as a servant in the home of Formosans.

The political domination of mainlanders, the use of the political apparatus to impose economic burdens that fall most heavily upon the Formosans, and various forms of social discrimination have made the distinction between mainlanders and Formosans apparent in almost every aspect of Formosan life and have kept alive the hatreds and antagonisms that arose from the bloody suppression of the revolt of 1947. As a result, most Formosans believe that they are being exploited for external political ends. They feel that they are unjustly subjected to the political

---

[20] One Formosan college graduate who served as a lieutenant in the Nationalist army between 1956–58 reported that while 40 per cent. of the soldiers in his division were Formosan (a division of the Nationalist army normally consists of about 12,000 men), there were only 12 Formosan officers in the entire division. Ng Jiurian, " A Formosan Officer's Memoirs," *Formosan Quarterly*, Vol. 1, No. 3 (January 1963), p. 81.

and ideological controls of a totalitarian organisation that they had no part in creating and one in which they cannot effectively participate, and have thereby become involved in the civil war of a nation with which they do not feel identified. Through military conscription and exorbitant taxes, the Formosans are forced to support an oversized military establishment and bureaucratic apparatus which subsists on the myth that it is the " national government " of China in " temporary " exile. As a result of a situation not of their own making, the Formosans are thus faced with the ever present danger of war and required to subordinate the economic development of the island to the military and political ambitions of what they consider to be an alien ruling group.

The Formosan reaction to the dominance of the mainlanders is severely limited by the totalitarian political controls exercised by the Kuomintang. While the Formosan independence groups in exile do not have a visible political following in Formosa, there is no doubt that the Formosans overwhelmingly favour the establishment of an independent republic, which many still hopefully expect will be realised through the intervention of the United States. Meanwhile, Formosan nationalist sentiment is expressed (in private conversations) in various theoretical and practical arguments which try to show that the Formosans are not and should not be considered Chinese and in relatively trivial ways such as the preference for the term " Formosan " rather than the Chinese term " Taiwanese." It is also expressed in various forms of " cultural nationalism " which attempt to distinguish Formosan from Chinese. In the absence of a truly distinctive Formosan cultural tradition, Formosan " cultural nationalism " has taken the form of the continued use of the Japanese language and the maintenance of a variety of Japanese social habits and styles of life. For the older generation of Formosans the use of the Japanese langauge and Japanese customs is largely a matter of habit. For younger Formosans it is usually a deliberate effort to assert their Formosan identity.[21]

For Formosan intellectuals " cultural nationalism " has also meant turning back to the Formosan past. For the Formosan who does not want to be considered Chinese, it is reassuring to believe that Formosa has had a history of its own significantly different from that of mainland China. While the Formosan nationalist view of the Formosan past is considerably overdrawn, as has been suggested above, the assertion that

[21] A characteristic example of this attitude has been described by a former Formosan member of the Kuomintang army: " In the Nationalist Army the use of the Japanese language was not permitted, but we Formosans used Japanese loudly on purpose. It was not by accident that we wrote letters in Japanese. We knew our letters were censored but we wrote them in the prohibited language intentionally. It was not from our love of Japan that we used Japanese, but the use of it certainly had a nuisance value as our tiny means of retaliation against the Nationalist regime." *Formosan Quarterly*, Vol. 1, No. 3 (January 1963), p. 80.

Formosa has had a distinctive history independent from that of the mainland is largely valid for the period since 1895.

Formosan resentment against the present régime and the desire for independence is also reflected in comparisons that are frequently made between Japanese and Kuomintang rule. There is undeniably a great deal of romanticisation in the Formosan view of their Japanese past, although there seems to be solid support for the assertion that the Japanese administration, while stern and harsh, was less corrupt and less arbitrary than the present government. Whether the Formosans were actually better off under the Japanese than they are now is less important than that most articulate Formosans believe this to be true.

Thus the cleavage between Formosans and mainlanders, originally created by the Japanese, has been widened rather than narrowed by the re-imposition of Chinese rule. This cleavage is reinforced by the attitudes of the mainlanders towards Taiwan and the Formosans. For most mainlanders Taiwan is still a foreign land and the Formosans are " the natives." If the expectation that the Kuomintang will " recover " the mainland has become increasingly less real, most mainlanders in Formosa still think that by one means or another they will eventually return " home." Many try not to think about the problem at all. Few, however, are reconciled to finding roots and remaining in Formosa. While the Formosans tend to think of the mainlanders as interlopers, the foreign observer is more likely to be struck by the pathos of their plight.

Although personal relationships between members of the two groups, are not, for the most part, overtly hostile, there are storehouses of chauvinistic terms and attitudes on both sides. While Formosans justly complain of the arrogance of the mainlanders, the Formosans themselves have their share of contempt for the mainlanders. Close friendships between Formosans and mainlanders are rare, even among college students where relatively favourable circumstances for such friendships might be expected to prevail. Intermarriage between Formosans and mainlanders is also uncommon. When such marriages do take place they usually arouse the hostility of the families of both partners and are predominantly marriages between mainland men and Formosan women. This latter is a further source of Formosan resentment.

The gulf between the mainlanders and the Formosans is deep but it is not necessarily eternal. Given time and the evolution of a more favourable political situation, it is conceivable that the younger generation could effect a genuine integration between the two communities. In the long run, however, such a development presupposes a willingness upon the part of the mainlanders to merge with the Formosan majority in an independent Formosan nation. At the present time there is little evidence that any such disposition exists. The political ascendancy of the

Formosans would of course mean the demise of the present régime, a fact which explains why the Nationalist government is so sensitive to the whole question of Formosan-mainlander relations, and why it reacts with particular violence to any political tendency that seeks a genuine reconciliation between the two groups.

Even the most liberal and democratic-oriented mainlanders have yet to come to terms with the demands of Formosan nationalism. Shortly before the suppression of the *Free China Fortnightly* in 1960 and the imprisonment of its editor, Lei Chen, an editorial in that periodical stated with very great courage and candour that "the majority (of Formosans) generally feel that their rulers are foreigners." [22] But the main thrust of the editorial was to deny that there were any differences between Formosans and mainlanders other than those created by the present system of one-party government. A similar point of view is taken by Chinese "third force" groups in Hong Kong and elsewhere, who argue that the Formosans' independence movement is basicaly an anti-Kuomintang political struggle rather than a movement of the Formosan nation against the Chinese. [23] Yet the fact remains that most Formosans conceive of the relationship between the mainlanders and themselves as not simply a matter of political differences between rulers and the ruled, but national differences between foreign colonial overlords and subject population. While the oppressive character of Kuomintang rule was the catalyst for the emergence of Formosan nationalism, the basis for this nationalism had been laid during the period of Japanese rule. The intensity of the Formosan belief that mainlanders are aliens and the tendency for Formosan opposition to the political rule of the Kuomintang to take the form of national opposition to foreign rule and a desire for national self-determination cannot be explained except with reference to the profound social and economic changes that occurred under Japanese colonial rule and Formosa's long separation from the mainstream of modern Chinese history. Thus the attempts of liberal mainlanders such as the ill-fated Lei Chen to win Formosan support for a genuine opposition movement are not only doomed to political repression but they are also severely handicapped by the suspicion of many Formosans that even the most liberal mainlanders seek only to use Formosa as pawns in mainlander (that is to say, foreign) politics.

Taking the generally accepted definition that a nation, in the final

[22] " Taiwan-jen yü ta-lu-jen " (Formosans and Mainlanders), *Tzu-yu Chung-kuo* (Free China), Vol. 23, No. 2 (July 16, 1960), p. 36.
[23] See, for example, Cheng Nien-hua, " Shih-lun so-wei Tai-wan tu-li yun-tung " (An Examination of the So-Called Formosan Independence Movement), *Hai-wei lun-t'an* (World Forum), Vol. I, No. 12 (December 1960), pp. 2–7.

analysis, is a body of people who feel that they are a nation,[24] there seems little doubt that the Formosans are eminently qualified for nationhood. Certainly the Formosans have a strong sense of common identity and believe that they belong together. Within the narrow confines of the existing totalitarian political structure they have done everything possible to prove that this is so.

As with other modern nationalisms, the sense of Formosan national identity is felt most strongly by the middle-class intellectuals. But as in other nationalist movements, particularly in Asia, the intelligentsia has served to both mould and articulate the feelings of much wider sections of society. The degree of popular support and the sense of national solidarity that appeared in the Formosan revolt of 1947 compare very favourably with the nationalist movements that arose in the former colonial territories of South-East Asia during and after the Second World War.

Even on the basis of the objective elements that are usually associated with the ideal model of a nation, a good case can be made for Formosan independence. The Formosans traditionally have lived on a well-defined territory and shared a common economic life. They speak the same languages and even have a distinctive language pattern; although the use of Mandarin is becoming increasingly widespread, both Formosan and Japanese remain " native " languages that are learned and spoken in the homes of most Formosans. For the better part of a century, moreover, the Formosans have shared a common historical experience that was and is different and separate from that of mainland China. The Formosans, of course, are ethnically identical with the Chinese and have no truly distinctive culture of their own. But, as many Formosans are quick to point out, the ethnic, cultural and even linguistic identities between England and the American colonies did not prevent the American War of Independence.

Professor Rupert Emerson has defined a nation as " a community of people who feel that they belong together in a double sense that they share deeply significant elements of a common heritage and that they have a common destiny for the future." [25] While there is no doubt that the Formosan people feel they belong together and that they share a common heritage, even the most ardent Formosan nationalists realise that the fate of Formosa is in the hands of outside forces—the evolution of Kuomintang politics in the first instance and the future policies of the United States and Communist China in the final analysis. The more realistic advocates of an independent Formosan state privately admit that

24 For an excellent discussion of the " elements of nationhood," see Rupert Emerson, *From Empire to Nation* (Boston, 1960), pp. 102–131.
25 Emerson, p. 95.

the long-term prospects are not bright and that an independent Formosa might be only a transitional stage to an eventual accommodation with the mainland. But the nationalist leaders want independence for their people (and power for themselves) now. They are reluctant to take too long a look into the future. Thus whether the Formosans have a common destiny for the future as a separate national entity, and, perhaps equally significant, whether the Formosans truly feel they have such a common destiny, remain questions which cast considerable doubt on the viability, though certainly not the validity, of the Formosan claim to nationhood.

A Formosan's View of
The Formosan Independence Movement

By ONG JOKTIK

THE ancestors of the contemporary Formosans abandoned the Chinese mainland with its poverty and inequalities, in the latter half of the sixteenth century, and emigrated to Formosa in order to open up and settle in new territory. Yet they have had little independence. The Dutch East India Company conquered Formosa and used it as a commercial base between 1624 and 1661; Koxinga and his supporters expelled the Dutch in 1661 and used Formosa as an anti-Manchu base until 1683; then the Manchus of the Ch'ing Dynasty gained control of Formosa until 1895; the island was ceded to the Japanese in 1895 and it was not until the collapse of Japan in 1945 that the Chinese Nationalist Government was able to rule Formosa.

During the long centuries of foreign rule the Formosans often resorted to impulsive and instinctive rebellions when they could no longer bear oppression. Some of these rebellions were on a relatively large scale. For instance, the Buwet rebellion in 1652; the rebellion led by Cu Jitkui in 1721; the rebellion of Lim Songbun in 1787; the Te Tiauchun rebellion of 1870. Yet these were peasant uprisings; they cannot be considered independence movements in the strict sense of that term.

THE NATIONALIST MOVEMENT UNDER THE JAPANESE

The Formosan nationalist movement in the modern period was born when all military resistance to Japanese imperial control had failed. The market economy and the spread of education which the Japanese brought to Formosa was a stimulant to a growing sense of nationalism. The spearhead of the movement was a group of young students who had studied in Tokyo. In 1920 they began publishing a journal called *Taiwan Seinen* (*Young Formosa*), in which they attacked the dictatorial government of the Formosa Government-General and called for Formosan autonomy. Subsequently the Formosa Bunkakyokai (Formosa Cultural Association) was organised on the island itself, and attempts were made to inculcate nationalism among the masses. Farmers and factory workers were organised to this end and, eventually, a Formosan Communist Party came into existence.

163

Sturm und drang characterised the Formosan nationalist movement under the Japanese. However, it was thoroughly crushed by the Japanese after the Manchurian Incident. The leaders of the movement were arrested and imprisoned or killed. Those who evaded arrest escaped either to the continent or to the Japanese islands; those who remained behind only had the choice of silence. The destruction of this movement in the thirties was followed by the Second World War, which brought general poverty to the people on Formosa.

FORMOSA UNDER THE CHINESE NATIONALISTS

The Formosans received the news of Japan's defeat and the return of the island to Chinese rule with mixed feelings. While Japan's defeat may have been welcomed, how far the Chinese " fatherland " could be relied upon to satisfy Formosa's aspirations was open to question. Almost immediately after the war a group of pro-Japanese Formosan politicians began planning for Formosa's independence. However, in the immediate post-war confusion, American policy was by no means clear cut and there was no hope of support from defeated Japan. Without mass support they soon fell easy prey to the Nationalists who came to occupy Formosa. The Chinese Nationalist officials and troops who arrived in Formosa behaved arrogantly and oppressively, as though they were victors dealing with a defeated nation. The Chinese took over all administrative organs and industrial equipment, which were distributed among the members of the Central Government, the provincial government, the Nationalist Party and the various financial interests which had accompanied the Nationalists to Formosa. The corruption and immorality which characterised the Nationalists on the mainland was brought to Formosa. The Formosans saw their island ruled by avarice and violence. The Chinese soon proved that they had neither the efficiency nor the honesty which had been the mark of Japanese rule on Formosa. The Formosans began to say that " the dogs have gone but the pigs have come to replace them. Dogs are to be feared, but at least they protect you from thieves. Pigs can only eat." Within less than eighteen months after the return of Formosa to Chinese rule the Formosans rose in revolt under the slogans " Chinese go home," and " Formosa for the Formosans."

The mass uprising which began in Taipei on February 28, 1947, spread rapidly through the island. For a period of one week the Formosans controlled the entire island, except for the Chinese military bases. In many areas " Committees to manage February 28 affairs " were organised and expected to serve as models for autonomous government. In addition, most of these committees subscribed to the " 32 Demands," something like a Formosan Bill of Rights, drawn up by Ong Thiamting.

The revolt, as reflected in the " 32 Demands," sought independence or, at least, autonomy for the island. In my opinion, this was the beginning of the contemporary Formosan Independence Movement.

The rebellion ended in total failure. Local political leaders and youth groups were ignorant of Chinese politics and were deceived by the promises of the Nationalists. When reinforcements arrived from the mainland the Formosans were immediately crushed. Over 10,000 Formosans were either executed or imprisoned. This costly failure has three basic explanations: (1) The rebellion was, like previous rebellions in Formosan history, spontaneous. There was no planning or central control. (2) The Formosans could expect no foreign assistance. The United States was supporting the Nationalist government and Japan was impotent with defeat. (3) The Formosans underestimated their enemy. While they knew that they could not rely on Ch'en Yi, the Governor of the island, to redress their wrongs, they felt that Chiang Kai-shek in Nanking would assume the task of correcting the injustices against which they complained.[1]

In the aftermath of the revolt the Formosan independence movement was driven underground and its outlook veered sharply to the left. Many students and other young people who had escaped execution or imprisonment by hiding in the cities and villages began to join the Communist Party. Lack of organisation was widely recognised as the primary reason for the failure of the February rebellion. The Communist Party alone had considerable experience in underground organisation. (The reader will recall that the Communists were often the core of the resistance movements in Europe and in China during the war.) The young people had confidence in the Communist Party, because it had fought with the people against the Nationalists during the rebellion. They felt that once they, together with the Communists, had overthrown the Nationalist régime, they would be able to agree on a settlement with the Communists on a basis of friendship and equality, in which the Chinese Communists would recognise Formosa as an autonomous region and eventually guarantee its independence.[2]

In addition to this movement of young people, a group of native Formosan political leaders who had survived the February 28 holocaust sought to isolate Formosa from the Chinese civil war and to prevent the Nationalists from escaping to Formosa where, these leaders felt, the Nationalists had no legitimate right to govern. They secretly tried to work

[1] For details of the February 28 Rebellion, see *Taiwan Chinglian*, February 1960, special edition.
[2] A similar approach can be found among Formosans who remained in Japan after the war. They hated the Nationalists and wanted to rely on the Communists, using their faith in the " Fatherland's Communists " for moral support, as a means of escaping from their social isolation in Japan.

through the members of the American diplomatic corps on Formosa, but their efforts were crushed by Chiang's régime, which needed Formosa as a place of refuge. In December, 1948, Chiang Kai-shek appointed Ch'en Ch'eng, the present vice-president and prime minister, Governor of Formosa. Chiang Ching-kuo, Chiang Kai-shek's elder son, was appointed director of the Nationalist Party headquarters on the island. In May 1949 Chiang Kai-shek himself moved to Formosa. The Nationalists ruled with an iron grip to prevent any repetition of the incident of February 28. Chinese and Formosan Communists were arrested and shot; Formosan nationalists were imprisoned and often executed on the pretext that they were connected with the Communists.

In the year following his flight from the mainland Chiang Kai-shek was confronted by both Formosan resentment and American abandonment. But, fortunately for him the Korean War, which began in June 1950, shifted American policy from neutrality *vis-à-vis* Formosa to active support of the Nationalists. As a result, Chiang could thoroughly suppress the Formosans and strengthen his own régime with American aid.

THE PROVISIONAL GOVERNMENT OF LIAO WEN-YI

A group of Formosan political leaders escaped to Hong Kong when the February 28 revolt collapsed. In the summer of 1948 they organised the League for the Reliberation of Formosa, and on September 1 they presented their first petition to the United Nations in the name of 7,000,000 Formosans. The petition requested that Formosa be placed under UN trusteeship and that the island be granted independence in the future. Their organisation was, however, shaken and split by the swift Chinese Communist victory on the mainland. Some of them, like Hsieh Hsueh-hung and Lin Mu-hsun, felt that it would be easier to liberate Formosa through the Chinese Communists and, accordingly, left Hong Kong for Peking. On the other hand, the pro-American group, centred on Liao Wen-yi (Thomas Liao), moved to Japan in search of a more congenial environment for their activities.

The history of these two groups is full of lessons for the Formosan independence movement. Hsieh and his group were purged in Communist China in 1958 as rightist counter-revolutionaries who were tinged with " regional nationalism." Those who escaped this purge were rudely awakened from their rosy illusions. Confronted with ugly realities, they had nowhere to turn. The Chinese Communists who, during the February 28 incident called on the Formosans to overthrow the Nationalists, now feared nothing more than the resurgence of a similar movement. Today they rely on the Chiang Kai-shek family to suppress the Formosans while they call for reunification of Formosa with the mainland.

However, if in the future the Chinese Communists should decide that the collapse of the Nationalist régime is imminent and unavoidable, they might try once again to woo the island's population through those Formosans still alive in Peking. In that event, if the United States should continue its policy of supporting the Nationalists, the Formosans might turn to the Chinese Communists like a drowning person clutching at a straw.

On the other hand, Thomas Liao, who had moved to Japan, succeeded in joining his supporters and friends in the Formosa Democratic Independence Party, which was organised in February 1950. In 1955 he organised a Provisional Government in Tokyo with himself as President. However, the situation in Formosa never developed to his advantage and the lack of money and competent personnel led to internal friction in his group. As a result not only was he unable to influence American or United Natnons' policy he could not even influence the Formosans.

The Chinese Nationalists and Communists both contributed to undermining the organisation of the Provisional Government. The Nationalists secretly dispatched agents to Japan to harrass the Provisional Government. At the same time, Chiang insisted that the Japanese strictly control Formosan activities. To some extent this backfired, since it aroused the interest of many Japanese journalists in the independence movement. The Chinese Communists, in their turn, surprisingly accused the United States and Japan of publicly supporting Thomas Liao. While this was an excessive complement to Liao, it must be understood as an action intended to forestall any possible US or Japanese assistance to the independence movement or to Liao himself.

Some American and Japanese observers have correctly evaluated the Provisional Government. For example, an editorial entitled " When Chiang Goes," in the *New Republic* on June 18, 1962, said that " In Tokyo there is a militant though still largely ineffectual independence movement which seeks a non-Chinese Formosan Republic." Certainly the Provisional Government has so far been ineffectual. While the Nationalist slogans of return to the mainland have been fading year by year, and when the Chiang régime's internal collapse cannot, despite massive American assistance, be forestalled for ever, it is natural that Formosans and those Japanese interested in Formosa wonder why Liao's movement has been unable to build up a more effective organisation.

Unfortunately, much of this responsibility lies with Liao himself. Like any pioneer, he was self-confident to such an extent that his self-confidence became his shortcoming. He cherishes the illusion that in time America will establish and maintain his power. Consequently, many competent and influential Formosans have criticised Liao and his organisation. Men like Ong Jauthuan, Khu Jinghan, Ngou Cinlam and myself have either left Liao or refused to join him in the first place.[3]

A NEW POLITICAL PARTY ON FORMOSA

Formosan politicians on Formosa, quiescent after the failure of the February 28 revolt, began to resume their political activities following the crisis of 1954, which included the bombardment of Quemoy and the Nationalist withdrawal from the Tachen islands, and the Bandung Conference in April 1955 when the Chinese Communists began their peace offensive. As long as the Nationalists regarded themselves as the legitimate government of China and pursued a policy aimed at the reconquest of the mainland, the Formosans could not but be influenced by Chinese Communists actions. Once the crisis was passed, many Chinese on Formosa relapsed into passivity. They were haunted by their desire to return to the mainland, and this desire was reinforced by a feeling of desperation. In time, they began to whisper about reunification of the Chinese Nationalist and Communist Parties. This shook the Nationalist régime. At the same time, foreigners in Taipei were seriously concerned over the possibility of an uprising in the army. It was under these circumstances that Formosan politicians resumed activity, cautiously watching the moves of both the Nationalists and the Americans.

The Formosans sought to organise a political party to compete legally with the Nationalist. Such organs of government as the Legislative Yuan, the Examination Yuan, and the Provincial Assembly, are simply show windows for a " Free China " appealing to the United States for assistance. The Central Government is overwhelmingly dominated by Chinese mainlanders. The only arena for Formosan political action is the Provincial Assembly, which does not even constitute, in reality, a consultative organ for the provincial government. Nevertheless, the Formosan politicians decided to continue their struggle through elections although they knew that, revolution aside, they could not hope to achieve even their minimal aims of real home rule. This, in effect, continued the unsuccessful movement for a Formosan Assembly which had taken place thirty years before under the Japanese.

At the same time, some Chinese liberals, led by Lei Chen, also

---

[3] Ong was a reporter for *Asahi* before the war, escaped to Hong Kong after the February 28 Revolution, where he energetically worked for UN discussion of the Formosa problem. Died in Tokyo, 1951. Khu is secretary of the League for the Reliberation of Formosa; now active in Japan in writing and business. Ngou is a practising doctor in Yokohama, long worked with Thomas Liao as vice-president of the Provisional Government; resigned at the end of 1962, became chairman of the Democratic Independence Party. I was a teacher before the war in a Tainan high school; went to Japan via Hong Kong after the February 28 Revolution; am now a lecturer at Meiji University and do research on the Formosan language; organised the Formosan Association in 1960; am now its leading spokesman.

accepted the need for political action within the " constitutional " framework of the Chinese government. They reasoned that Nationalist collapse was inevitable so long as the régime was intent upon the reconquest of the mainland. To avoid this collapse, the government must change its basic policy, reform its entire structure, reduce the military establishment, and institute democratic reforms throughout the island. Consequently, a political party would have to be organised to these ends. However, for the many Chinese who worked for the government such a solution was tantamount to cutting off their livelihood. Lei Chen and others had, therefore, to seek collaborators among the Formosans. In this they were encouraged by Chester Bowles' idea of a Sino-Formosan Republic.

The resumption of the Communist bombardment of Quemoy in 1958 can be considered a kindness to the Nationalists, bringing it out of its lassitude. The Chinese Communists called on the Chinese on Formosa for co-operation and warned them against the Americans who intended to deprive them of even their last place of exile. Because of this, the new party movement was temporarily postponed under government pressure, but revived again in 1960. It was called the Democratic Party and Lei Chen was named chairman. One of the party's Formosan supporters, Kao Yü-shu, former mayor of Taipei, pointed out significantly that the proportion of Formosans to Chinese on the organisational committee was 8 to 2, which reflected approximately the ratio of Formosans to Chinese in the population at large. The government could no longer remain silent. Lei Chen was imprisoned and tried and sentenced on false charges. The *Free China* fortnightly, which reflected the new party's policies, was suppressed. The Government categorically banned the new party. The Formosans were once again forced into silence.

THE FORMOSAN ASSOCIATION

While the Nationalists were taking action against the new party on Formosa, Formosan students in Japan organised their own political movement in Tokyo in February 1960. They had been repeatedly critical of Thomas Liao's Provisional Government but, for lack of leadership, had been unable to take independent action. At this point I decided to support them. I had taught some of the more vocal Formosan students now in Tokyo when they were at high school on Formosa. Together we organised the Taiwan Chinglian (Youth) Associates, later renamed The Formosan Association. Believing that steady propaganda work and secret organisation were the most important activities at the time, the Association began to publish *Taiwan Chinglian* in Japanese and the *Formosan Quarterly* in English. Through these organs it hopes to acquaint Japan and the United States in particular, with the basic problems of Formosa.

The Association, which includes over 800 Formosan students in Japan and receives moral and economic support from some 25,000 Formosan businessmen in Japan, squarely challenges Nationalist propaganda and American support for Chiang's régime, including Washington's support for the Nationalist's representation in the United Nations. Because Formosans in Japan maintain close contact with Formosa itself, the Association's ideas and activities are being implemented inside Formosa as well.

It is not surprising that it is students in exile who are giving voice to the Independence Movement today. Although departure or escape from Formosa is very difficult now, two important groups of political refugees continue to make their way abroad. On the one hand, Nationalist officials who have lost hope in the future of Formosa have been sending their sons to the United States and are preparing to follow. On the other hand, there are Formosan youths who leave their country to study abroad because conditions at home have become intolerable.

On Formosa, college graduates cannot take the required examinations for studying abroad until they have completed a year-and-a-half to two years of military training. Then they face a stiff competition before they can leave the country. Abroad, they are enrolled in graduate schools for an average of over two years. Formosan nationalist associations among students abroad are based on the friendships and ties established at home in high school, college, or in the army.

The 600,000 troops on Formosa are as much directed against the Formosan population as against the Communists across the water. The Nationalist-American alliance is itself a basic source of political as well as economic capital for Chiang Kai-shek. However, there is a fatal flaw in the scheme of continued Nationalist domination of Formosa: the composition of the army is changing from year to year. The troops brought to Formosa by Chiang Kai-shek are ageing. Discharged from the army, they have been settled in the mountainous countryside or driven into the city slums. Young Formosan soldiers, equipped with American arms, have been drafted in their place. In short, the army, the mainstay of the Chinese régime, is itself steadily becoming less Chinese in its composition. Amid this the Chinese sense of helplessness and decadence is increasing, while in contrast self-confidence of the Formosan population is rising.[4]

At the same time, many Formosan youths in Japan and in the United States, are acquiring the skills upon which the future of Formosa depends. If they can organise themselves effectively, they may be able to play a leading role when the final Chinese crisis on Formosa occurs.

[4] For a description of the moral conditions among discharged soldiers, see the *Formosan Quarterly*, Vol. 1, No. 4, April 1963.

List of Contributors

Lucy H. Chen, former editor of the Formosan literary journal *Hsien-tai Wen-hsüeh* (Modern Literature), is now studying literature in the United States.

Shinkichi Eto is Associate Professor of International Relations at the University of Tokyo.

Lewis Gilbert is a journalist based in Hong Kong, with long experience on both the Chinese mainland and Formosa.

Sheppard Glass is a student of the Formosan economy, with many years of experience in the area.

Akira Iriye, a specialist on American Far Eastern policy and Far Eastern diplomatic relations, is an instructor in the History Department at Harvard University.

John Israel is Assistant Professor of History at Claremont Men's College, California.

Ong Joktik is a Formosan intellectual now in exile in Tokyo. He is the founder and leader of *The Formosan Association,* which publishes *Taiwan Chinglian,* a monthly journal of the independence movement.

Joyce K. Kallgren is a Junior Research Political Scientist at the Center for Chinese Studies, University of California, Berkeley.

Donald Klein of the Asia Foundation is currently at the Union Research Institute, Hong Kong.

Mark Mancall teaches at the East Asian Research Center at Harvard University.

Mei Wen-li is a writer living in Formosa.

Maurice Meisner is a Research Fellow in East Asian Studies at the East Asian Research Center, Harvard University.

Jonathan Mirsky is an instructor in Chinese at the University of Pennsylvania, Philadelphia.